Disciples and Discipline

Disciples and Discipline

European Debate on Human Rights
in the Roman Catholic Church

Edited by:

Caroline Vander Stichele
Ad van der Helm
Bert van Dijk
Rik Torfs
Svetko Veliscek

Leuven
1993

ISBN 90-6831-547-1
D. 1994/0602/1

CONTENTS

PART III

Introduction

Until the end of the Second World War, churchleaders had difficulties dealing with the principle of liberty, democratic structures and the concept of a constitutional state. In this respect the Second Vatican Council was a turning-point. It declared: "Therefore, by virtue of the gospel committed to her, the Church proclaims the rights of man. She acknowledges and greatly esteems the dynamic movements of today by which these rights are everywhere fostered."(Gaudium et Spes [1965], no. 41) Nine years later, in 1974, the papal commission *Justitia et Pax* saw the consequences for the Roman Catholic Church itself and called for an act of self-examination. How are we dealing in the church with the fundamental rights of every person? The European Conference for Human Rights in the Church has taken this call for self-scrutiny seriously. During its second meeting in 1991 the decision was made to publish a book on the European situation of human rights in the church. An editorial committee was formed, consisting of Bert van Dijk, Ad van der Helm, Rik Torfs, Svetko Veliscek and Caroline Vander Stichele. They elaborated the concept of the book, gathered information and collected articles and translations. Occasionally, editorial changes were made and every article was provided with a short introduction to situate it in the whole of the book.

The European Conference, which took the initiative for this publication, is a network of organizations from various European countries, concerned with human rights in the church. Organisations from Germany, the Netherlands, Belgium and France gathered for the first time in 1990 in Huissen (the Netherlands) and decided to start more intensive contacts. In 1991 a second meeting was held in Eschborn (Germany), where representatives from England, Ireland, Italy and Switzerland were also present. The next yearly meetings took place in Chur (Switzerland, 1992) and l'Arbresle (France, 1993). The Conference has expanded to include also members from Austria, Luxemburg, and Spain. The Conference established contacts with the American Association for the Rights of Catholics in the Church and the Coalition of Concerned Catholics in Canada.

With this book the European Conference wants to present a study on the problem of human rights in the church. The purpose of the book is not to present an overall picture of the problem, but the variety of its

aspects. Therefore, experts from different European countries have been
invited to contribute to this project. They present their own analysis of
the problems under consideration. By giving them the floor, the Conference hopes to bring the issues discussed to the attention of the church
community.

To speak about the violation of human rights in the church may seem
exaggerated and even disrespectful, when one takes into consideration
the gravity of violations taking place in so many areas of the world.
However, when the right to lead a life worthy of a human being is considered to be fundamental, then not only its most flagrant violation, but
also the continuation of structures that form an obstacle to the implementation of that right can be seen as a violation of human rights. This
is for instance the case with the attitude of the institutional church
towards women and homosexuals. In a broader sense this is also the case
with the way in which the Roman Catholic Church as an institution tries
to maintain and even expand its power over its members, especially
those who in one way or an other are dependent on it. This approach
explains the wide perspective of the book.

The book consists of three parts. The first part has an introductory
character. In the first chapter Ad van der Helm makes an analysis on the
basis of reports from the associated countries about the situation in their
country. This analysis results in a first overview of the most important
problems dealing with justice and unjustice in the Roman Catholic
Church of today. The second chapter, a coproduction by Erik Borgman,
Bert van Dijk and Theo Salemink, is more historical in its approach. It
presents the development of civil society and the notion of justice,
resulting in human rights as its radical and critical expression. The reluctance of the church to acknowledge some of the fundamental human
rights in society as well as inside the church itself, is also questioned.
The third chapter is written by Rik Torfs and describes the different traditions existing in today's Western European legal culture. He draws
attention to the role of the law and the view of law within the discussion
on human rights in the church.

In the second part of the book concrete issues concerning human
rights in the church are studied by prominent scholars from different
European countries participating in the European Conference. The contribution of Ida Raming gives an overview of the situation of women in
the structures of the Catholic Church and discusses the arguments used
to justify the ongoing discrimination of women. Raffaele Botta analyses
the situation of employees in tendency organizations and looks at the
role labour law plays and could play. Another problem, treated by

Antoon Schoors, is that of married priests. Their situation is described and the reasons for the continued defense of obligatory celibacy are discussed. The recent nomination of controversial bishops is the focus of Peter Hebblethwaite's contribution to this book. According to him the present system cannot endure and more responsibility should go to the local churches. Klaus Lüdicke discusses the problem of legal protection in the church. Besides reluctance on the side of church hierarchy there also seems to be a lack of interest to obtain legal protection. Through a historical analysis of church documents, Jan Jans demonstrates that freedom of conscience and research as imposed after the Second Vatican Council implies a return to a pessimistic anthropology. A particular problem is tackled by Knut Walf, namely the German church tax system. In his article he demonstrates that there is more than one reason to oppose this way of financing the church. The situation of gay men and lesbian women as it developed in the Netherlands, is the topic Jan van Hooydonk treats. He sketches the evolution that took place in the course of this century and sees reasons for hope. Finally, Luciano Zannotti describes the impact of the process of Italian democratic development on the relation between the Catholic Church and the state in this country.

The third and concluding part of the book presents more general, underlying topics. Karl-Wilhelm Merks looks at the anthropocentrism of human rights and observes an inconsistency in the attitude of the church. In his contribution Ruud Huysmans investigates how a just use of the power of governance is possible in the church and sees some possibilities for the future. Marie Zimmermann analyses the notion of democracy and looks at its reception in the church. According to her there still exists an anti-democratic mentality in the church.

In the name of the editorial committee I want to express our gratitude towards all those who have contributed to this book: the authors, but also the translators whose names are mentioned at the end of each translated article. Special thanks go to those whose names are not explicitly mentioned, but who have also contributed to this book: John Fennessy, Susan Roll, Keith Carlon and Ward Kennes for proof-reading texts; Miriam Schoors for her indispensable help at the last moment and Knut Walf, who supplied us with the snappy citations on the opening page of this book.

Caroline Vander Stichele
November 15, 1993

SURVEY ON HUMAN RIGHTS
IN THE CHURCH

AD VAN DER HELM

*The debate on human rights in the Roman Catholic Church demands
in the first place a survey of the difficulties that occur in different European countries. On the basis of national reports from several countries,
completed by inquiries about others, Ad van der Helm, who did special-
ized studies on Catholic Church law and human rights law, draws this
survey in order to show the underlying issues such as the so-called
nature of the church that is sometimes considered imcompatible with the
concept of human rights and religious freedom.*

The concept of human rights has become a well-known notion
throughout the world since the Second World War. It has developed into
an issue of substantial political influence and into the object of important
international conferences like the Conference on Security and Cooperation in Europe (CSCE). No country can withdraw itself from the discussions on human rights without being called to accountability by other
countries or by the competent international organisations. Also public
opinion plays a role in these matters which cannot be ignored. Organizations like Amnesty International understand the possible effects of the
public opinion and succeed in mobilising it.

The inevitable risk in the discussion on human rights is that the concept
can easily be applied without a clear definition. This explains why working
on the development and reinforcement of the respect for human rights is a
lengthy and laborious process. Different ideas about human rights are possible and the instruments for the protection of human rights differ a great deal
in procedures and efficacy. They can be complicated and expensive, and
there is the fact that these instruments of protection function with great difficulty. For example, the procedures of the European Commission and the
European Court of Human Rights in Strasbourg take a great deal of time
and money before they pronounce judgment. One can doubt the effects of
these instruments of protection when it takes about ten years before cases
come to an end. Still, the principle remains that these procedures create a
jurisprudence which cannot be ignored. Unquestionably this has a preventive effect on the governments of member states of the convention.

Dealing with human rights, one enters into a complicated discussion that not only touches different categories of human rights, but complicated systems of protection of human rights as well. One right does not equal the other. The right to inviolability of one's body differs from the right of future generations to a clean and liveable earth. Some rights demand that the public authorities refrain from action, others on the other hand require an active intervention in order to protect them. Moreover, rights are not protected to the same degree in the different systems that actually function throughout the world[1]. The European system, with 32 member-states, is generally considered as the most far-reaching of all.

These considerations make us hesitate to propose an elaborate and clear-cut definition of the concept of human rights. At this moment we only can describe human rights as a number of claims that human persons can assert towards other persons and public authorities. These claims are formulated in juridical texts and are claimable in different degrees according to the system of human rights in force. A distinction also has to be made between the juridical effects of human rights and the ethical ones. The Universal Declaration of Human Rights of 1948 is quite limited in the juridical sense, though it is the most famous document. More important — on the juridical level — are the Conventions of 1966 on political and civil rights on the one hand and on economic, social and cultural rights on the other, which are lesser known than the Universal Declaration. Apart from a number of rights these conventions also contain the juridical instruments to accuse nations if they do not respect the articles of the conventions. If a nation refuses to sign, it cannot be forced to observe the conventions; this does not exclude moral pressure. This moral pressure meets the resistance of what is called national sovereignty: to what extent is it permitted for a nation to criticize the internal situation of another country? Often nations invoke national sovereignty which does not allow other nations to meddle with their internal affairs. But is this meddling never justified?

As far as the Roman Catholic Church is concerned, it is striking that the Holy See, subject of international law, repeatedly affirms the principles of the 1948 declaration without signing it or signing other international conventions. The only international agreements signed by the Holy See are the four Geneva conventions and their protocols (1949)

---

[1] Apart from the universal system of the international covenants of 1966, there is the American Convention on Human Rights (1969), the African Charter on Human and People's Rights (1981) and the European Convention for the Protection of Human Rights and Fundamental Freedom (1953).

and the convention against all forms of racial discrimination (1965). Yet the Second Vatican Council (1962-1965) has laid the foundations for a more effective support for the respect for human rights. *Gaudium et Spes* and *Dignitatis Humanae* are ineffaceable milestones. But as we asserted earlier, speaking of human rights demands as well that we transcend the level of principled pronouncements. It demands actual and effective protection of human persons, their convictions and ways of living. Then we may ask the question once again, also to the Roman Catholic Church: what about this level?

The lengthy dicussion about the compatibility of human rights within the church and of a (more) democratic structure of church government with the 'nature of the church' is set aside here for a moment. In spite of the large number of publications there is still no worldwide consensus in these matters that could instigate the ecclesiastical legislator to modify radically the structure of church government so that we can speak of a democratic government or a system of protection of human rights within the church. Apart from this discussion, one can register worldwide dissatisfaction as far as the legal situation is concerned of Catholics who are in a specific position in the church, as employee or theology professor, pastor or nurse in a Catholic hospital, etc.

The influence of the Catholic Church is wider than only the influence of a religious organisation; in some countries it has a tremendous influence on the public opinion and it functions as employer of others than its ministers. In several countries we made an investigation concerning local issues, problems and tensions and the possibilities of handling conflicts as well[2].

The dissatisfaction that we observe is disrespect for the fundamental rights of human persons and Catholics at least according to the judgement of the people and organisations concerned. Yet the code of canon law (1983) established a list of rights among its rules of law, but church authorities find it quite difficult to realise these rights and to give them a reasonable substance. It goes too far today to speak of human rights within the Catholic Church because the ways of enforcing these rights are quite limited. There are no independent institutions where one can lodge a complaint. There is no possibility of a really free judicial judgement. Yet the fundamental rights of Catholics in the code of canon law

---

[2] In some countries organisations linked with the Dutch *Acht-mei-beweging* drafted a national report, namely Germany, Great Britian, France, Italy, Ireland and the Netherlands themselves. As far as other countries are concerned the editorial committee made their inquiries.

offer us the opportunity to evaluate the actual situation in different countries in different matters.

1. Religious Freedom or Freedom of Ecclesiastical Institutions

The first issue that draws our attention is the relation between church
and state. The separation of these two can never be an absolute one for
the churches are not allowed to disobey the civil law and they can only
enjoy the freedom permitted by civil law. Originally the idea of separation of church and state was inspired by the estimation that the church
authorities had too much influence on national political relationships.
The Catholic Church resisted this idea for a long time: the alliance
between throne and altar would be broken. Only with the Second Vatican Council was this attitude of resistance transformed into a positive
assertion.

Today one can observe the process that the Catholic Church invokes
more and more this separation of church and state in order to safeguard
its 'specific nature' from the intervention by the civil law or even to
withdraw itself from the regulations that are generally accepted and
applied in the state. This is even more the case in the area of human
rights that still are in full development. The Catholic Church seems to
use the separation of church and state to minimalize state influence in
matters of human rights on the ecclesiastical relationships. The space
thus created by the separation of church and state varies from one country to another. Countries like Germany, Italy and Spain have signed a
concordat with the Holy See that allows the Catholic Church to organise
its internal affairs according to its own rules to a very large extent. By
concordat ecclesiastical laws are incorporated into civil law[3].

In the Federal Republic of Germany this situation explains that
employees in Catholic schools, hospitals, etc. are employees of the
Catholic Church (this is the same for the Protestant Churches) who can
be appointed and fired according to the criteria of the church itself. State
labour law and juridical protection do not apply to this category of workers. The German state has given a large competence to the churches in
many social matters together with the necessary finances which explains
why the churches have become the second largest employer (with over
600.000 workers). The Catholic church uses this autonomy in order

---

[3] According to the content and the juridical value of the document, we can distinguish
different kinds of concordats, cf. J.-B. ONORIO, *Le Saint-Siège dans les relations inter-
nationales*, Paris, 1989, pp.200-201.

to fire divorced and remarried people and homosexuals as is common practice in Germany. It is questionable whether this is a legitimate use of the liberty given to the churches by concordat. In fact in Italy the situation as far as it concerns teachers of Catholic schools is the same: they are fired if they remarry after divorce or express dissident opinions.

It is not impossible that church and state implement a different set of juridical rules and norms, but the responsibility of the state concerns all citizens. This responsibility watches over the equality of all citizens: the situation of citizens belonging to one group should not be substantially worse than the situation of other citizens. The specific status of churches and their autonomous institutions granted by the new code of civil law in the Netherlands aims at the internal ecclesiastical relationships and cannot be the justification of substantial inequality before the law e.g. in labour law[4].

In other countries there is less liberty for churches: this should be the case for France where the church is subordinate to civil law and labour law as regards its internal affairs. Freedom of religion guaranteed by the constitution though provides a possibility to escape the rules in force. The French Catholic church has in fact no other legal existence than the diocesan association and *de facto* associations. The diocesan association is the legal form in French civil law of Catholic dioceses. The resident bishop is its president and its scope limited to financial management (budget, property and employment) and does not encompass the diocese as a whole. Furthermore labour law governs the employment of laypersons by ecclesiastical institutions. The validity of letters sent by the bishop that contain a ecclesiastical mandate or mission is doubtful when the labour contract has another content — especially concerning the duration of the contract[5]. But still, even in this situation, the ecclesiastical authorities find ways to impose their own criteria: the diocesan association is completely dominated by its president, the local bishop. Most of these associations hesitate to employ laypersons directly in order to evade the legislation on employee councils.

In Italy the legal situation of the Catholic Church is under the dominating presence of the pope, bishop of Rome, as president of the Italian episcopal conference. By the new 1989 law on the state payment of the clergy, the bishops have more influence on the payment of priests, which

---

[4] J.J. OOSTENBRINK, *Een dienstbetrekking van 'godsdienstig karakter'*, in *Een stellig annotator. Opstellen aangeboden aan Dr. J.R. Stellinga*, Zwolle, 1982, p.88.

[5] In 1992, the French bishops state in their most recent document on lay ministers that withdrawal of the *lettre de mission* is not a sufficient legal reason to dissociate a labour-contract. There is no clear legal statute yet for lay ministers in France.

reinforces the episcopal influence on the priests themselves[6]. A reduction in personal liberty is felt by a certain number of Italian priests. Priests and religious who abandon their ecclesiastical statute without permission of the Holy See do not receive any state pension. This also explains the fact that employment of lay persons is still unthinkable in this situation.

Another variation can be found in Ireland. There is no concordat, nevertheless there is no real separation of church and state. The Catholic Church is the most privileged religious institution and its influence on the public opinion is immense. And one only has to think of the legislation on abortion to discover the influence of the Catholic Church, which limits the individual liberty of decision-making. This ecclesiastical influence is clearly visible also in Catholic schools under strong domination of priests and religious. This domination forces teachers to give Catholic religious instruction without reference to their own religious convictions.

2. Fundamental Rights Threatened

One of the rights and freedoms that is most severely threatened is the free expression of opinion. This has another juridical value in church law than in civil and international law, because it is stated in a less absolute manner. It is linked with obedience to the ecclesiastical authorities. Still it is of fundamental importance that Catholics can make known their needs and desires to the ecclesiastical authorities. Obedience never eliminates the proper responsibility of each individual christian (can. 212 §1 and 2). It is not only a freedom, but even an obligation if these opinions concern the well-being of the church. In spite of this important right of christians, boundaries are quite narrow: when the opinions differ too much from what is officially held as Catholic doctrine, people can be sanctioned for the expression of their opinion. Sanctions are very often imposed in the area of labour law (i.e. dismissal from ecclesiastical office). On the other hand in order to avoid these sanctions people tend to submit themselves to a kind of self-censorship (Belgium, Great-Britain, France).

In canons 215, 216 and 299 the freedom of association is laid down. Many associations of Catholic christians are private organisations and

---

[6] This law is an execution of the new 1984 concordat and the 1985 law on financial relations between the Italian states and the Catholic Church.

obtain corporate capacity by civil law. In all countries one can discover tremendous activity by all kinds of organisations. Also public associations are numerous, e.g. *Justitia et Pax, Pax Christi*. In Germany the *Zentralkomitee der Deutschen Katholiken* is a representation of traditional lay-organisations since the 19th century. Lately it begins to free itself from the strong influence of the German bishops. It reproaches them that they try to refuse the dialogue[7]. The private associations can raise controversial issues more easily than public associations can.

The freedom of theological education and research is formulated in canon 218. But in England a Catholic theological institution, the Corpus Christi catechetical institute, is closed down because of the theological views which were held there. Individual theologians are also hindered in their profession. The worst problem is that personal files are treated in secret: the individual concerned is not clearly informed about the allegations made against him/her. The same is the case in the Netherlands as far as the fusion of theological institutions is concerned. A number of professors of theology have to leave because the number of posts is reduced. The dogmatic orthodoxy which is finally submitted to the judgment of the diocesan bishop, and one's private life are used as criteria for dismissal as soon as it is allowed by the fusion procedures. There is some protection by labour law but procedures for merging several theological institutes into one facilitate the ecclesiastical authorities in getting rid of certain professors.

In Luxemburg Catholic religious education is privileged compared to Protestant and Jewish religious education in spite of constitutional neutrality of the state. It is included in the official syllabus of the state school (99,9 % of primary and 80 % of secondary schools are state run). Where religious instruction is not conducted by clerics or members of religious institutions education teachers are paid by the state.

Recently a German bishop refused to give a permission to teach — a *nihil obstat* / no objections declaration — to a feminist theologian who was presented unanimously by a Catholic faculty in a State (!) university[8]. Also in Austria professors of Catholic theology depend on ecclesiastical approbation: only if they received a canonical mission from the bishop will they be paid by the state.

In France there is no civil law protection in ecclesiastical theological institutions. The *instituts catholiques* have a pontifical status and cannot deliver university degrees recognised by the state government. The eval-

---

[7] This issue was raised during the discussion on a paper about pastoral matters.
[8] It concerned the theologian Silvia Schroer in Tübingen.

uation of theology professors is the responsibility of the high chancellor
or the local bishop. Only in Strasbourg, where the concordat of
Napoleon is still in force, professors of theology and canon law teach in
a state faculty; but here the ecclesiastical authorities can still impose its
veto on the nomination of these professors.

Lay persons are able to hold ecclesiastical offices, according to canon
228, and to teach the Christian doctrine, according to canons 229 §1,
759 and 766. The criteria for selecting lay persons evoke protests in several countries. In Germany the ecclesiastical authorities resort to con-
formist lay-persons instead of persons with a more critical attitude
towards ecclesiastical institutions. In the Netherlands several dioceses
try to stop the growth of the number of lay ministers. The arguments for
this policy are quite arbitrary: e.g. the policy of the diocese of 's-Hertogenbosch is not founded on the real competence of lay ministers. Even
in pontifical law in the 1983 code, there is no such basis. It is purely
based on the statistical relation between priests, deacons and lay ministers. Nowhere in juridical sources is this ever mentioned as a juridical
reason for refusing to nominate laypersons as ministers in the church. In
Great-Britain lay ministers remain quite rare; so the canons on lay participation in ecclesiastical offices seem quite irrelevant, unfortunately.

According to canon 278 also priests may invoke freedom of association, together or with others. Complaints about such organisations are
heard in several countries, but for many priests these associations are
considered as a way to cope with the aggravation of professional responsibility. As such the code offers a motive for creating an association of
priests in canon 275, pleading for a bond of brotherhood, which can
reinforce their bond as colleagues, and aiming at cooperation in the common purpose, pastoral work. In Germany we came across a specific
complication for priests: the risk of being betrayed to the ecclesiastical
authorities. Priests who disobey certain ecclesiastical rules because of
pastoral necessities, run the risk that conservative parishioners will
denounce them. Many bishops will not hesitate to take serious measures.
This violates the right of good reputation, which is a right of each Christian (can. 220).

In Italy the financial situation deteriorated since the influence of the
Italian episcopal conference became stronger by the 1989 concordat.
Still the financial policy of dioceses is inscrutable. One can also hear this
complaint in France. Irrespective of purely ecclesiastical norms for the
administration of temporal goods (can. 1284), the code suggests that the
ecclesiastical institution for the administration of those goods take a
juridical form that is valid in civil law as well (can. 1274 §5). With this

suggestion common rules for a proper administration of goods, among others publicity, are also relevant for ecclesiastical administrators. In France the local bishop is automatically president of the diocesan association (i.e. the civil law form of all French dioceses apart from Strasbourg and Metz) and he nominates the other members of the association: the financial situation and policy is by no means the object of public control or debate. In 1991 the diocese of Lyon published its financial survey. It was the first diocese in France (of the 95) ever to do so.

In Germany and Austria, the financial resources of the church are incomparable to those of France. This is due to the system of ecclesiastical taxes levied by the state government, the *Kirchensteuer,* and the financing of the Catholic and Protestant institutions of which we spoke already. Generally this wealth of the churches is considered as the reason why ecclesiastical authorities show little interest in a dialogue with groups of Catholics about the administration of these temporal goods. There is no need for them to create a bond of confidence with Catholics in financial matters in order to stimulate their generosity. Anyhow, Catholics (and even non-Catholic and non-Christian tax payers) are forced to contribute financially!

One has to add the complications of labour law. Canon 1286 is quite clear though very lapidary in its formulation: ecclesiastical administrators must meticulously observe the civil laws pertaining to labour and social policy. In the Netherlands a great deal has been achieved in the labour law for lay ministers and especially in non-ecclesiastical institutions. In ecclesiastical institutions primarily fundamental juridical — apart from theological — differences remain between clerical and lay ministers; secondly church authorities can still impose their criteria for dismissal quite easily. But a procedure for arbitration has been developed which without any doubt has a strong preventive value. The heart of the procedure is the arbitration committee nominated by the two parties, whose decision is absolute for the litigants, whether it is the bishop, the employer or the employee. In Germany employees of Catholic institutions, not only lay ministers, are more vulnerable because of the fact that these are public institutions with their own labour law. But in Germany there is a category that is more independent: the teachers of religion in civil service. They can lose their bishop's permission to teach but not their job. In Austria and Italy payment by the state of teachers of religion depends of the canonical mission given or refused by the local bishop. In France lay persons working in pastoral jobs are numerous, but still the French episcopal conference has not yet succeeded in issuing a covenant specifically for lay ministers in spite of the fact that proposals have been made since 1990.

As we already remarked, canon law is very limited in its possibilities for claiming fundamental rights. On the other hand ecclesiastical authorities have hardly any practice in leaving their own judgments for a juridical examination by a more or less independant institution to see whether they observe canon law. The only administrative appeal is the appeal to a higher authority and finally to the Apostolic Signatura. This procedure has the same problem as the international systems for the protection of human rights: they take a great deal of time. Moreover the outcome of the procedure is actually quite predictable for there is no real separation of legislative, executive and judicial power in the church's juridical system.

A typical English remark is that canon law has a lot of Roman law features. Especially due to its autocratic character, that means that the statute is the main source of law and that the legislator has a decisive influence on the development of the law system. This strikes countries like England and Wales because of their different law tradition: the common law. In these law systems jurisprudence has a far more important influence on the development of juridical notions and rules. From their position common lawyers can relativize more easily this Roman law caracter of canon law. The existence of different law systems indicates a historical juridical development that bears a certain contingency in itself. Apart from this, the remark shows the importance of a law culture: law is not only a set of rules and a number of definitions and procedures but also a culture influencing the (non-)development of certain juridical notions and mechanisms. This law culture will be discussed in a following chapter.

3. Perspective on the Future

Diocesan synods, which are open to lay representation — even by majority — and which may discuss any issue, are regarded as a hope of a progress toward more democracy within the church and as a breakthrough of fundamental rights and freedoms. In France there is an impressive experience of 50 synods held over the last twenty years. They usually involve thousands of people over several years, who experience free expression and debate, as well as democratic methods. A particularly fruitful synod was the one held in the diocese of Evreux (North West of Paris) where the democratic approach was explicit on the side of the bishop himself — Jacques Gaillot — and which has set up representative assemblies at all three levels of the diocese and improved the inner and outer communication. Yet as a rule, the changes brought in by synods remain thin and the risk of disillusion cannot be excluded. Another example is Paris, where such a synod is lacking. Instead of a synod the archbishop started a *marche de l'évangile*. In this way the meaning of the synod as a general assembly has been twisted into a march for which the archbishop determines the direction. Still the diocesan synod is considered in France as a very important way of imposing some changes. In Austria several bishops are restraining pastoral councils at diocesan or parish level. It seems they are afraid of the changes such meetings could effect. In Italy the diocesan synods are severely controlled by the hierarchy.

In other countries diocesan synods are a rare phenomenon. There are private associations of Catholics that try to renew ecclesiastical life. In Great Britain there is the National Council for Lay Apostolate and several women movements, traditional ones like the Union of Catholic Mothers and the Catholic Women's League and progressive ones like the Catholic Women's Network and the Catholic Lesbians Sisterhood. Also very active is the National Board of Catholic Women which is a consultative organ of the English bishops.

In Italy the base communities form an effective network of critical engaged Catholics. Organised in a *Comitato nazionale di legame*, they try to establish an alternative church that abandons power and privileges engaging itself with the poor in society. The base communities take care of persons who are sanctioned by the ecclesiastical authorities in one way or another. In Germany two of the eldest organisations focusing on human rights within the church are the *Oekumenische Arbeitsgruppe Homosexuelle und Kirche* and the *Komitee Christenrechte in der Kirche*. The exclusion of the first one together with other organisations from the official *Katholikentag* in 1980 led to the establishment of a *Initiative Kirche von Unten* assembling about 50 critical Catholic and ecumenical groups and organising since 1992 *Katholikentage von unten* to include women expressively parallel with the official biannual *Katholikentage*. Also groups more obedient to the hierarchy start to protest, e.g. the *Verband der katholischen Buchhändler und Verleger* protested against an attempt of the archbishop of Cologne, Cardinal Meissner, to declare a boycott of a bookseller who had invited for a lecture by Drewermann.

In the Netherlands three groups are energetically working for the renewal of the church: the *Landelijke Beweging Open Kerk*, the *Mariënburgvereniging* and about one hundred organisations that joined the *Acht-Mei-Beweging*. The latter assembles each year about 12.000 people on a national meeting and puts the issue of human rights on its agenda

of activities. This led to several publications concentrating on the
present-day situation in the Netherlands as far as human rights within the
church are concerned. Whereas in the Netherlands some 1400 priests
and lay ministers have joined *Verenigingen van Pastoraal Werkenden*
(clerical and lay ministers), comparable organisations in other countries
do not exist. In France, lay ministers are not inclined to claim their rights
as does the organisation *Droits et libertés dans l'église*. The periodical
Golias represents a group of critical Catholics and publishes detailed
information about hot items in the Catholic church of France and elsewhere.

4. Disrespect for Human Rights

It is commonplace to state that the great difference between human
rights in the church and in the state has its foundation in the different
nature of these entities. Whereas the individual person precedes the
state, and so his/her fundamental rights, in the church one first has to
become a member in order to enjoy rights as a Christian. We dismiss
this opinion for it is too small a basis for church membership.

Several arguments support our criticism. In the first place a vast
majority of Catholics became member by being christened as a baby,
without any personal decisionmaking. Secondly, even the code itself
speaks of a divine vocation as a basis for membership of the church.
Christians are those who are called to exercise the mission which God
has entrusted to the church. In order to exercise this mission they are
incorporated into Christ by baptism and constituted as the people of
God. Becoming a member of the church is a personal religious act, not
just an administrative enrolment. Baptism is a sacrament creating a permanent liaison with the community of Catholics. Thirdly, the rights of
Catholics find their foundation in their human dignity and not in their
church membership[9]: the human person has the right to search for
his/her own way, the fact that he/she belongs to the church does not
eliminate this fundamental right. Finally the classic distinction of the
external and internal forum, also preserved in the 1983 code of canon
law, leaves room for a much more liberal practice than the actual practice of ecclesiastical authorities would suggest. The chapter on sanctions
in the church leaves room for remission in the internal forum i.e. in private whereas in the public (or external) forum a more rigid attitude is

---

[9] Vatican II: *Gaudium et Spes,* no. 26, 29, 41; *Dignitatis Humanae,* no. 6.

prescribed (can. 1355 and 1357). This traditional canonical distinction is an invitation to Catholics to carry a prudent judgment.

5. Ways of Action

Knowing that juridical procedures in order to claim the fundamental rights of Catholics in the church are very limited, there is no reason yet to despair. We can indicate some fields in which active intervention could be effective, though mostly only in the long term. Several times people try to claim fundamental rights in the church by appealing to a civil tribunal. In some cases this might be useful, one can think of labour law conflicts. When the conflict concerns internal ecclesiastical affairs however, like the admission to training in order to become a deacon, this seems hardly effective — which does not mean that any effort would be useless. Secondly, the possibilities of canon law are still not exhaustively implemented. One can think of the procedure in the Netherlands to treat doctrinal complaints against Catholic authors, which is really an achievement. The code of canon law (1983) proposes the creation of an administrative tribunal (can. 1733) for each diocese. A small number of episcopal conferences put it into practice [10]. The third approach would be a more dogmatic one, looking for the anthropological basis of the rights of Catholics within the church. This reflection was begun at the end of the Second Vatican Council, but invites much further development. The following chapters could be a contribution.

---

[10] Namely El Salvador and Nigeria; no European countries though. In the Netherlands the dioceses of Breda and Utrecht installed this kind of tribunal.

ROMAN CATHOLIC TRADITION
AND HUMAN RIGHTS

ERIK BORGMAN
BERT VAN DIJK
THEO SALEMINK

Democratisation of the governmental set-up, more freedom for the laity, freedom of opinion for theologians, freedom of conscience for all church members, equality as to sex and sexual orientation: there is many a plea for them, and in several places experiments are carried out, but there is no breakthrough yet. The hierarchy is afraid of 'human rights in the church', of 'protestantization', and most of all afraid of losing its specificity. But, according to Borgman, van Dijk and Salemink, this seems to be a historical mistake.

On July 14, 1789 the Bastille of Paris was stormed and the French Revolution started. A good month later, on August 26, the new regime proclaimed the 'Declaration of the Rights of Man and of the Citizen'. Its first sentence testifies to a revolution in the concepts of right and politics: "From their birth on people are free and equal; social differences can only be based on the common good". This does not mean that France took the lead. On July 4, 1776 a former British colony, the United States of America, proclaimed its independence and declared that it based itself on a fundamental freedom and equality of all people. The American revolt against colonial power, and the French rising against absolutism, stand at the beginning of the gradual development of the constitutional state in the western world.

In the course of this process the term 'human rights' has become the epitome of a wide variety of rights with different characters. The first category is formed by the *classical human rights* which were formulated in the nineteenth century. They protect the citizen against a powerful state. Every individual can claim a fundamental inviolability as to his or her personal life and body; everyone is entitled to political influence, no matter what race, sex or religion. Everybody is equal for the law. Everyone can claim freedom of conscience and freedom of speech. In the twentieth century, especially in the context of socialism, a new category developed: *social human rights*. They concern the right to work, to health, the right of association, and others. Finally, in recent years attention is paid to what are called | *solidarity rights*: | the rights to peace, development, survival, or an uncontaminated environment[1].

Behind this thematical subdivision lies a historical problem. In this article we simply accept this broad and heterogeneous use of the term 'human rights' and do not take part in the extensive specialists' debate whether such a broad concept is legitimate. Our contribution is historical. We shall outline the developments in the concept of those rights that figure in *present day* discussions about human rights, paying special attention to the ideas found in Roman Catholic circles. As a result we shall, for example, qualify the social commitment of catholics following Pope Leo XIII's encyclical *Rerum Novarum* (1891), as a commitment to social human rights. We shall find, however, that the Catholic Church of the nineteenth century was still so much obsessed by the all-out fight against the classical human rights that the term itself received strongly negative connotations and that the entire concept of human rights was rejected.

1. Man Was Born Free, and Everywhere S/He Is in Chains

Just over two hundred years ago the French Revolution meant the decisive breakthrough of a new way of thinking about European society. The feudal theories, rejected by this Revolution, presupposed a fixed order in which every individual has his or her place. In this world there are some that pray, some that fight, and some that work; from the beginning, it was said, mankind had three sections: those that pray (the clergy), the fighters (the nobility), and the third estate of peasants and craftsmen.

Now this feudal theory, as historian G. Duby shows in his book *Les trois ordres*[2], was from the beginning and first of all mainly a *way of thinking*. The feudal concept of order does not reflect an actual 'natural' harmony in medieval society, as was often supposed in the nineteenth and the first half of the twentieth century. Recent studies show us a very chaotic and centrifugal medieval society. It is exactly in periods when the unity of this society and the harmony between the three estates are in greatest jeopardy, that the feudal concept of order is most cherished. But

---

[1] R.J. DUPUY, *The Right to Development at the International Level*, Alphen aan de Rijn, 1980; F. TANGHE, *Sociale grondrechten tussen armoede en mensenrechten*, I. and II, Antwerpen, 1986-1987; A.K. KOEKKOEK, e.a., *Grondrechten*, Nijmegen, 1982.

[2] G. DUBY, *Les trois ordres ou l'imaginaire du féodalisme*, Paris, 1978.

from the fourteenth century onwards medieval society was fundamentally changed. The economic structures were transformed, centralistic states were born, with absolute sovereigns. These revolutions, irreversible from the sixteenth century onwards, led to fundamental changes in political thinking. New political theories were published about the absolute power of the sovereign (N. Machiavelli; Th. Hobbes), and as a reaction theories arose which formulated the rights of the people apropos the sovereign and the state. In the seventeenth and eighteenth century this resulted in founding the state on the natural rights of everyone and on the common interest (J. Locke, Ch.L. de Montesquieu). This new approach, abandoning the theory of 'order' and basing itself on individual people as 'free and equal beings', was applied in the French Revolution.

The pathos of the later French Revolution is probably best expressed by French philosopher J.J. Rousseau. His book *Du contrat social* (The Social Contract) of 1762 opens with the famous sentence: "Man was born free, and everywhere he is in chains". This is a contradiction that makes clear that social changes are needed to redress man's original freedom. The solution, according to Rousseau, lies in a society in which free consensus and contracts make all people equal *vis-à-vis* the law. In this way, he thinks, a society can develop of free and equal individuals promoting the common good. Thus Rousseau articulates the utopia of the modern democratic state and society. This state does not derive its powers from God or the dignity of the sovereign, but from those that are governed by the sovereign or the state. Free and sovereign human beings, making history themselves and enjoying inalienable rights, are the source of political power.

This utopia has penetrated into modern history because in 1789 it resulted in a political revolution[3]. The rising of the French bourgeoisie is directed against an order based on parentage and custom. The opposite conviction now is that all men are born free and equal and that any social order is only legitimate if, in dialogue with critical reason, it can prove its usefulness. But this principle of universal equality, also expressed in the notion of human rights, has in fact led a double life in the actual history of the past centuries. To be sure, the ancient hierarchical order is challenged by the appeal on freedom, equality and brotherhood, irrespective of birth, estate or class, culture, sex or religion, but it

---

[3] G. BEST, "The French Revolution and the Human Rights," in G. BEST (ed.), *The Permanent Revolution. The French Revolution and its Legacy 1789-1989*, London, 1988, pp.101-127; N. HAMPSON, "The French Revolution and its Historians," *Ibid.*, pp.211-234.

remains — as has already often been pointed out — the social class of the French bourgeoisie which forwards this claim. For, first, the French Revolution is emphatically a *national* revolt, a *French* revolution and no worldwide revolution. In the name of a universal humanity a political turnover within the boundaries of one single country is carried through. And the export of the political ideals of this revolution is, in the nineteenth century, also an export of French state power. It can be maintained that the concrete absolutist shaping of the national state, leading in Europe to such terrible and bloody consequences up to this day, starts in 1789[4].

In the context of this article, however, another matter is even more important. Although recent studies have thrown more and more light on the complicated events round 1789, the final conclusion still is that the French Revolution is the uprising of *only one social class*: the bourgeoisie, composed of the entrepreneurs of a thriving capitalist economy, of the new executives of state officialdom so much expanded in this absolutist atmosphere, and of the new intelligentsia of authors and philosophers who earned their living by generating ideas[5]. On the one hand they wished to see their growing social power translated into political power, on the other they sought to use the modern state power for their own purposes. That the French Revolution was intimately connected with the interests of just one class becomes clear in the fact that, despite the introduction of parliamentary government in many European states which was stimulated by the French Revolution, it is only as late as the First World War that the right to vote is given to those who have no possessions.

2. Human Rights for the Powerless

The notions of freedom and equality, and of universal human rights, led a double life. For after all they turned out not to confine themselves to the nationalist ideology of one class. Also for other classes, groups and people in other countries they proved applicable as a legitimation of their struggle for emancipation. Not, this time, an emancipation from the feudal order, as the bourgeois did, but an emancipation from domination by the bourgeois, or by the patriarchate, or by the colonizing western world. In the nineteenth century the labour class used them to underpin

[4] C.C. O' BRIEN, "Nationalism and the French Revolution", *Ibid.*, pp.17-48.
[5] T.C.W. BLANNING, *The French Revolution. Aristocrats versus Bourgeoisie?* Basingstoke, 1987.

its claim for general suffrage, and women's movements followed suit[6].

It is not illogical either that, in the middle of the nineteenth century, the labourers' movements touched the sensitive spot of nationalism. Labourers, they said, have no possessions and so no native country. "Proletarians *of all countries* unite" is the last sentence in the *Communist Manifesto* by K. Marx and F. Engels (1848). In the second half of the nineteenth century the socialist movement claimed political rights for the labourers. In this same period women started making a stand for their political freedom. The bourgeois women's movement, strong in the USA and Britain, advocated equal rights for women. The socialist women's movement made out a case for general suffrage and so for women's right to vote. On July 4, 1876, at the centenary celebration of the Declaration of Independence, the National Woman Suffrage Association offered American vice-president Thomas W. Ferry a *Declaration on the Rights of Women*. This declaration only applies human rights on women, and this is already radical enough: at this historic moment these women do not ask the government a special favour, no special privileges, no special laws. They say they just ask for justice, for equality, they require that all civil and political rights which the citizens of the United States of America enjoy be also guaranteed to themselves and to their daughters[7].

In the twentieth century, finally, the peoples of the so-called 'Third World' rose against the privileges of white westerners. This century became the century of national liberation wars against western colonial powers; in less than fifty years the European world empires were broken down. In addition, within the western superpowers minority groups revolted against their subordination, the black people in the USA after 1945 being the clearest example.

Just because of their radical option for universal human equality, human rights turn out to be the source of an ongoing emancipation of all social groups, and to function as a border post against the usurpation of power by central authorities. When, in discussions about human rights, reference is made to human nature — men are *by nature* free and equal,

---

[6] W. ABENDROTH, *A Short History of the European Working Class,* London, 1972; E.J. HOBSBAWM, I: *The Age of Revolution. Europe 1789-1848*; II: *The Age of Capital. 1848-1875*; III: *The Age of Empire. 1875-1914,* London, 1962, 1975 and 1987; W. HOFMANN, *Ideengeschichte der sozialen Bewegung des 19. und 20. Jahrhunderts,* Berlin/New York, 1974; I. WALLERSTEIN, *Historical Capitalism,* London, 1983.

[7] H. SCHRÖDER (ed.), *Die Frau ist frei geboren. Texte zur Frauenemanzipation,* II: 1870-1918, München, 1981.

and are *by nature* entitled to ... — this reference should not primarily be understood as the unshakeable foundation of those rights, but as an attempt to create a court of appeal against existing constitutional or common law. In other words: a balanced definition of human nature is less important than the fact that this concept curbs the prevailing legal systems. As the socio-political and economic systems changed, the violations of human dignity turned out to take place in ever different fields. In reaction to this, in the course of time new categories of human rights were formulated.

In the middle of the nineteenth century K. Marx subscribes to Rousseau's pathos of the preceding century: "Man was born free, and everywhere he is in chains". Having made this link, he exposes the weak spot in Rousseau's line of thinking. Man? Where do we find this independent and free individual, whose individual rights should be respected? What gain is there if people acquire political freedom, but die of famine, as was often the case in the Europe of Marx's days and still happens in many Third World countries? Man, Marx says, is an aggregate of social relationships; man, that is the world of men.

Marx raises a point that in the twentieth century also received pride of place in the debate about human rights. Human rights can not be only a matter of guaranteeing political freedom or legal equality. People are also entitled to a decent existence, to work, to a minimum income, to health, to education, to existence as minority groups. So the issue is also: social human rights within a society, and solidarity rights everywhere and in every nation. Article 23 of the Universal Declaration on Human Rights (1948) accordingly mentions the universal right to work.

There exists, however, a tension between the classical human rights and the more recent social human rights. The right to have work and economic security can clash with the classical right to property. The history of the socialist movement shows us this never-ending struggle for these social human rights. Christian social democracy, too, sometimes and with varying vigour, defended social human rights, and a similar commitment is found in the liberal movement. The post-war welfare state, developed in several European countries after World War II, is an attempt to safeguard the citizen's social human rights within the framework of a national state. Since then we have been familiar with the vocabulary of the rights to have a minimum income, to get unemployment benefits, or financial support in illness or old age. A global equivalent of this is the right to receive development aid, although it should be added that the international solidarity rights between the rich North and the poor South have so far hardly been recognized, let alone been effectuated.

During the Eighties Europe and the USA showed a tendency to return to a more conservative government policy laying stress again on the classical human rights such as the right to property, rather than on the social human rights. No longer a border post against the unlimited exercise of state power, the classical human rights become a means to defend the established privileges against those people who, in their turn, want to draw a line.

3. The Defensive Attitude of the Catholic Church

On the eve of the French Revolution in most European countries the Roman Catholic Church still fully clung to the feudal concepts, and operated in close connection with the economic and political order of the *Ancien Régime*. The church was a political and a religious power at the same time. The democratic revolutions and the political doctrine of human rights at the end of the eighteenth century were looked upon by the church as simultaneously theological heresy and political treason. Especially for the higher church executives, mainly recruited from the nobility, the changes meant a traumatic shock. In Italy is was very keenly felt. The political changes in the wake of the French Revolution directly affected Pope Pius IX's secular power and threatened the Papal States. In 1870, during the French-German war, the popes' secular power came to a definite end[8].

Against this background the leaders of the Roman Catholic Church vehemently opposed the new liberal states, the principles of popular sovereignty and a democratic constitutional state, and liberalism as a philosophy; in short: they opposed the practice and the theory of the classical human rights. As early as 1791 Pope Pius VI said the freedom of opinion and action which national conventions assigned to people as inalienable rights, were a blatant revolt against the rights of God the Creator. In his encyclical letter *Mirari Vos* (1832) Pope Gregory XVI called the revolt against the monarchs a revolt against God, a new slavery, and an old heresy which from Luther to the Valdenses had asserted that nobody must be dependent any more. This position was also taken by Pope Pius IX in *Quanta Cura* and *Syllabus Errorum* of 1864.

All the same, the nineteenth century confrontations of the Roman Catholic Church with the modern civil states led to a new view on the

---

[8] *1789: The French Revolution and the Church* (Concilium 1989 no.1); K.-E. LÖNNE, *Politischer Katholizismus im 19. und 20. Jahrhundert,* Frankfurt am Main, 1986.

relationship between church and state, and on their respective characteristics. It was formulated in the doctrine of the *societas perfecta*, in which
the church defined itself first of all as a 'perfect society' — without
claiming moral or religious irreproachability. The church is seen as a
society completely independent of any other society, and having its justification in itself. The church is a world of its own. This doctrine
implies that the state is also a 'perfect society', with its own objectives
and its own justification.

So there are two separate worlds, with their own patterns. It is useful
not to forget the modernity of this doctrine, and to realize it means that
the church adapted to nineteenth century circumstances. In the feudal
concept secular and ecclesiastical powers were not imputed to separate
domains, but church and state were seen as two powers within one single social entity, the highest and final authority falling to the church. But
the doctrine of the *societas perfecta* opposes the rise of the modern secular state which knows just one social reality, classifies the church as a
private organization, and brings to bear its ordering and regulating activities also in those fields that the church used to claim for herself. That is
why the popes of the nineteenth and twentieth centuries defend the
'inalienable rights of the church' against modern liberal and later also
fascist states. The development of an internal statute book (the Codex of
1917) is a logical consequence of the church's self-image as a perfect
society.

The vindication of the rights of the church took several forms in nineteenth and twentieth century Europe. The best-known model is the *Kul-
turkampf* (Italy, France, Germany), an open confrontation with the state.
In other countries, The Netherlands among them, a pragmatic cooperation with the new liberal state was worked out. There, new legislation,
guaranteeing amongst other things religious freedom, gave Catholics
and Protestants equal status for the first time since the Reformation, and
allowed Catholics to set up their own structures within the society (pillar or *verzuiling*)[9]. But here, too, the church only partially identified
with liberal society.

The rise of the modern market economy, the emphasis on technologi-
cal innovations, the formation of big industrial enterprises, the creation
of new class antitheses replacing the 'orderly distinction' of the three
estates, the unlimited accumulation of capital, the internationalization of

---

[9] H. RIGHART, *De katholieke zuil in Europa: Een vergelijkend onderzoek naar het
ontstaan van verzuiling onder katholieken in Oostenrijk, Zwitserland, België en Nederland,* Amsterdam, 1986.

trade, the politics of colonization, in short, the nineteenth century growth of industrial capitalism: it meant a clash with traditional Catholic thinking as well as with the new political system. What was happening ran absolutely contrary to the ecclesiastical doctrine on usury and the church's notion of labour as based on the order of creation. The capitalist system presented itself as a radical reversion of the long-held Christian ethics of economy. For from the first century onwards Christianity had its reservations concerning the pursuit of material gain. This reservation is already visible in the Gospel judgement that one cannot serve God and mammon (Mt. 6:24; Lk. 16:13) and the verdict ascribed to St.Paul that the love of money is the root of all evils (I Tim. 6:10).

When in the nineteenth century Catholics started taking an active interest in the new 'social problem', their approach was strongly anticapitalist. The new economic system was rejected precisely since it destroyed the social and religious nature of man. The outstanding spokesman in this field was Wilhelm E. von Ketteler (1811-1877), who became bishop of Mainz in 1850. From 1848 on he spoke insistently about *Die Großen sozialen Fragen der Gegenwart* (Great Social Questions of Our Time), the title of a collection of six Advent sermons preached that year in Mainz cathedral. He sharply attacks the asocial consequences of the unbridled capitalism of his days, appealing to the theology of St. Thomas Aquinas and especially the latter's doctrine of the value of labour. The Catholic religion, he says, forbids treating human labour as merchandise. Von Ketteler also thinks that the traditional reaction to social problems, viz. charitable deeds, is no longer sufficient in the new period of history. Labourers, also those who are Catholics, should organize themselves in order to counterbalance capitalism with humaneness, and it is the state's duty to take legal measures to protect the social rights of the labourers against the devastating influence of the 'free market'. In summary: in contrast to its reservations about the classical human liberties, in the field of social human rights the Catholic Church has from the very beginning taken a rather radical stand.

At the end of the nineteenth century this anticapitalism was given a new dimension when Pope Leo XIII published his encyclical letter *Rerum Novarum* on the 'social question' in modern capitalism[10]. The

---

[10] D. DORR, *Option for the Poor: A Hundred Years of Vatican Social Teaching,* Dublin/New York, 1983; R. JEURISSEN, *Gods kinderen en de machten: Het Vaticaan en de Wereldraad van Kerken over internationale economische verhoudingen, ontwikkeling en bevrijding 1965-1985,* Utrecht, 1986.

pope acknowledges there is a new time and a new form of economy, but simultaneously he sharply criticizes the violation of basic social human rights. Labourers, he says, fall victims to the inhuman practices of their masters, and to unrestrained competition. Usury and the profit motive meet with no mercy. "In addition, just a few people have gained almost complete mastery in the labour market and in trade in general, so that a tiny group of financial magnates have imposed the yoke of slavery on the immense mass of proletarians." [11]

In the Thirties of the present century this approach led to a dramatic deadlock. In the eyes of the Roman Catholic Church the consequences of the economic recession were unacceptable because they were contrary to the basic social rights. The socialist alternative was also unacceptable. So the church devised a third way between free market and statism. The encyclical *Quadragesimo Anno* (1931) proposed an economic reorganization which does not affect private property, but on the other hand leads to a political structuring of the economy that respects social justice. This is, however, a political structuring that supposes a corporate state, i.e. a state founded on an organic national unity that is not split up by opposing interests. Now this aspect links Catholic thinking with the antidemocratic movements of the interbellum, and they cash in on this [12]. This shows us something of the ambiguity which has always characterized the Catholic resistance against capitalist economy.

4. Ambiguity

In Catholic circles capitalism met with widespread and sometimes even radical criticism, but this criticism was not only inspired by solidarity with its victims. Compassion and economic insights were intricately bound up with other elements. For example with the fear of an economic market mechanism which might expel religion from socio-economic life and from the hearts of the members of the new labour class. And consequently also with the fear of the socialist movement which was looked upon as a dangerous antireligious competitor. But the central factor was possibly the nostalgia for an era in which the church was still in the centre and in which economic relationships were still small-scale and neatly arranged; a nostalgia for the medieval estates, which from the very beginning gave Catholic anticapitalism a restorative ring.

[11] *Rerum Novarum*, no. 2.
[12] T. SALEMINK, *Katholieke kritiek op het kapitalisme 1891-1991. Honderd jaar debat over vrije markt en verzorgingsstaat,* Amersfoort/Leuven, 1991.

The modern reader may see this most clearly expressed in the Catholic position concerning women[13]. In the period before World War I the women's movements — the so-called first feminist wave — focused on equal rights for women and men. The cry for political and legal equality led, in a number of countries, to the formation of non-denominational, 'neutral' women's organizations and to campaigns for suffrage. From the beginning the Catholic Church was very diffident about this. In the second volume of his *Lehrbuch der Nationalökonomie* (1908) Jesuit priest Heinrich Pesch, the leading thinker on Catholic social doctrine before World War I, writes that men and women are really equal as regards their fundamental human essence and the final purpose of human existence, the communion with God. But they are different because of their natural characteristics, a physical, intellectual and mental individuality which suits the natural sexual differences and the ensuing special roles of each sex. He claims this is not a value judgement and does not suggest any inferiority of woman: woman is equal to, but by nature basically different from man. Nevertheless his observations on the female nature lead to a vehement rejection of equal rights for women, the aim of the first feminist wave. Quite a number of prominent catholic authors followed this line and advocated an 'organic suffrage' in regions, municipalities and families: because man is the head of the household, it is only he who gets the right to vote: it is a 'paterfamilias suffrage'.

Now this resistance against legal equality can be seen as consistent with the general Catholic opposition to the classical human rights. But the fact that, at a relatively early date, the church was sensitive to social human rights does not imply an empathy for the feminist struggle on behalf of women's social human rights. The idea that women are entitled to paid work, an income of their own, economic security and independence, collided with the traditional and theologically underpinned Catholic conviction that woman's role is a receiving and nourishing one, and that woman is destined for labour in childbed, nursery and housekeeping. Not a right to work was at stake here, but a duty. And although in the Sixties within the ecclesiastical context a feminist theology and a militant feminist movement were born, in some church circles the fundamental uneasiness regarding women's fight has persisted to our days, as is seen for instance in Pope John Paul's encyclical *Mulieris Dignitatem* of 1988 [14].

---

[13] W. BEINERT (ed.), *Frauenbefreiung und Kirche: Darstellung, Analyse, Dokumentation*, Regensburg, 1987.

[14] T. SALEMINK, E. BORGMAN, "Katholieken en de eerste feministische golf," in B. VAN DIJK, L. HUIJTS, T. VERSTEEGEN (eds.), *Katholieke vrouwen en het feminisme. Een onderzoek door de Acht Mei Beweging*, Amersfoort/Leuven, 1990, pp.14-35.

In recent years historians have sketched a new profile of Catholicism in the nineteenth and the first half of the twentieth century, and in this the ambiguity is explained. Swiss author Urs Altermatt[15] and Flemish author Staf Hellemans[16] see Catholicism as a social movement of its own within the conflicting modernization process of modern history. It reflects the internal divisiveness of modern thinking, and the shaky foundations of faith in progress and the action based on it, which nonchalantly victimizes many people. Catholicism generated a strong feeling of uneasiness regarding liberalism, and regarding the rise of modern economy and modern society. As such it was the social movement of a Catholic group within the infrastructure of modern civil society. It made use of the modern state, general suffrage, the right of association, the achievements of the constitutional state, and the new social civil rights.

It is especially Altermatt who works out the paradox of 'an anti-modernism using modern means'. In his view Catholicism as a social movement, and the social denominationalism it gave rise to in many countries, formed a counter-society and even a ghetto. But it is exactly this counter-society which contributed a great deal to the integration of Catholics in modern society. Catholics came together in separate organizations, but there they learned how to function in modern institutions such as a trade union, a political party, an interest group. The churches did set up organisations of their own, but in them Catholic lay people were trained in autonomous and independent action. "Although from the start Catholic organisations had a defensive set-up," Altermatt says, "they helped Catholics to enter a pluralist and democratic society."[17] Altermatt alludes here to developments after World War II, when the so carefully constructed Catholic ghetto was torn down and Catholics became full participants in modern society. Human rights, too, were approached differently[18].

5. After 1945

The Second Vatican Council (1962-1965) means a radical reversal in what the church thinks of parliamentary democracy and political liber-

---

[15] U. ALTERMATT, *Katholizismus und Moderne. Zur Sozial- und Mentalitäts-geschichte der Schweizer Katholiken im 19. und 20. Jahrhundert*, Zürich, 1989.

[16] S. HELLEMANS, *Strijd om de moderniteit. Sociale bewegingen en verzuiling in Europa sinds 1800*, Leuven, 1990.

[17] U. ALTERMATT, *Katholizismus*, p.62.

[18] E. BORGMAN, B. VAN DIJK, Th. SALEMINK (eds.), *De vernieuwingen in Katholiek Nederland. Van Vaticanum II tot Acht Mei Beweging*, Amersfoort/Leuven, 1988.

ties. This reversal can be seen as the formalization of what the church learned when fascism ruled Europe and dictatorial regimes dominated a number of Third World countries. After the experience of fascist dictatorship which subjected everything and everybody to the state, no flirt with authoritarian or corporative forms of government would be acceptable. As had already happened in Protestant circles, in the Catholic world, too, it was realized that the concept of humanity created as the *imago Dei* (the image of God) was done more justice to in a democratic constitutional state than in an authoritarian regime.

In Vatican II's pastoral constitution *Gaudium et Spes* the swing in ecclesiastical thinking is shown in one single sentence: "It is therefore obvious that the political community and public authority are based on human nature and hence belong to an order of things divinely foreordained; at the same time *the choice of government and the method of selecting leaders is left to the free will of citizens*" (no.74). The constitution also discusses the right to revolt against an unjust authority, a right not unknown in Catholic tradition. The council acknowledges freedom of religion and freedom of conscience for everybody. In the encyclical *Populorum Progressio* (1967) these themes return, but this time from out of the perspectives of the Third World. The right to national self-government is vigorously defended.

Because it accepted democracy and no longer rejected political freedom, in the Sixties the church could also welcome a mixed economy and the welfare state. In the encyclical *Mater et Magistra* (1961), the constitution *Gaudium et Spes* (1965) and the encyclical *Populorum Progressio* (1967), the solution for the problems of capitalism is no longer sought for in a specific Catholic 'corporative economy', but in an association with a secular and composite view of a 'caring state' that guarantees the citizens' social rights, both nationally and internationally (welfare state). The concept of humanity as God's image is used to advocate a modern constitutional state that not only safeguards political freedom, but also social human rights and solidarity rights. In this context a theologically elaborated 'option for the poor' is increasingly brought to bear, although official ecclesiastical statements are less outspoken than for example liberation theology.

During the Eighties the central church authorities led by Pope John Paul II very often pronounced on political and social issues. And increasingly reference was made to 'human rights'. This can also be seen in the most recent social encyclical *Centesimus Annus* (1991), published on the centenary of the first social encyclical *Rerum Novarum* (1891). But in *Centesimus Annus* the ambiguity we discussed before is clearly present. There is a permanent misgiving that in our modern world after the fall of the Berlin Wall religion and morals will suffer. In Christian-democratic circles, too, there is much talk of a 'moral vacuum' and the need for a 'moral revival' given the fact that both liberalism and socialism are facing a crisis.

It is a remarkable development that, in recent years, also the defence of human rights *within the church* has been embarked upon[19]. Exactly because in its official pronouncements the Roman Catholic Church had started to lay so much stress on human dignity and the inviolability of the human person, founding this on the notion of humanity as God's image, and also because with many ups and downs the political liberties had been accepted and social human rights had been defended at an early date, it stands to reason that also within the church the faithful can claim the fundamental rights the modern constitutional state tries to guarantee for them: the inviolability of the human person; equality as to race, sex and sexual orientation; carefulness in procedures; equality of rights; participation and co-responsibility; social justice; freedom of conscience and opinion; freedom of action; respect for privacy. And all those rights should hold good for both clergy and laity, the two 'estates' current canon law distinguishes inside the church.

Here, however, the Catholic Church is burdened by undigested history. Whereas in recent history most Protestant churches in Western Europe carried through a democratization of their structures, on the basis of its fundamental diffidence regarding modernity the Roman Catholic Church hermetically screened off its structures against the entry of civil ideas about human rights and political rights. For this church looked upon itself as a specific and autonomous society alongside civil society, with a code and governmental structures of its own. Civil human rights did not apply inside the church since the church was supposed to belong to a different order of things. The documents of the First Vatican Council (1869-1870) elaborately formulated this anti-modern-state approach. True, Vatican II liberated the church from its isolationism vis-à-vis civil society, but there was no comparable internal development.

Democratization of the governmental set-up, more freedom for the laity, freedom of opinion for theologians, freedom of conscience for all church members, equality as to sex and sexual orientation: there is many

---

[19] E. BORGMAN, B. VAN DIJK and T. SALEMINK (eds.), *Recht en onrecht in de R.K. Kerk. Een onderzoek door de Acht Mei Beweging*, Amersfoort/Leuven, 1989.

a plea for them, and in several places experiments are carried out, but there is no breakthrough yet. The hierarchy is afraid of 'human rights in the church', of 'Protestantization', and most of all afraid of losing its specificity[20]. But this seems to be a historical mistake. The acceptance, after 1945, of human rights in the fields of politics and social relationships has liberated the church from its defenselessness against anti-democratical political trends, and made it possible for it to join others in their efforts for social human rights. In the same way an internal recognition of human rights is indispensable if the church is not to suffer from dramatic sectarianism and loss of social significance. If the church proclaims that all people are equal and have an inviolable dignity, and if it bases these convictions on human being created in the image of God, the present era of history requires the acceptance by the Roman Catholic Church of political and social human rights, both in civil society and the church.[*]

[20] P.A. ARNS, "Kirche und Menschenrechte in Lateinamerika," in J.B. METZ and P. ROTLÄNDER (eds.), *Lateinamerika und Europa: Dialog der Theologen,* München/Mainz, 1988, pp.146-156; J. HULSHOF, "Christenen en de vrijheid van anderen. Mensenrechten als hermeneutisch probleem in de katholieke traditie," in *Tijdschrift voor theologie* 32(1992) 31-56; K. WALF, *Vragen rondom het nieuwe kerkelijk recht,* Hilversum, 1988.

[*] Translation by R. Bunnik

CULTURE OF LAW

RIK TORFS

Within the wondrous world of canon law discussions about law, more often than not, tend to deal with other things. They are no more than thinking exercises about the relationship between canon law and theology. At first sight such an approach may raise some eyebrows. After all, reflections about essence and functioning of secular law are certainly not limited to considerations about the relationship between law and ethics, or about possible cross-links between law and philosophy. But according to the Flemish canonist Rik Torfs there is an historical explanation for the zeal with which canonists fling themselves upon the relationship between law and theology.

1. Law and Theology

As a rule the Code's predecessor, as early as 1917, was interpreted in quite a positivist vein. The rule of law stood by itself. Normally no questions were asked about why the legislator had made it, or which theological roots it had. *Dura lex, sed lex.* This practice caused canon law to become an ill-loved discipline, which hardly elicited any spontaneous interest. Links between law and ideas were practically non-existent. The real theological knots remained outside the canonists' competence. Juridical tricks, such as laying surprising cross-connections, were unthinkable. The canonist was expected to concentrate on the text, and particularly on its historical roots.

The change-over occurred at the Second Vatican Council. From then on rules of law required a sound theological basis. The present Code of Canon Law (1983) is built on the same principle. Pope John Paul II, in his apostolic constitution *Sacrae Disciplinae Leges,* writes that, in a sense, the new code ought to be seen as a great effort to rephrase the doctrine of Vatican II, its conciliar ecclesiology in particular, in terms of canon law [1]. In theory of law, too, the discussion boils down to the

---

[1] Apostolic Constitution *Sacrae Disciplinae Leges, A.A.S.,* 25 January 1983, Vol. LXXV, Pars II, p.VII.

question about the relationship between canon law and theology. There
is the school of Navarra which holds that law and theology are to be
clearly distinguished, although there is an external relationship. For
church authority, in both policy making and doctrine, does in fact super-
vise canon law. The school of Munich holds a different view, with no
essential difference between canon law and theology. They are both theological disciplines with different methods only[2].

To outsiders this discussion, together with a good many other opinions, for that matter, may look funny at times. It is purely academic, and
it does not always seem to take into account that law — irrespective of
its relationship with theology — may have a story of its own to tell. The
specific dynamism of law is, in fact, continuously overlooked. A climate
enabling all attention to be focussed upon the theological positioning of
canon law, also accounts for a number of quite rudimentary and static
views of canon law. Thus some years ago a member of the hierarchy
made the following comparison during a congress of canonists: "In the
body of the church there is for me this (limping) image: theology is the
brains, spirituality is the heart, pastoral care is the face (listening, speaking, seeing, smelling, tasting, ... and is being seen, listened to, and felt)
and law is the skeleton."[3] Law as the skeleton. Our profession suddenly
looks desperate. How can one spend one's life thinking about it and
ceaselessly caring for it?

It is only natural that there should be moments when even the most
pronounced theologically engaged canonist, or the policy orientated specialist can no longer shun deeper questions about law. For deeper questions do not only refer to theological principles.

2. Various Law Traditions

Present canon law, mainly found in the 1983 Code of Canon Law, has
been predominantly influenced by Roman law and by the Western continental law tradition. Nothing to be ashamed of, of course, although one
might conceive of a law system, pertaining to the universal church,
which was also inspired by other law traditions. From time to time, say,
at an international congress, there is a *culture shock* suddenly throwing

---

[2] For further details and for the description of other schools, see M. WIJLENS, *Theology and Canon Law. The Theories of Klaus Mörsdorf and Eugenio Corecco*, Lan-
ham/New York/London, 1992, pp.11-22.

[3] See an intervention in R. TORFS, P. DE ROO and H. WARNINK (ed.), *De
katholieke identiteit van instellingen en organisaties in het recht*, Leuven, 1990, p.13.

new light upon the implicit suppositions of the ecclesiastical law system. Why should canon law's main props be the legal texts, as is the case with the continental traditions? Might it not be just as well in line with the Anglo-American law culture, to pay more attention to the administration of law and to the precedents it creates? Does not a more analytical approach offer a number of opportunities, like a sharper attention for concrete cases, which by a more synthetic, continental approach might remain a little under-exposed?

In a paper he presented to a congress about fundamental rights within the church the Canadian canonist Germain Lesage proposed a more inductive way of arguing, illustrating it by a beautifully apt quotation from the late British prime minister Harold MacMillan: "Latin minds begin by intellectual planning. They give shape to the landscape by roads and towns, aquaducts and villas. The model they create is transferred from paper onto the soil. Non-latin minds create their projects by allowing them to develop slowly according to the natural features of the land. Thus an irregular mosaic is created in full harmony with hills, vegetation and waterways."[4]

This quotation aptly illustrates my point. The Anglo-American *common law* system, by preferring the precedent as the basis for its judgments, develops from case to case. The rule of law is not so much the product of a universal juridical principle than the generalization of a concrete solution. In each case the judge looks for the *ratio decidendi,* the binding rule of law from earlier cases in order to reach a solution. The rule of law, although being a general one exceeding the particular case, remains closely connected with the concrete circumstances from which it developed. Both judges and lawyers argue inductively[5]. The Western continental tradition works quite differently, which means in a deductive way, using abstract principles. The rule of law has often been drawn up in abstract terms by the legislator in order to comprise all possible future cases. So this procedure is quite the reverse, as is perfectly illustrated by the MacMillan quotation.

The preceding text offers unmistakable proof that the question how to deal with ecclesiastical law has not been adequately answered once the

---

[4] G. LESAGE, "Les droits fondamentaux de la personne dans le perspective du 'Common Law'," in E. CORECCO, N. HERZOG and A. SCOLA (eds.), *Les droits fondamentaux du chrétien dans l'église et dans la societé,* Fribourg/Freiburg i.B./Milano, 1981, p.848.

[5] See F. GORLE, G. BOURGEOIS and H. BOCKEN, *Rechtsvergelijking,* Gent, 1985, p.177; M.A. GLENDON, M.W. GORDON and C. OSAKWE, *Comparative Legal Traditions,* St. Paul (Min.), 1985.

law has been given its place in theological thinking. Juridical approaches vary widely. There are certainly more than just the continental and the Anglo-American ones; one could think of the *palaver* and the conciliatory model that comes with it from Bantu law. Theologically speaking it is hard to see that one or the other idea of law should be inferior or superior. The Anglo-American law tradition is no further from God than the continental one. Nor is there any radical option in the Gospel for the Western continental system of law. Yet one finds it hard to ignore the impression that the continental approach suits an institution like the church well (herself its partial off-spring in her structure). Clear rules of law seem to offer more stability than the always slightly woolly and elusive world of jurisprudence. A system much given to palavering will sooner tie up with a dialogical church model than with the hierarchical system we know at present.

Should one now conclude from all this that canon law, inheritor of the continental tradition, is a norm-giving entity from which an unchangeable answer can be produced to each concrete problem? Still canon law as the skeleton? I do not think so. For one thing the church's preference for the continental model is only implicit. It should not — at any cost — be accepted as the sole frame of reference. For instance in the field of marriage law a guiding role can be observed of the Rota jurisprudence, where link-ups with the Anglo-American tradition are recognizable. It is in the very field of marriage law that canonical law practice has developed furthest, producing various thorough juridical discussions. For another thing, the very existence of a rule of law does not justify the conclusion that it should be unequivocal. It does not say what it says. This statement does not exclusively hold good for poetry. The fact that a rule of law constitutes a norm does not exempt it from the principle that it is only communicable by language. I should like to dwell for a moment upon one concrete aspect typical of the wording of such norms.

3. Open Law Norms

The CCL canons contain a good many open law norms. Concepts like 'scandal', 'public welfare', 'just punishment', 'respect', 'obedience' can hardly be called by any other name. Whence this glut of open, multi-interpretable law norms? Two factors are decisive.

First, there is the inescapable observation that canon law has to do with the juridical organization of a religious community. This implies that themes other than trading bills and tax papers take centre stage.

Faith demands a different, more ambiguous vocabulary. This way of thinking is also recognizable in ecclesiastical law. But to settle for the idea that the particular character of the church implies the use of specific vocabulary reveals a smugness found in *sui generis* reasonings shunning all comparisons.

There may be a second cause for the massive presence of vague law norms in canon law, viz. the absence within the church of the separation of powers. No doubt canon 135 §1 (CCL) states that governing power is divided into legislative, executive and judicial powers. But the significance of this paragraph is very limited: governing powers are *distinguished, but not separated*. There is a technical distinction between them, but in actual fact they are all in the hands of one central figure: the bishop within his diocese, the pope within the universal church.

Of course I am aware that separation of powers is no unequivocal concept. There is a difference between Locke who gives the legislator pride of place, and Montesquieu who — through a sociological analysis of driving social forces — develops a juridical theory of the state about the functions to be fulfilled in order to make the community realize its esprit[6]. Moreover, the idea of the separation of three independent powers has been overtaken. As early as 1921 the Dutch specialist of constitutional law C.W. van der Pot wrote that the system had long become obsolete because of, among other things, the increasing blurring of legislative and executive tasks within the European parliamentary democracies[7].

But what is, undoubtedly, to remain characteristic of the separation of powers is the idea of balance and control, for the sake of which impartial and independent administration of justice in particular is highly respected. Exactly that is missing in the church. There is no independent judge to pore over legal texts in case of a concrete dispute. In order to keep his ideas intact and to implement them in society the legislator is given a free hand not to issue crystal-clear and sharply outlined law norms. Why should he bother to write down technically faultless norms, if he is himself the one who later, then in his capacity of supreme judge, interprets the range of these very same norms? The judiciary is not independent, there is no control, so why bother to go to such extreme lengths? Again, as the separation of powers is missing, the legislator not only is not at a disadvantage by the fact of vague law norms, he in fact profits by it. The legislator wields the executive power as well, so the

---

[6] On this topic see J. WITTEVEEN, *Evenwicht van machten,* Zwolle, 1991, pp.50-51.
[7] C.W. VAN DER POT, *De verdeling der Staatstaak,* Haarlem, 1921, p.8.

more open a rule of law is, the more room for policy-making he has as an executive. Tight rules would only hinder him in devising his policy.

From what has been said up till now it appears that the massive presence of open law norms in canon law is due to two causes. First, the specific character of a religious community produces open norms. Secondly, the absence of a separation of powers within the church excuses the legislator from making sharply defined laws. On the contrary, in his capacity of executive he profits by rules of law shrouded in vagueness.

Does all this mean that the entire system with its vague norms is no more than an instrument in the hands of a hierarchical authority holding all powers in a single hand? This would be a false conclusion. Although the existence of numerous open law norms is explained by the church's concentration of powers, their presence cannot be put to good use by the hierarchy only. Open law norms are open to everybody; the ordinary lay person can profit by them. Law norms are there, whatever the reason why they are as they are. The law text holds pride of place. This idea is, indeed, expressed in CCL canon 17 which contains a guideline how a legal text should be interpreted: "Ecclesiastical laws are to be understood in accord with the proper meaning of the words considered in their text and context. If the meaning remains doubtful and obscure, recourse is to be taken to parallel passages, if such exist, to the purpose and the circumstances of the law, and to the mind of the legislator."

So the legislator's intention comes at the bottom end of an enumeration which opens with the proper meaning of the words. The meaning of canon 17 can be agreed with, irrespective of the question whether this proper meaning exists at all, or whether every accepted meaning does not, at least implicitly, carry a value judgment with it. The legislator's will must not take precedence. The legislator is expected to know how to express his intentions verbally. This is no new idea. A most authoritative author like Francisco Suárez (1548-1617) already wrote that a law does not originate through the legislator's will, but through its words[8]. That is what is so attractive about laws. For whatever the intentions that gave rise to the CCL, and however undemocratically decisions were reached, at a certain moment, on 25 January 1983, it was promulgated; ten months later, on the first Advent Sunday, it became law. From that moment on a book of law has a life of its own. This tends to be forgotten. As was mentioned before: the monopoly the hierarchy enjoys in creating the law, is often unjustly and implicitly still assumed at the level of its interpretation.

---

[8] F. SUAREZ, *Tractatus de legibus ac Deo legislatore,* Antwerpen, 1613, 1, VI, C.1, n.13.

Although the Code of Canon Law is issued by the pope – the well-known Dutch canonist Ruud Huysmans in his many publications consistently calls it "the papal book of law"[9] – it can, of course, be read on quite different levels. Open law norms facilitate its reading.

4. Canon Law at Three Levels

Roughly speaking the CCL can be approached on three levels: macro-, meso- and micro level. The first is to assume the position of the pope and his staff. One observes that the Holy Father still has considerable room for policy making. His is the highest, complete, immediate and universal power within the church, which he can freely wield at all times (can. 331). This to our modern ears somewhat pompous sounding list of powers is more than just a piece of rhetoric. Canon 333 §1 grants the pope legal precedence over all particular churches and groups. So he does not only hold power over the church as a whole, but he can also, personally and directly, interfere anywhere in a decisive manner. Canon 333 §3 suppresses any glimmer of doubt about this by stating that there is no appeal nor recourse against any papal statement or decree. Reading the CCL from this angle, at macro level, makes one feel that whoever happens *not* to be pope (and there are quite a few of those in the church) will find himself with no more than a few crumbs.

But it is also possible to look at the code from a meso perspective, viz. from the bishop's position. What can he do, in legal perspective, if he wants to make room for liberating structures? He certainly holds far more trump cards than most bishops seem likely to assume. For one thing the bishop is the interpreter of the universal law. For the very reason that a great many law norms are somewhat vague, quite a few possibilities may be detected. Just one example: in canon 861 §2 it says that, if the ordinary minister, the bishop, priest or deacon is impeded, the local ordinary can nominate others to administer baptism in a valid way. Now the question is what should be understood by "is impeded". Here the discussion is open. Does it mean that within a range of fifty kilometers no cleric is to be found? Or that possibly present clerics must be on holiday or ill? Or could it mean that — for the sake of efficient pastoral care — clerics must not be overburdened with duties that can be performed just as well by a pastoral worker? This last interpretation is legally flawless.

    [9] E.g. in R.G.W. HUYSMANS, *Het recht van de leek in de rooms-katholieke kerk van Nederland*, Hilversum, 1986.

But the bishop has a few more strings to his bow. He may issue particular laws inside his own diocese, although the possibilities are not
limitless. Canon 135 §2 in fine states in no uncertain terms that a lower
legislator cannot issue a law which is contrary to a law enacted by a
higher authority. Yet again this does not mean that in that case the
bishop is powerless over against universal law. In his capacity of executive he still has quite a few possible routes open to him. The CCL (1983)
strongly widens the bishop's authority to provide dispensation from universal law [10]. Whereas according to canon 81 CCL (1917) the bishop
could not in principle dispense from universal laws, the present canon 87
§1 states the very opposite: "As often as he judges that a dispensation
will contribute to the spiritual good of the faithful, the diocesan bishop
can dispense from both universal and particular disciplinary laws established for his territory or for his subjects by the supreme authority of the
church. He cannot dispense, however, from precedural or penal laws or
from those laws whose dispensation is especially reserved to the Apostolic See or to another authority."

Apart from what is said here there are some more limitations to the
bishop's power of dispensation. Canon 85 states that dispensations are
only possible regarding merely ecclesiastical laws; and canon 86
exempts from dispensation all laws containing essential constituant elements of juridic institutions or acts. Moreover, no dispensation is
allowed without a just and reasonable cause (can. 90). But even if dispensation should be impossible, the bishop is not helpless. He can resort
to go-slow action. Without actual rejection of the law itself, the bishop
can reduce its application. With regard to certain duties as a member of
the executive he can adopt a kind of sluggishness. For instance, in order
to prevent an anti-feminine effect of deacons in the liturgy he could proclaim a moratorium in the ordination of deacons, something already
practised by the former bishop of Seattle, Hunthausen, and by bishop
F. Sullivan of Richmond. Although this latter practice is still liable to
discussion [11], there is no doubt that at meso level, within the bishop's
power, there are quite a few creative possibilities. To put it briefly, there
is a strategy in four stages: interpretation of the law, particular laws,

---

[10] On this topic see R.G.W. HUYSMANS, "The Significance of Particular Law and
the Nature of Dispensation as Questions on the Rule of Papal Law," in J. PROVOST and
K. WALF (eds.), *Ius sequitur vitam. Studies in Canon Law Presented to P.J.M. Huizing*,
Leuven, 1991, pp.44-45.

[11] Some canonists advance, not mistakenly, that this moratorium is incompatible
with canon 1026, that strictly forbids to deter a candidate who is canonically suitable for
receiving ordinations.

dispensation and go-slow action. Not a bad packet at all. But as a matter of course, its successful application depends entirely on the bishop's personality.

Next to the view of the law from both macro (pope) and meso (bishop) levels the same code can be read from a micro level, viewed from the individual faithful's angle. The central issues of such a way of reading the law are the duties and rights of all christian faithful (can. 208-223). It is my sincere conviction that these sixteen canons (some of which have only ecclesiastical relevance without any connections with basic secular legal rights) possess all possibilities to be the liberating launching pad of positive church renewal. If it was the legislator's intention to achieve a structural status quo, it was a mistake to include canons 208-223 in the CCL. For all their vagueness they are a Pandora's box, certainly from a conservative ecclesiastical point of view. A number of rules are there, but they might turn out to be explosive. The principle of equality is no longer a mere ornament as soon as it becomes juridically relevant (can. 208). How far does the right of association extend (can. 215)? And what about the right and the duty to express one's views (can. 212 §3)?

Meanwhile it should be clear by now that the law in general and the CCL in particular can be approached from different angles, owing to the numerous open law norms found in them. The result of legal investigative processes will be qualified depending on the angle of approach (macro/meso/micro), without one result being juridically more correct than the other. The point of departure may decide the outcome of the legal argument but not its correctness.

5. Juridical Consequences and Theological Compromises

So far an effort has been made to focus upon the dynamism of the law. The fact that canonical theory of law almost exclusively dealt with canon law's theological statute, and all but completely ignores its own basic rules and opportunities, does not mean that these have nothing to offer. The implicit option for a form of canon law typical of the continental law tradition is less innocent than it looks: it is an option which guarantees the authorities the highest degree of control. But even within a mainly continental type of law system a good deal of room for creative activities remains, through — among other things — open law norms which abound in the CCL. A dynamic view of law further also means that the CCL, although conceived in an undemocratic manner, need not in its interpretation be a continuation of that process. On the contrary, the CCL can be approached on three different levels, the last of which being that of the individual faithful with the duties and rights of all christian believers as its basis.

Critics might react by saying that these levelwise readings of the CCL certainly look interesting, but that they might, within the code itself, cause some sort of short-circuit. Can one, without risk, consider all juridical consequences of the rights and duties of all christian faithful without somewhat impairing the highest, complete, immediate and universal ordinary power in the church, the pope's power? It must be feared that one cannot get round the economic scarcity principle. More rights for the faithful means less power for the hierarchy, even if there is the fullest possible harmony between the two.

These non-imaginary short-circuits, the clashes and collisions that arise, cannot automatically be blamed upon a levelwise approach of the law, or upon the law in general. They are the result of the theological compromises that are found in the Council documents of Vaticanum II. For instance, in the constitution on the church the Vaticanum I doctrine of papal primacy is found alongside the doctrine of the collegial structure of the church ministry. The second chapter of that same constitution about the people of God reflects the *communio* ecclesiology, whereas the third chapter outlines a hierarchical ecclesiology. One can agree with Ernest Henau that these are no compromises in the negative sense of the word. Henau calls for understanding for the difficult and delicate task to realise simultaneously two at first sight incompatible intentions[12].

To understand this is easier for the theologian than for the canonist. The theologian tends to sublimate the contradiction with lyrical fervour; he transcends it by what he usually calls an enriching implementation, or a higher synthesis. The canonist sees things differently. He knits his eyebrows as soon as he is confronted with the absolute papal power on the one hand (can. 331) and with the duties and rights of all christian faithful on the other (can. 208-223), norms which come close to general human rights. The law is at times a pitiless mirror. Rhetoric has to give way to the simple logic of the scarcity principle.

Theological ambivalence, however, provides one more argument for a view of law which allows several angles and levels of approach in equal manner. Even if one should hold the view that the law can, in an almost linear way, be deducted from the underlying theological mass of ideas, this view at once becomes quite relative if those theological roots go

---

[12] E. HENAU, *De kerk: instrument en teken van heil*, Leuven, 1989, p.32.

different ways among themselves. The law reclaims a piece of its liberty, causing the actual view of the law to become more important. This paves the way for different approaches, providing more room for dialogue structures, and for a gradually developing jurisprudence.

6. Conclusion

This contribution was aimed at drawing attention to the role of the law and the view of law within the discussion of human rights in the church. Far too often the discussion around this subject remains too theological. However, as has been pointed out, the law is a far from neutral element in all this. For one thing, there are a great many divergent law traditions. Canon Law is primarily based upon the Western continental tradition, but from a theological point of view it might have been the Anglo-American tradition supporting the system, with perhaps surprising consequences in the practical field. But even on the basis of the present Western continental tradition there is quite a bit of room for a variety of approaches, certainly in view of a wavering underlying theology. Whether the present code is looked upon from a macro, meso or micro point of view, theological orthodoxy has nothing to do with it. In this field the three angles of approach are legitimate. The present discussion is a juridical one. It is far more exciting than one would expect.*

---

* Translation by M. van Buren

WOMEN IN THE STRUCTURES OF THE CHURCH

IDA RAMING

Among the many diverse movements that, in the course of our century, have influenced theology and the life of the church, the women's movement has without doubt been one of the most important, if not 'the' most important. Its demands are a challenge to the church that we must not underestimate. According to German theologian Ida Raming it is of decisive significance for the future of theology and of the church if and how they react to this challenge.

What is the position of women in the Roman Catholic Church[1] and how are they regarded by their fellow Catholics? It was only during Vatican II (1962-1965) that these questions were asked explicitly and emphatically; and in the post-Council period an ever-increasing number of church members rallied to the women's cause.

The movement was sparked off by a personal initiative: in 1962 the Swiss lawyer G. Heinzelmann was the first woman to submit a proposal to the preparatory commission of the Council calling for complete equality of women in the church and the admission of women to all ecclesiastical functions, a demand that she based on a theological rationale. In 1963 her protest was joined by that of German women theologians (J.Th. Münch, I. Müller, I. Raming), who commented critically on the place hitherto allocated to women in the church and the estimation accorded to their contributions. The collected submissions and articles, including two by American authors, were published in a German and English bilingual pamphlet entitled *Wir schweigen nicht länger! Frauen äußern sich zum 2. Vatikanischen Konzil. — We Won't Keep Silence Any Longer* (Zürich, 1964).

1. Attitude of the Hierarchy

With a few notable exceptions, the bishops assembled in the Council were not prepared to heed the requests of the women. In the Council

---

[1] Cf. I. RAMING, *Frauenbewegung und Kirche*, Weinheim, 1991 (2nd ed.); also W. BEINERT (ed.), *Frauenbefreiung und Kirche*, Regensburg, 1987.

documents the question of women's role in the church is treated only in a very general way. The pastoral constitution *Gaudium et Spes* (no. 29) says: "with respect to the fundamental rights of the person, every type of discrimination, whether social or cultural, whether based on sex, race, color, social condition, language, or religion, is to be overcome and eradicated as contrary to God's intent." Yet we must not overlook the fact that this has not been implemented in the actual organization of the church.

The remaining Council documents referring to women in the church, few in number anyway, (e.g. the *Decree on the Lay Apostolate,* no. 9) discuss the place of women in the church only in the context of a new role of the laity, without even mentioning the question of women's ordination. However, the mere fact that the women's issue had been raised by the Council led to an increasing number of publications on this topic, and this in turn had an effect both at the grassroots level and at the level of the hierarchy.

Subsequently several national synods as well as the Roman Bishops' Synod tackled the question, which ensured that the discussion did not cease. Among the national synods was the Joint Synod of German Dioceses (1971-1975), which, in view of the pastoral situation, advocated the admission of women to pastoral offices, e.g. the diaconate, and proposed a commission which was to study the position of women in the church and in society. The German Conference of Bishops decided to constitute such a commission, and the result of its work was the basis of the joint pastoral *On the Position of Women in the Church and in Society*[2].

If we compare this document with earlier declarations of the hierarchy, even in our century, we find that it differs from its predecessors in its basically positive attitude towards the women's movement in the church and in society. The bishops base their arguments on the message of Vatican II and on Pope John XXIII's encyclical *Pacem in Terris,* which refers to women's emancipation as a sign of our times. This leads them to accept the basic equality of all human beings, as proclaimed by St. Paul in Gal. 3:27. They make a number of suggestions for implementing this principle, none of which have so far been put into practice[3]. "The

---

[2] (Verlautbarungen der deutschen Bischöfe, 30), Bonn, 1981.

[3] An example is the petition submitted by the German bishops to the Congregation for Church Reform asking that "women be admitted to all the functions of the priesthood common to all baptised persons, thus granting them equality". There has so far been no response from the Roman authorities. The same fate was suffered by an application to the pope to admit women to the diaconate. (Cf. *On the Position of Women,* pp.19.23 f.)

Church should be a model for a society in which men and women live together as partners with equal rights." By formulating this the bishops admit, at least implicitly, that the reality in the church is still far removed from their utopian target.

We cannot ignore the fact that the position of women in the church and the attitude of the hierarchy towards them as expressed in official declarations are still flawed by an inherent contradiction. On the one hand, women have been, ever since the days of primaeval Christianity, at the receiving end of the preaching of the faith; they have had access to baptism and to the Eucharist, they have been members of the 'body of Christ' and have shared the salvation that arises from all this. In this respect they are in no way inferior to men which the Vatican II Constitution *Lumen Gentium* (no. 32) affirms by saying: "Hence, there is in Christ and in the Church no inequality on the basis of race or nationality, social condition or sex... (cf. Gal. 3:28)." On the other hand there can be no question of equality between men and women in the institutions of the Catholic Church, with the result that there is a marked discrepancy between the unity and equality of the sexes in Christ as proclaimed in Gal. 3:27f. and the reality of the church as we know it.

This discrepancy is reflected in our liturgical services, which are after all, one of the most important ways in which the church expresses itself: While men, as priests and deacons, take the leading roles in the services, while they preach and administer the sacraments, women have been assigned the passive roles: apart from a small number who are allowed to read a lesson or assist with Holy Communion, they are confined to the receiving end of sermons and sacraments. They just make up the congregation. But that is not all. All liturgical prayers and chants are addressed to a God with exclusively male attributes. A well-known German hymn professes: "God is one in Three; the Father created the world, the Son redeemed us, the Spirit chose us". We should point out that *Geist*, the German word for 'spirit', is masculine. In many hymns and prayers the faithful are referred to as 'brother' or 'brethren'. To quote another German hymn: "To Thee, Father, we dedicate bread and wine, the gifts of the earth,... Let us, as Christ's brothers, share in this sacrifice". If women are aware at all of what these texts say, they must feel that they themselves are of no significance, either in transcendent reality or in the visible church.

2. The Impact of Canon Law

Women's activities, not only in liturgy but also in other areas of church life, are limited by canon law. According to Pope Paul VI, the reform of canon law, initiated by Pope John XXIII at the time of Vatican II, aimed at adapting it to the requirements of the modern world... and the needs of the people of God[4].

With regard to women, however, the new law code, which came into force on November 27, 1983, falls short of these aims. In fact, it takes over the traditional conception of a church structured according to status, which the code of 1917 claims to be based on divine order. Thus canon 207 §1 of the 1983 code sets forth that the differences between clerics and lay people were ordained by God. And canon 212 §1 makes quite clear that this means subordination of one to the other: "Whatever the spiritual pastors, taking the place of Christ as teachers of the faith or as leaders of the Church, enjoin must be accepted by the faithful, who should be mindful of their responsibility, which includes Christian obedience." This does not accord with the conception of the "people of God", revived by the Council, which implies the equality of all members of the church.

But this conception was not the guideline for the 1983 CIC. According to canon 1024 women have a subordinate status and owe obedience to those in authority in the church, as their sex bars them from sacramental ordination and thus from the diaconate, the priesthood and the episcopate. This provision is taken verbatim from the earlier code, which says: "Ordination is restricted to baptised men" (can. 968 §1 CIC 1917 = can. 1024 CIC 1983).

The exclusion from the above-mentioned offices means that women can not be responsible for pastoral work. Since they are not ordained they cannot have any powers of jurisdiction in the church, and any share they might have in decisionmaking is strictly limited under the terms of canon law (can. 129 and can. 274 §1 CIC). Moreover they are deprived of influence in the realms of doctrine and morals as well as in legislation.

Here are a few exemples to show what this means in practice: A woman cannot preside at the celebration of the Eucharist; even a convent has to call in a male priest. Women cannot hear confession; even this highly personal function cannot be carried out without a man in the

---

[4] Paul VI's address of 20 Nov. 1965. Cf. Editor's Preface to the American Edition of the CIC, 1983, p.XV. Also R. PUZA, "Strömungen und Tendenzen im neuen Kirchenrecht," in *Tübinger Theologische Quartalschrift* 163(1983) p.163.

leading role. Women are excluded from decision-making in questions of doctrine, e.g. at councils. The New Code of Canon Law was worked out exclusively by men. Thus the equality of the sexes, which women can claim by virtue of belonging to the people of God and which is affirmed in canon 208, is drastically curtailed. The perversion of the human mind that inspired canon 1024 is reflected in a comment by Norbert Ruf (1983): "Unbaptised persons and women cannot validly receive the sacrament of ordination."[5] Neither intellectual nor religious qualification, however high, nor baptism can enable a woman to overcome this obstacle. It is only sex that counts!

Not even among lay people do we find complete equality of the sexes. The closer you come to the altar the more restrictions there are for women. Canon 230 §1 reserves the functions of lector and acolyte to male persons. Women may exercise these functions on particular occasions, but not as permanent offices: they can act as Extraordinary Ministers of the Eucharist; they can baptize, they can even preach, but only during the liturgy of the word or before the beginning of mass (cf. can. 230 §3 and 767 §1). The wording of these canons makes clear that lay people may take over most of these functions only in the absence of an ordained cleric. In other words, lay people, especially women, serve as liturgical stopgaps.

The exclusion of women from ordination has far-reaching consequences even beyond the realm of liturgy. This appears clearly in the situation of women in theological faculties, both in Germany and elsewhere in Europe. In the past professorships of theology were reserved exclusively for priests, and even today this is still largely the case. Since 1972 women have been able to qualify for teaching positions in the faculties of theology in German universities, which means that, in principle, they can be appointed professors of theology; but as long as they are excluded from ordination, they will always be at a disadvantage when competing against ordained male colleages[6]. In fact, there are so far only two women incumbents of professorial chairs in university faculties of Catholic theology and only a small number at *Gesamthochschulen* (institutes combining traditional university courses with professorial training) and *Fachhochschulen* (professional colleges).

Thanks to differently structured university systems, women theologians have better chances in the USA and in the Netherlands. One of the

---

[5] N. RUF, *Das Recht der katholischen Kirche,* Freiburg, 1983 (4 ed.), p.239.

[6] Cf. I. MÜLLER, "Berufsperspektiven katholischer Frauen an deutschen Universitäten," in *Concilium* 21(1985) 454-460: Id., *Die Misere katholischer Theologinnen in den deutschen Universitäten,* Weinheim, 1987.

reasons is that in those countries, a doctorate in theology entitles you to a university appointment, which is not the case in Germany. Since the nineteen eighties a number of women have fulfilled the formal academic preconditions in theology for university appointment (*Habilitation*). It is evident, however, that if they take a critical stance on the treatment of women in the church or tend to teach feminist theology, they stand very little chance of being given the Roman 'nihil obstat' and thus of getting a professorial chair. Owing to the lack of women's influence on theology the entire academic field in this discipline is determined by male attitudes. So here we have another domain where women seem almost nonexistent.

Has the new Code of Canon Law, compared with its predecessor of 1917 and with the pre-Council period, not made any progress with regard to women? This question cannot be answered with a simple no. A few provisions that discriminated against women have been abolished. Among them are canon 742 §2 (CIC 1917), which regulates emergency baptism. In the ranking of persons allowed to administer this sacrament women were relegated to the last place. Similarly, the prohibition for women to enter the sanctuary (can. 813 §2 /1917) has been cancelled. Further positive amendments, few in number anyway, are clearly due to the shortage of priests. Thus, lay people, even women, can take over certain pastoral duties in parishes without a priest (can. 517 §2). Furthermore lay people, including women, can be on the panel of a collegiate church court (can. 1421 §2); they can act as judges in collegiate church courts (can. 1421 §2) and also as church attorneys and marriage advocates (can. 1435) or as trustees of church property (can. 494 §1; 537 and 1282). They can be members of councils with consultative functions, such as parish councils and pastoral councils. We might sum up by saying: The changed position of women in society has not "simply passed over the Church without leaving a mark", but the "decisive changes still remain to be made"[7].

In 1987 the seventh Bishops' Synod, dealing with "the vocation and mission of lay people in the Church and in the world twenty years after the Council", did not bring about a revision of the status of women in canon law. The *propositiones* of the Synod fail to state clearly the equality of men and women in serving at the altar as lectors or acolytes. Nor did they follow up the suggestion that women should be admitted to the diaconate. The only activities recognized as "enhancing women's

---

[7] R. PUZA, "Zur Stellung der Frau im alten und neuen Kirchenrecht," in *Tübinger Theologische Quartalschrift* 163(1983) p.110.

personal dignity" are consultative functions, the preparing of material that is to be used in decision-making and preparatory work for pastoral documents and missionary activities[8]. Apart from that the Apostolic Letter published after the Synod contains only very general recommendations, such as: "It is necessary that the Church recognize all the gifts of men and women for her life and mission, and put them into practice."[9]

3. Justifying Different Roles

Let us now see how the hierarchy justifies the discrimination against women, especially their exclusion from ordination.

If we examine the official documents published by the church since the Council, we shall find a stereotyped line of argument running through all of them. On the one hand they proclaim the equal dignity of men and women, and on the other hand they refer to the specific traits of female nature, which are then used to justify the allocation of different functions to men and women. Here are a few typical examples: "equality is in no way identity, for the church is a differentiated body, in which each individual has his or her role. The roles are distinct, and must not be confused."[10] "Men and women should contribute to the life of the Church according to their specific gifts and share responsibility in the Church and in society. Notwithstanding their different functions men and women have, in principle, the same responsibility and the same rights."[11]

Such statements are generally followed by urgent admonitions against egalitarianism. "Equal rights must not lead to egalitarian and impersonal levelling... The result would be that women would lose their feminine qualities, even their personalities. ... Today we must achieve a closer cooperation of men and women in society and in the Church, so that they may contribute towards the building up of a new world, each according to their specific gifts and creative talents."[12]

---

[8] Cf. *Christifideles Laici.* Postsynodal declaration by Pope John Paul II, 1988, no. 49 and 51.

[9] *Christifideles Laici,* no. 49.

[10] *Inter Insigniores.* Declaration of the Congregation for the Doctrine of the Faith on the Admission of Women to the Priesthood, October 15, 1976, no. 6 (*Origins* 6[1977] no.33, pp.518-524)

[11] "Mann und Frau sollen ihre je eigenen Gaben in das Leben der Kirche und ihrer Gemeinde einbringen und gemeinsam Verantwortung in Kirche und Gesellschaft übernehmen. Unbeschadet ihrer unterschiedlichen Aufgaben haben Mann und Frau grundsätzlich die gleiche Verantwortung und die gleichen Rechte." *Gemeinsame Synode der Bistümer der Bundesrepublik Deutschland,* Freiburg, 1985 (6 ed.), pp.611-612.

[12] "Die Gleichberechtigung darf nicht zu einer egalitären und unpersönlichen Einebnung führen... Das Ergebnis wäre unangebrachte Vermännlichung oder aber

To justify the different roles allocated to the sexes in the church, the hierarchy cannot quote any injunctions given by Jesus. There is no passage in the gospels where he is reported to have entrusted different functions to men and women, nor did he teach that women should be subordinate to men, which was the conception of some of the disciples of the Apostles, rooted in Judaism or in other ancient cultures. Nevertheless, the hierarchy avers that the established allocation of roles is based on God's 'order of creation and redemption'. This idea is expounded in *Mulieris Dignitatem,* an Apostolic Letter by Pope John Paul II, published in 1988[13]. It claims to give us the "anthropological and theological bases that are needed in order to solve the problems connected with the meaning and dignity of being a woman and being a man" (no.1). The Pope interprets certain biblical texts (e.g. Gen. 1:27f., 2:18-25; Matth. 22:16; Luke 1:49; John 2:25) in such a way that the traditional role of women appears as part of God's act of creation, based on His 'eternal plan', and Christ is seen as a 'witness' of this divine order (no. 25). After all, in appointing his twelve Apostles, he chose only men; and at the so-called 'institution of the Eucharist' he again instructed only men to "do this as a memorial of me" (no. 26). Similar arguments are used by the Congregation for the Doctrine of the Faith in their declaration *Inter Insigniores* of 1976[14].

Mulieris Dignitatem does not take into consideration either the fact that Jesus could not simply ignore the social conditions of his time and was therefore not "completely free and independent" in his choice of the Twelve, or the symbolic significance of the twelve Apostles as representing the progenitors of the twelve tribes of Israel who were, of course, all men. What the Apostolic Letter says is that Jesus chose only men because in this way he wanted to "express the relationship between man and woman, between what is 'feminine' and what is 'masculine.' It

---

Persönlichkeitsverlust (der Frau)... Heutzutage geht es vor allem darum, zu einer immer größeren und engeren Zusammenarbeit zwischen Männern und Frauen in Gesellschaft und Kirche zu gelangen, damit sie alle in ihren besondern Reichtümern und schöpferischen Kräften zum Aufbau einer Welt beitragen." PAUL VI, *Wort und Weisung im Jahre 1976,* Vatican City, pp.175-176.

[13] *Mulieris Dignitatem,* no. 1. (Origins 18[1988] no.17, pp.262-283) See also *Christifideles Laici,* no. 50.

[14] *Inter Insigniores,* no. 2. According to P. HÜNERMANN, "Roma locuta — causa finita?" in *Herder-Korrespondenz* 31 (1977) p.209, the declaration itself qualifies this statement by saying that the practice of the Church... constituted only a very low degree of dogmatic obligation and that the arguments based on Scripture and tradition were of limited relevance. See also K. RAHNER, "Priestertum der Frau?" in *Stimmen der Zeit* 195(1977) 291-301.

is a relationship willed by God both in the mystery of creation and in the mystery of redemption" (no. 26).

Moreover the pope interprets the analogy between the matrimonial relation between man and woman and the relation between Christ and his church, set forth in Eph. 5, as confirming the relation between the sexes characterized above. Though there is no basis for this in the text of the Epistle, the analogy is taken to signify that holding office is the male part and making up the flock the female part. The conclusion from all these 'premises' is that women "cannot receive the sacrament of orders and therefore cannot fulfill the function of the ministerial priesthood" [15]. It is especially for the sacramental service of the Eucharist that a male priest is required, for he acts *in persona Christi,* thus expressing in a sacramental manner the act of redemption, in which Christ is the bridegroom and the church his bride [16].

Let us now look at another theological justification of the traditional role of the sexes in the church. Official declarations have recently used Mariology as one of their key arguments in this issue. According to *Mulieris Dignitatem* Mary demonstrates, in an exemplary and most sublime fashion, the "two dimensions of woman's vocation": motherhood and virginity. "Mary is the 'new beginning' of the dignity and vocation of women, of each and every woman" (no. 11). But instead of seeing Mary as 'typifying the Church' as a whole, she is stylized into typifying the lay person [17]. This is, without doubt, a non-biblical anachronism, as the distinction between clergy and lay people can be dated no farther back than the third or fourth century. It was reinforced by the feudal order of the middle ages. The restriction of Mary as the 'archetype of the Church' to the lay element shows the male-centered view with which theologians want to keep women in their subservient positions.

4. Ancient Roots

If we look at the history of the church we see the ancient roots of the subordination of women that 'modern' reasoning, consciously or unconsciously, tries to conceal. The necessary limitations of the present article permit only the tracing of a few representative lines of development.

---

[15] *Christifideles Laici,* no. 51.

[16] *Mulieris Dignitatem,* no. 26; *Christifideles Laici,* no. 51.

[17] Cf. John Paul II, Encyclica *Redemptoris Mater,* no. 26 and 46. A critical analysis of the encyclica is given in I. RAMING, *Frauenbewegung und Kirche,* p.61 ff.

The depreciation of women goes back to the Hebrew Bible and beyond. To illustrate this we can quote such passages as the creation of Eve, who was shaped out of Adam's rib, the fall of man, initiated by Eve's transgression (Gen. 2 and 3), and God's words "Your desire shall be for your husband, and he shall rule over you" (Gen. 3:16), which was erroneously taken to express a divine punishment. The interpretation that these passages were given in the course of church history drastically reinforced the idea that women were both biologically and ethically inferior to men. Women were considered 'secondary works of creation', i.e. not directly created by God, and thus more susceptible to temptation.

The biblical texts quoted above were given a definitely discriminatory twist in some of the apostolic and post-apostolic letters, e.g. in I Cor. 11:3-10 and in I Tim. 2:11-14. It is especially in the latter passage that we find the ontological and ethical inferiority of women proclaimed for the first time in a christian document. Moreover the author of this letter draws practical consequences for the position of women in the christian community: "A woman must be learner, listening quietly and with due submission. I do not permit a woman to be a teacher,... for Adam was created first, and Eve afterwards; and it was not Adam who was deceived; it was the woman who, yielding to deception, fell into sin". Furthermore the admonitions to the christian families in Col. 3:18; Eph. 5:22-33; 1 Pet. 3:1-6, enjoin the subordination of women to men, thus reflecting a development that gained ground in the first half of the second century.

The principle of woman's subordination in marriage and the family was extended to the christian community. Whereas women participated actively in early missionary work (cf. Rom. 16:1 ff. and Gal. 3:27 f., the early christian baptismal rite), their position was debased as christianity gradually adapted to patriarchal society and, at the same time, developed more rigid institutions. Early christian constitutions, e.g. the third century Syrian *Didascalia* and the fourth century *Apostolic Constitutions,* retain and even extend the prohibition of women teaching laid down in I Tim. 2:11 ff. Further stages of development can be traced through the fifth-century *Statuta Ecclesiae Antiqua* and the twelfth-century *Decretum* of Gratian right up to the Codex Iuris Canonici of 1917 and the CIC of 1983, where canon 767 §1 again forbids women to preach. Moreover, the early middle ages revived the purity prescriptions of the Hebrew Bible (Lev. 12:1 f. and 15:19 f.), which were based on the idea that women became unclean through certain physical functions, e.g. childbirth, thus barring them from church offices and from sacred rites.

The disdain of women, which is at the bottom of the prohibition against teaching, appears in its most drastic form in the declaration that woman was not created in the image of God (cf. I Cor. 11:7). This tradition can be traced from Ambrosiaster (fourth century) — "Woman must veil her head because she was not made in God's image" — via the *Decretum* of Gratian (12th century) and Thomas Aquinas (13th century) — "Man is woman's origin and end, just as God is the origin and end of creation as a whole" — and other theologians and canonists, e.g. Huguccio, who saw the reason for woman's exclusion from ordination in her biological deficiency, right up to the *Malleus maleficarum,* the 15th-century handbook on witchcraft. In the manner of a theological summa, this handbook gives a survey of all anti-feminist arguments throughout the epochs of secular and ecclesiastical literature. It comes to the conclusion: "Thus woman, being prone by nature to doubt the tenets of the faith more readily, is also prone to deny the faith more readily, which is the basis of witchcraft" [18].

Are not all these negative ideas about woman and her nature passé? What have they to do with the estimation of woman and her position in the church of today? Do not church documents of recent years, such as the Apostolic Letter *Mulieris Dignitatem* (1988), emphasize the dignity of woman and expressly refer to her as the image of God? True. But where are the consequences of all these grandiloquent assertions of woman's dignity?

An ever-increasing number of Catholic women feel that the assertion of the hierarchy — women have the same dignity as men but are barred from ordination — tend to obscure the issue and are therefore counterproductive. The inherent contradiction that this argumentation tries to conceal, cannot be overlooked: On the one hand scientific enquiry, especially concerning human procreation, and progressive anthropology have rendered the traditional Aquinas-style conception of woman's inferiority untenable. On the other hand the status of woman in canon law, especially her exclusion from ordination, is still basically mediaeval. It is based on the conception of female inferiority, which was handed down from century to century. As long as this is so, all assertions of woman's dignity and of her being created in the image of God are mere words that cannot hide the enormous credibility gap.

Women should be familiar with the history of their oppression if they want to assess their place in the church today and see through the

---

[18] "Also schlecht ist das Weib von Natur, da es schneller am Glauben zweifelt, auch schneller den Glauben ableugnet, was die Grundlage für Hexerei ist." J. SPRENGER, H. Institoris *Der Hexenhammer,* Darmstadt, 1974, p.348.

specious justification of their present-day position, which makes light of their degradation. This should be one of the tasks of pastoral work today. It must be remembered, however, that the long history of discrimination has left women with a feeling of inferiority that may go as far as self-contempt. Indifference, indolence and resignation have blunted many women's sense of honour, thus making them incapable of fighting for their liberation. This explains why so few women have so far been prepared to make this laborious effort. Yet, in spite of all obstacles, it will be possible to find the way from servitude to freedom, trusting in the power of God. The memory of Jesus and the auspicious beginnings of christianity will encourage us and give us the strength to make St. Paul's assertion that "in Christ there is neither male nor female" become reality in the life of the church. By making church practice conform to this basic tenet, women (and perceptive men striving for justice) will humanize men and women and bring us closer to the coming of God's kingdom, which, even now, we can feel to be 'at hand'. *

---

* This chapter is based on I. RAMING, "Die Frauen in der Kirche," in *Stimmen der Zeit* 208(1990) 415-426, which has been slightly modified. Translation by O. Stein.

APPLICATION OF LABOUR LAW

RAFFAELE BOTTA

The general organization of religious associations and denominational authorities within limits of tendency organizations appears to have gradually become the most usual and efficacious instrument by which to exclude - partially or totally - the activities of these associations and authorities from the labour law sphere. According to Italian Canonist Raffaele Botta, this is not only true of Germany, where 'Tendenzschutz' has long-since been subject to legislative discipline, but also in other countries such as France, Spain and Italy where that type of discipline has been traditionally lacking.

On the one hand, tendency would add to the worth of the fiduciary dimension of labour relations between the organization and the secular employee such as to exclude the applicability of the provisions governing individual dismissals to this latter. It concerns particularly the provision concerning obligatory reinstatement of the illegitimately dismissed worker and the irrelevance of the worker's religious opinions on the formation, implementation and resolution of labour relations. On the other hand supposing that the worker was also a member of the association, tendency could not become subject of a community of purpose between employer and employee such as to exclude the configurability of work relations themselves instead, not even alongside, of the necessarily prevailing associative relations.

In Italy, there may have recently been a legislative recognition of the importance of tendency which excluded applicability regarding non entrepreneur employers who carry out non-profit making activities of a political, trade union, cultural, educational nature or pertaining to religion or worship[1]. Yet it extended the sanction of reinstatement of the illegitimately dismissed worker to the so-called minor business concerns.

Actually safeguard of tendency would not appear to form the reason for the different sanctions (which substantially involves reimbursement of damages instead of reinstatement in the place of work) for illegitimate

---

[1] L. 11 May 1990, N° 108, art. 4, 1st paragraph, second part.

dismissal of an employee of a tendency organization. And indeed, the area of partial exemption from the strong stability regime of the place of work is identified in relation to the circumstance by which the activities of a political, trade union, cultural and educational nature or pertaining to religion or worship be carried out in the absence of entrepreneurial characteristics and on a non-profitbearing basis, while any ideological inspiration would appear to be substantially indifferent. The previously mentioned area of exemption therefore appears to be solely reserved to non profit organizations rather than tendency organizations.

The above indicates the failure of the tendency organizations to coincide with employers, towards whom the so-called real safeguard of the worker is not applicable. This failure is also demonstrated by the fact that the real safeguard regime (reinstatement in the place of work) or that of obligatory safeguard (reimbursement of damages alone) is applied to the so-called tendency enterprises, with reference to the employment levels established by law alone, although entrepreneurial nature and profit-making scope could coexist with ideologically oriented activities.

And that is not all. Regarding the system safeguarding against illegitimate dismissal, the law does not even distinguish between workers with tendency tasks and workers with neutral tasks. This would seem to strengthen the assumption that tendency should be considered substantially irrelevant when it comes to the applicability of a certain type of safeguard against individual dismissals to workers employed by such an organization.

1. The Problem of Dismissal

As has developed in doctrine and jurisprudence, the problem of dismissal in tendency organizations has, indeed, been reduced to that of an exceptional justification of the withdrawal of ideological or religious discrimination generally evaluated as illicit almost par excellence. Dismissal in these cases is only justified and considered acceptable if strictly limited to those cases in which ideological loyalty of the employee means unreserved authenticity of the performance. On the one hand, this forces those situations in which tendency, invoked as possibile justification for dismissal, actually becomes the instrument and distinctive mark by which to create a protected market for substantially commercial activities[2]. On the other, those workers with so-called neutral

---

[2] Such as tourist activities organized and managed by a trade union, or educational or shelter and care activities managed by a religious organization.

tasks, unfit to characterize, from a qualitative aspect, the working per-formance according to ideological contents complying with the tendency asserted by the employer, are excluded from the regime of exception from the common discipline governing dismissal.

The Italian law N° 108/1990 therefore does not appear to resolve the true problem, i.e. if tendency can constitute just cause for dismissal of an ideologically unloyal worker. Actually, it declares discriminating dis-missals to be in any case void, regardless of the utilized motivation and subject to real safeguard whichever number of employees are employed by the employer (art. 3). This is a provision of generalized significance which is undoubtedly considered applicable to tendency enterprises or profit-making tendency organizations but which, according to many, albeit in the absence of explicit indications and with certain limitations, should be considered applicable to tendency organizations which are mere non-profit organizations.

Once again, all this would appear to indicate an increasingly relevant safeguard of the worker which could indeed be weakened in the case of ideological labour relations. But this is only the case where the tendency conditioning these relations is qualified, i.e. when it is one of those deci-sively indicated by the law, and pure, i.e. not contaminated by an entre-preneurial typology of the organization or, in any case, by a profit-mak-ing scope. The discretionary and justificatory element of the privilege would, therefore, appear to be identified in the ideal scope of the activ-ity, but qualified by the merit of the activity itself. Almost as though the legislator had wished to code a sort of hierarchy between ideal scopes, worthy of major or minor regulatory consideration[3].

The ascertained increase in the safeguard of the worker cannot fail to reduce the areas of importance of tendency in labour relations, particu-larly accentuating the unescapable and direct possibility of reference to the worker's tasks. It is, in fact, evident that while, within the framework of an entrepreneurial organization, the tendency pursued by the employer drops to accessory character level, the same tendency, which must also be qualified, within a non profit organization can effectively pervade the entire company structure. The intensity of the relation between tendency and tasks is, therefore, more important in the former than in the latter case. Here, the pervasiveness of the tendency can objectively limit the area of neutrality of the tasks themselves.

---

[3] P.G. ALLEVA, *L'ambito di applicazione della tutela*, in F. CARINCI (ed.), *La disciplina dei licenziamenti. Dopo le leggi 10 8/1990 e 223/1991*, Naples, 1991, p.61.

To consider a dismissal for ideological unloyalty as justified can, therefore, only be the result of an interpretation inspired by a particular caution, mindful of the concrete and specific tasks of the dismissed worker. This is even truer when it involves a tendency enterprise - not an organization - or when an off-the-job behaviour of the dismissed worker must be evaluated.

Recently, however, the most frequent justification for dismissing the secular employees of denominational organizations or institutes actually appears to be the way the workers behave in their private lives. Dismissal of a teacher in a Catholic school was considered legitimate in France because the teacher had divorced and remarried[4], while an assistant sacristan was dismissed owing to his ascertained homosexuality[5]. In Ireland, dismissal of a teacher in a Catholic school was considered legitimate because the teacher in question entertained romantic relations with a married man and had become pregnant by him[6]. In Italy, two teachers working at different Catholic schools were considered to have been legitimately dismissed after they had celebrated civil weddings[7].

The Italian cases are rather interesting, not only because of their singularity, but also because they involved teachers with neutral tasks (an English teacher in one case and a physical education teacher in the other). Neither had they publicized the private behaviour which led to their dismissal[8].

---

[4] Cass., Ass. plen., 19th May 1978, in *Gaz. Palais,* 1978, p.464.

[5] Cass. soc. 19th March 1991, in *Gaz. Palais,* 1991, II, *Jurisprudence,* p.599 with note by C. Pettiti.

[6] Case of Flynn v. Power, in *I.R.,* 1985, p.648.

[7] Cass., Sez. lav., 21st November 1991, N° 12530, in *Foro it.,* 1992, I, p.2155 ff., with note by G. AMOROSO, *Ammissibilità, o meno, del licenziamento c.d. ideologico nelle organizzazioni di tendenza;* Court of Florence, 28th February 1992, in *Foro it.,* 1992, I, p.2247 ff. Regarding previous specific edicts, it is worthwhile remembering the decisions of the Magistrate's Court of Palermo on 17th November 1979, in *Foro it.,* 1981, I, p.891, which judged dismissal of a primary school teacher in a Waldensian school unjustified, considering primary school teaching neutral *by definition* in relation to tendency; and of the Magistrate's Court of Milan on 8th January 1980, in *Riv. giur. lav.,* 1981, II, p.204, which considered the dismissal of a drawing teacher, who was living *more uxorio* with the mother of a pupil, ordered by a religious school as equally unjustified, affirming that this behaviour was to be considered insignificant in relation to the labour relations.

[8] The CCNL (National Collective Labour Contract) applicable to the previous cases was that AGIDAE for personel employed by institutes managed by ecclesiastic organizations in which art. 7 establishes in the 1st paragraph that "recruitment is made according to written application where the party in question declares that he is aware of the educational tendency and catholic character of the Institution", while the 3rd paragraph states that "tutors are guaranteed freedom of teaching in order to train learners in observance of the moral, civil and religious conscience of the same and in compliance with the constitutional regulations and training proposal of the institute". However, the only "ideological" sanction established in this particular CCNL is that against the "circulation of periodicals or printed matter contrary to the educational principles of the institute and catholic morals".

However, according to the judges, the merely civil celebration of their weddings amounted to behaviour which questions the ideological line of the school, inducing the teacher to fail in his/her contractual obligations whereby his/her role of teacher had to conform with the dictates and values of the Catholic school, also regarding his/her private conduct, as public expression of compliance with those moral principles, propagation of which he/she had previously supported[9]. In this case, it would be worthless to claim neutrality of the tasks since the cultural line, oriented towards basic options, is evinced whichever the function of the teacher may be[10].

The fact that the teacher celebrated a civil wedding is, therefore, defined actual contractual unfulfilment without investigating whether the circumstance and choice of that particular form of marriage was due to a possibly changed religious conviction and if the choice itself was in some way publicized, explained to the pupils as unquestionable belief, with consequent damage to the image of the institute. Equally apodictically, the supposed unfulfilment is defined serious without indicating the reasons for which it is to be considered as such. By and large, it would appear to be the duty of the worker to bring even the more intimate areas of his/her life in line[11] with the tendency of the employer. This, therefore, would appear to demand total servitude.

No one disputes the fact that safeguard of denominational identity of groups or organizations is an essential aspect of achieved social pluralism, but it is not a totem or, worse, a convenient shield by which to violate the workers' rights. This is especially valid when these are freedom rights and when a behaviour pertaining to private life and not to fulfilment of work is involved, also considering the progressive depersonalization of labour relations which has become the legislative guideline of the past thirty years.

Even if one wished to admit that the significance, in tendency organizations of the worker's private behaviour in the public sphere of the labour relations could be more clear-cut, I do not think there can be any doubts as to the need to evaluate exceptionally important private facts according to objectivity and specificity principles. These facts must also

---

[9] Cass., Sez. lav., 21st November 1991, N° 12530, cit., loc. cit.

[10] Court of Florence, 28th February 1992, cit., p.2249.

[11] "This is because (affirms a well known sentence of the Federal German Constitutional Court) the churches' credibility can depend on the respect shown by their members for church order once they have entered the church's employ, this also affects their way of life. All this by no means 'clericalises' the legal situation of church employees. Rather it is exclusively a question of the substance and scope of their contractual obligations to show loyalty."

be in close and direct connection with the particularity of the relations and with the specificity of the tasks carried out by the worker. They must possess a notable incidence potential on the way in which the work is carried out. The facts must always therefore be sifted by the judge. Although this, more than in other cases, may be conditioned by the ideology of the judge himself, it may never result in a non-critical acceptance of the employer's evaluation, almost as though an inadmissible unquestionableness in merit were sanctioned in relation to an equally inadmissible magisterial right to withdrawal [12].

This would be all the more so were the employer, while remaining a tendency organization, to act for profit-making reasons or through a company organization, as a private Catholic school where fees corresponding to market values had been effectively paid, could undoubtedly be defined. It would, in fact, truly mean blindfolding one's eyes to reality to deny that the previously mentioned school possessed an entrepreneurial character. It would almost be as though a consistent productive activity in private teaching possessing ideological characterization, because of this very ideological characterization was unable to imply the designation of entrepreneur for those carrying out this activity just because it was ideologically characterized. Other entrepreneurs supplying the same type of teaching would unquestionably pertain to the category of entrepreneurs, while they are requiring the same fees and obtaining the same profits but without the ideological description of the product [13].

It is worthwhile remembering that in a sentence of 27th March 1985 N° 47 [14], the Spanish Constitutional Court was able to clearly affirm that the right to establish an educational set of ideas is not unlimited but has

---

[12] V. CARBONE, *Questo matrimonio "civile" non s'ha da fare!*, in *Corr. giur.*, 1992, p.167.

[13] S. NESPOR, *Organizzazioni di tendenza e imprese con etichetta di tendenza*, in *Lavoro 80*, 1989, p.892. For the configurability of the private, also denominational school as enterprise, see R. ROMBOLI, *Libertà di insegnamento e organizzazione di tendenza*, in *Foro it.*, 1978, IV, p.318 ff.; M. COSTANZA, *L'attività scolastica è esercizio d'impresa?*, in *Rass. dir. civ.*, 1989, p.867 ff. Also see S. BERLINGO', *Scuole confessionali*, in *Enc. dir.*, XLI, Milan, 1989, p.923 ff., in particular p.926 f. for relations between importance of tendency and entrepreneurial organization of the schools, plus Magistrate's Court of Rome, (ord.) 10th October 1990, in *Dir. lav.*, 1991, II, p.155 f., according to which the association which manages a school for non-profit making purposes and following payment of fees must be considered industrial enterprise according to articles 2082 and 2195, 1st paragraph of the Civil Code, and is not excluded from the sphere of application of the real stability system in compliance with art. 4, 1st paragraph of L. N ° 108/1990. *Contra Cass.*, Sez. lav., 19th January 1989, N° 253, in *Corr. giur.*, 1989, p.409 ff. with note by G. CASTELLI, *Scuole private e Statuto dei lavoratori*.

[14] In *Rev. esp. der. constitucional*, 1985, N° 15, p.219 f.

its limits in the respect to the constitutional rights. It also implies that a simple disagreement of a teacher with a set of ideas of the centre may not be the cause for a dismissal, if it has not been exteriorized or stated in any of the educative activities in the centre. Thus, also regardless of the certain prevalence of safeguard of the worker over safeguard of the tendency when the dismissed worker carries out neutral tasks, it appears right to retain that, when a worker's decision pertaining to his private life does not become part of an alternative concrete ideological proposal to that of the employer, there can be no ideological conflict between worker and enterprise or tendency organization[15], unless the latter are recognized the right to not only claim doctrinal conformity from their employees, but actual evidence of real values[16].

2. Clergy in Ecclesiastical Organizations

There is no doubt in relation to secular employees of ecclesiastical organizations (and this is also true for that particular category of employees known as sacristans[17]) about the existence of common labour relations subject to labour law doctrine albeit with the already discussed difficulties concerning the qualification of the employer as tendency organization. However notable problems remain when the job is done by

[15] *Contra* Court of Florence, 28th February 1992, cit, p.2249, which considers it of no importance for the "private" behaviour of the tutor to have been made known to the pupils, since "the minimum of seriousness in the denominationally characterized educational activity" would have in any case have been jeopardized.

One could underline that the Apostolic Constitution on Catholic Universities, *Ex corde Ecclesiae* of 15th August 1990, in AAS, 1990, p.1475 ff. contemplates the contribution of both those belonging to other Churches and even that of non-believers towards the accomplishment of university tasks in observance of their religious freedom (see S. BERLINGO', *Enti e beni religiosi in Italia,* Bologna, 1992, p.176 n.118). If this contribution does not distort, one could say *ex lege,* the tendency of Catholic Universities, it is very difficult to believe that a private behaviour of the tutor (which, moreover, has remained exclusively such) is able to cause irremediable conflict with the tendency of the denominational school in question. *Contra* Court of Florence, 28th February 1992, cit, p.2249, according to which the fact that the school pupils are not necessarily of Catholic extraction is of no importance: "il fatto (according to the above mentioned sentence) non impedisce, ed in qualche misura rende più impegnativo il disegno educativo confessionale (associandosi alla missione di proselitismo perseguita dalla chiesa cattolica)".

[16] Regarding this «radical» prospect A. VITALE, *Lavoro e fattore religioso, cit.,* p.390.

[17] See G. DOLE, *Les professions ecclésiastiques,* Paris, 1987, p.201; P. LILLO, *Il rapporto di lavoro dei sacrestani,* in *Dir. eccl.,* 1987, I, p.709 ff. It is interesting to note that art. 15 of the National Collective Labour Contract in force in Italy for sacristans considers "cohabitation of the Sacristan *more uxorio* beyond the Sacrament of Marriage to be serious fact, giving rise to the resolution of the contract for just cause".

someone pertaining to the clergy, even though the work is identical to that carried out by secular employees[18]. These particular difficulties do not appear to be bound so much to the nature of the work, both because the work carried out by the clergy is often no different from that carried out by secular employees and because sacerdotal activity has also been considered possible subject of subordinate or autonomous labour relations[19]. Also the peculiar nature of the relations binding the clerical worker to his institute seems not to be relevant.

In relation to this the prevailing doctrine, backed by consolidated jurisprudence, excludes the possibility of work carried out by the clergy from being considered subordinate labour relations. This work would stem from the special relationship that binds the clerical worker to the institute, i.e. the work is carried out free of charge, rendered in order to attain the religious scope of the institute in question. These type of relations are very often compared to the typical ones in a family community where services, even when they can objectively be considered as work, are always presumed as being rendered free of charge; rendered, it is maintained, *affectionis vel benevolentiae causa*, a presumption that has also been extended to the so-called *de facto* family.

In reality, even if one is convinced there is a similarity between family community and monastic community, this would hardly be of use, at least in Italy, after the family law reform and the new provisions governing family concerns came into force in 1975. These tendentially excluded the presumption that services rendered amongst relations were to be considered free of charge[20], especially when relations collaborate in a family concern, even when the services involve housework. This type of situation can be considered prevalent in monastic communities which, in order to finance themselves directly or indirectly, carry out business activities in which the clerical members of the community are employed.

[18] See G. DOLE, *Les professions*, p.259 ff.; R. BOTTA, *Il lavoro dei religiosi*, Padua, 1984 about the subject and, lastly, L. FICARI, *Lavoro dei religiosi*, in *Enc. giur.*, XVIII, Rome, 1990, with extensive bibliographical references.

[19] Regarding Italy see Cass., Sez. lav., 20th October 1984, N° 5324, in *Foro it.*, 1985, I, p.807 ff. with note by N. COLAIANNI; Cass., S.U., 4th May 1989, N° 2081, in *Quad. dir. pol. eccl.*, 1990/1, p.399 ff., plus S. BERLINGO', *Enti e beni religiosi in Italia*, p.178. Also see EEC Court of Justice, Sect. II, 23rd October 1986 (case 300/84), in *Foro it.*, 1987, IV, p.131 ff., which applies the notion of "unpaid worker" in compliance with art. 1, lett. a), 4th paragraph of EEC regulations N° 1408/71 to the missionary priest who receives sufficient payments from third parties for his activities to fully or partly take care of his needs.

[20] M. PAPALEONI, *Lavoro familiare*, in *Enc. giur.*, XVIII, Rome, 1990, p.7; M. TANZI, *Impresa familiare: I) Diritto commerciale*, in *Enc. giur.*, XVI, Rome, 1989, p.1 ff.

One could, however, interpret the objectively working services of the clergy as cases of unpaid labour considered, not without disagreement, admissible[21]. There is no doubt that entry in force of the outline law on voluntary employment[22] induces one to seriously reflect on the fact that there are interests recognized by the Italian State as being no less worthy of safeguard than that of retribution and fit to characterize the dealings and exclude them from the attractive provisions governing the typical case of subordinate labour relations. In truth, the services rendered by someone subscribing to a voluntary organization do not appear to be similar or assimilable to the services rendered by a clerical worker to the benefit of his institute: these latter services are, as a rule continuous and full time. They amount to fulfilment of a juridical obligation correlated to true subordinate relations strengthened by an absolutely superior duty to obey and submit to hierarchial powers. They are often carried out within the framework of true entrepreneurial activities. By and large, they enable clerical workers to earn their upkeep, the only payment in living means for the work they carry out which is compatible with the peculiarity of their status.

In actual fact and especially if one views the matter according to the provision outlined by the Italian Constitutional Court with sentence N° 108 of 9th June 1977[23], labour relations between the clerical worker and his institute are not excluded because the services the former renders in favour of the latter are objectively work, but because it would not be possible to consider the institute as third party in relation to the clerical worker[24], as the service rendered by this latter should be considered fulfilment of obligations pertaining to the associative relations.

---

[21] L. MENGHINI, *Nuovi valori costituzionali e volontariato. Riflessioni sull'attualità del lavoro gratuito,* Milan, 1989, p.50 ff. On unpaid work for all see R. SCOGNAMIGLIO, *Lavoro subordinato: I) Diritto del lavoro,* in *Enc. giur.,* XVIII, Rome, 1990, p.13 f.

[22] L. 11th August 1991, N° 266.

[23] By issuing this sentence, published in *Dir. eccl.,* 1978, II, p.108 ff., the Court declared the constitutional illegitimacy of the sole art. of law N° 392 of 3rd May 1956 in the part where it excludes church workers who render subordinate work services to the organizations indicated in art. 29 lett. a) and b) of the Lateran Concordat from subjection to the obligatory national insurances for invalidity, old age and tuberculosis. The Court retained that the above mentioned illegitimacy "only exists if the activity of the church worker is carried out in the employment of 'third parties', category in which the religious congregation or order in question could never be considered part".

[24] In Belgium, jurisprudence thus considered that labour relations were only possible if the employer was not the institute to which the clerical worker belonged (Cass. 25th January 1982, in *R.D.S.,* 1983, p.85).

3. Subordination of Employees in Tendency Organizations

The matter yet again poses the problem of compatibility between subordinate labour relations and associative relations. The positive solution to this problem (an opinion actually shared by many in both doctrine and jurisprudence) is of much less interest if the right importance is given to the tendency, typical of labour law, to expand its sphere of intervention wherever it is necessary to safeguard circumstances and relations which, although without all the characteristics of subordination in the technical sense, do amount to an "alienation" of physical or intellectual human energies which can still be considered part of the omnicomprehensive constitutional concept of employment.

Indeed, the fact that art. 35 of the Constitution obliges the Italian State to safeguard employment in all its forms and applications, can reasonably attenuate interest in an extensive interpretation of subordinate employment such as to prevent an unequal safeguard of other working performances. This is even truer now that the deep changes that have occurred in the working world (e.g. the development of the services sector and computer work which have, for example, created many perplexities concerning the traditionally defined boundaries between subordinate employment and self-employment, urging the development of provisions to unify the safeguards) lead one to deny the existence of a unitary notion of subordination in employment and to propose the configuration of different types of subordinate employment instead. All the more so if one considers that safeguard of those who, making a living from their work, find themselves in conditions of need cannot be considered as a gracious activity of the State nor remain entrusted to the categories in question, but which forms a necessary expression of the solidarity of the entire collectivity, with its constitutional guarantee in the combined provision of articles 35, 1st paragraph and 38, 2nd paragraph of the Constitution: thus the social security system appears set to decidedly overcome the sphere of subordinate employment to extend to all categories of workers, to all citizens who earn their living through their work. This because the purpose of social welfare achieved by paying benefits has now become the guarantee of income and no longer that of retribution[25].

---

[25] M. PERSIANI, *Diritto della previdenza sociale,* Padua, 1989, p.14 s. S. BERLINGO', *Enti e beni religiosi in Italia,* p.179 would appear to agree about recovery of elements in labour relations to the benefit of clerical workers, especially in relation to social security.

On the other hand, an increasingly more incisive intervention of the church has developed during the more recent years in defense of employment and the worker. This was first achieved with the Encyclical *Laborem Exercens,* then with the establishment of the Labour Department in the Apostolic See (ULSA) and, lastly, with the Encyclical *Centesimus Annus,* which also strongly urges the State to strengthen the welfare conditions of the citizen who earns his living through his work and to promote a conception of the enterprise as "joint and several community" in which the participation of all is guaranteed. In particular, it is interesting to underline how the apostolic Letter dated 1st January 1989 which established ULSA [26] explicitly defined that particular community formed by all those men and women, priests, clerical and secular persons, who render their services in the Departments and Organizations of the Apostolic See, in the service of the universal church as working community. Thus a labour law doctrine interpretation of the services rendered by clerical workers should no longer arise a prejudicial diffidence if characteristics of human labour include the existence of a prerogative of the person, a duty, a right and, lastly, a service.

4. Social Protection of Clergy and Religious

In this way, I feel that one can finally outline a correct prospect by which to safeguard the activities carried out by clerical workers in fulfilment of the constitutional precept which requires that all working citizens be guaranteed the right to means fit for living requirements in the case of illness, invalidity and old age. And, indeed, there are many countries in which the social security system has also been extended to church workers. Thus a Luxembourg law of 14th May 1974 associated members of religious organizations working in welfare with the social security system. Similarly, French law N° 78/4 of 2nd January 1978 established a series of guarantees against the various social risks to the benefit of ministers of worship and church workers who are not obligatorily subject to a different social security system[27]. Lastly, a Spanish

---

[26] In *AAS,* 1989, p.145 ff. See N. DE MARINIS, *L'istituzione dell'ULSA e la gestione dei rapporti di lavoro presso la Sede Apostolica,* in *Dir. lav.,* 1989, p.243 ff.

[27] In relation to this, one should underline that Cass. soc. 20th December 1990, in *La Semaine Juridique,* 1992, II, *Jurisprudence,* 21844, established that "doivent être affiliés au régime général de la Sécurité sociale des religieux qui, lors d'interventions ponctuelles effectuées à la demande d'un établissement d'enseignement catholique, exercent des disciplines d'ordre profane distinctes de leur function sacerdotale ou religieuse et se trouvent placés sous la dépendance juridique et administrive de l'établissement".

law of 29th December 1981, Royal Decree N° 3325, established that church workers who resided and normally carried out their activities on Spanish territory would be subject to the special social security system for self-employed workers.

Draft bill N° 564 was presented on 6th May 1992 to the Chamber of Deputies in Italy. This proposed to extend the field of application of the social security system to include a category which, justly, possesses the rights to take part in the system itself, thus preventing citizens who have dedicated their activities and work in favour of the community from remaining unprotected in case of need[28]. Examination of the bill would indicate a complete system of safeguard for church workers pertaining to the services they render: church workers employed by third parties would, by and large, be recognized as equal to conventional subordinate workers and would enjoy the social security safeguards typical of this category to which they were extended by law N° 392 of 3rd May 1956. Those who work directly in favour of the institute would benefit from the social security safeguards guaranteed them by the establishing Fund, but always in relation to the service they render, i.e. not because and as they are members of the institute but since they are subordinate workers in a broad sense. The bill thus, in my opinion correctly, takes note that the problem of safeguarding the individual cannot be simply resolved according to the voluntariness by which the relations were established and the possibility of withdrawal from these relations. This is because one must first establish whether the individual can renounce certain of his guarantees of freedom and dignity within the sphere of relations that are actually difficult to renounce and within which he in any case carries out his activity and develops his personality[29]. In these cases, safeguard of the citizen can only be an unrenounceable duty of the State, which cannot consider itself bound by a possibly different denominational (evaluation and) qualification of the objectively working activity rendered by churchworkers to the benefit of both third parties and the institute to which they belong.

Approval of such a bill would finally ensure that church workers, who do not in this way cease to be citizens, are afforded those safeguards they are due in relation to the services they render. This could perhaps

---

[28] The report emphasizes the seriousness of the situation of those members who leave the institute, "who are forced to face life without any previous insurance coverage, since can. 702 c.j.c. fails to recognize their right to receive anything in relation to services rendered" (in relation to this point consult R. BOTTA, *Religiosi (diritto ecclesiastico)*, in *Enc. dir.*, XXXIX, Milan, 1988, p.755).

[29] M.C. BIANCA, *Le autorità private*, Naples, 1977, p.31.

have been ensured by just a little more courage and less denomination-alism on the part of jurisprudence[30].

In fact there has always been a tenacious resistance on the part of the state towards permitting general application of civil labour laws to the relations that these authorities establish with their secular and clerical employees when running and in order to run their various activities (schools, hospitals, hotels, publishing companies, etc.). Traditionally this attitude is justified by the undeniable specificity of the church and the unrenounceable safeguard of its autonomy. Yet canon 1286 obliged church authority administrators to comply with the civil laws pertaining to labour and social policy.

It is probable that the invincible repulsion towards considering cleri-cal employees as workers on the same level as the other employees of the institution is mainly based on a certainly unacceptably misunder-stood assimilation between work and worker. It would be manifestly incompatible with the dignity of the clerical status of a worker if he or she would be demoted as subject of a right contractually guaranteed by the employer.

Although the above mentioned repulsion is much more attenuated in secular employees, there seems to be an - unconfessed - prejudice towards the compatibility between management of a company activity and the religious nature of an organization. This would force these rela-tions to be at least partly exonerated from the application of civil labour laws, especially those pertaining to dismissal, and with greater incisive-ness in relation to other individuals, also qualifiable as non-entrepre-neurs, since recognition of the tendency expressed by these organiza-tions towards their similar condition would in any case prevail.

---

[30] A *denominationalism* which, moreover, appears to be limited to cases concerning the Catholic Church. On the other hand, the following principles are surprisingly affirmed in a case involving the Dianetic institute Association: 1) the religious scope of the asso-ciation would be unable to ascribe a different nature to the labour relations established with the association itself "even though through person also possessing the capacity as associate"; 2) "by now it is considered a consolidated principle that the status of the cler-ical worker and priest loses its importance in comparison with the general character in the provisions of art. 38 N° 2 Cost., also in relation to services rendered by individuals belonging to religious orders of the Catholic Church, since only the status of the worker is taken into consideration". Thus Cass., Sect. I, 9th May 1990, N° 3788, in *Quad. dir. pol. eccl.*, 1990/1, p.395, which refers to Constitutional Court sentence N° 108 of 1977 to back up the above mentioned conclusions.

MARRIED PRIESTS

ANTOON SCHOORS

One of the unprecedented facts of our time is the massive exodus of catholic priests which started in the late sixties and before long took the shape of a real 'priest-drain'. This movement has not yet come to an end, although during recent years the number of those who 'have given up' the ministry has dropped considerably in most European countries. The main reason for this drop is that there are not many priests left. The vast majority of those who leave say that their decision is connected with the problem of celibacy. According to Antoon Schoors, the circumstances under which priests leave the priesthood, the legal procedures, the situation of those involved and, as a matter of fact, the main reason for the movement, viz. obligatory celibacy, has something to do with human rights. In fact, he states, the majority of these priests do not resign the priesthood, but are thrown out because of their marriage.

Although the Code of Canon Law recognizes the freedom of all the christian faithfull in choosing their state of life (can. 219), the legal practice in the Catholic Church shows that this rule of law is quite senseless when priests are concerned. They cannot change their state of life without losing their ecclesiastical position. Let us first look at the legal procedure which leads to dispensation of the obligation of celibacy and at the canonical situation of the dispensed priest[1].

1. The Canonical Situation

Before Vatican II the regulations were very stringent: dispensation from celibacy for priests was practically never granted. Thus the 1917 Code of Canon Law made no provision for dispensation from celibacy and a document published by the Commission for the Authentic Interpretation of the Code of Canon Law in January 1949 is scarcely better: dispensation remained extremely exceptional. The rules of 1964, accord-

---

[1] For this part of my article I am much indebted to dr. R. Torfs, professor of Canon Law at the Katholieke Universiteit Leuven, who allowed me to make use of a lecture he gave on the subject.

ing to which my own dispensation procedure in 1969-70 was conducted, were secret — they were published only in 1971, when they were no longer in force — so that the party concerned did not know them and was practically defenseless. Their approach to the case was strictly judicial and had nothing humane about them. I remember that the *officialis* who questioned me was rather embarrassed: he apologized for the sometimes painful questions and he helped me in formulating the best possible answers. Among other things, these norms provided that "the marriage was to be celebrated in the presence of the local ordinary himself without witnesses and notary and its record must be preserved in the secret archives of the curia".

Since the rules of January 1971, fully published only in April 1972, the approach is no longer judicial but administrative. But quite a few conditions concerning secrecy, the domicile of the dispensed and the exercise of a number of functions, remain attached to dispensation. Under Pope Paul VI, dispensations were granted rather easily, especially after the episcopal synod of 1971. But Pope John Paul II (*feliciter regnante*) felt called upon to abandon this more humane approach. As early as October 14, 1980 new norms were promulgated by the Congregation for the Doctrine of the Faith. They are more restrictive than those of 1971: "A dispensation from celibacy should not be considered as a right which the Church must recognize indiscriminately as belonging to all its priests." "With the exception of cases dealing with priests who have left the priestly life for a long period of time and who hope to remedy a state of affairs which they are not able to quit, the Congregation for the Doctrine of the Faith shall in processing the examination of petitions sent to the Apostolic See accept for consideration the cases of those who should not have received priestly ordination because the necessary aspect of freedom or responsibility was lacking or because the competent superiors were not able within an appropriate time to judge in a prudent and sufficiently fitting way whether the candidate really was suited for continuously leading a life of celibacy dedicated to God."[2] To prove that at the time of ordination the necessary freedom or responsibility was lacking, the petitioner is almost compelled to make the judges of the Congregation believe that he is or at least was mentally not fully balanced.

According to the 1980 rules a dispensed priest is no longer allowed to preach a homily or to act as extraordinary minister of Holy Communion (as lay people can according to can. 910 § 2). He can no longer exercise

---

[2] Cf. J.A. CORIDEN, e.a. (eds.), *The Code of Canon Law. A Text and Commentary*, New York, 1985, p.234.

a directive office (*officium*) in the pastoral domain, a rule which, in fact, does not exclude *all* pastoral work, as the former norms did. In a seminary he cannot assume any task (*munus*), be it that of a professor or an administrator or even a technician. A dispensed priest is apparently extremely dangerous for the well-being of the seminarians. Also in other institutions of higher education which are under ecclesiastical authority the laicized priest is not allowed either to hold an executive office or to teach. And that is much more rigid than the former norms which made a distinction between 'profane' programmes and faculties or institutions where theology was taught or religious education was given. Only humble or administrative tasks are open to him. Even in institutions that are independent of the ecclesiastical authority he should not teach theology or any closely related courses. And also in church controlled schools of a lower level directive tasks or teaching are forbidden, which again is a position worse than under the rules of 1971 in which this interdiction was limited to teaching religion. In schools independent of the church authorities the dispensed priest is no longer entitled to teach religion. And finally he must live in a place where his former status is not known, although the ordinary of the place where he lives can dispense him from this obligation.

The question now is whether all these rules have been replaced by the new *Codex Iuris Canonici* (CIC) of 1983. Canon 6 §14° stipulates that the new Codex abolishes all disciplinary laws concerning a matter which is completely regulated by this Codex. Is this the case with regard to the canonical status of the dispensed priest? An important counterargument is that the dispensation papers always contain a series of conditions, so that one can state that on this point the Codex is not complete, and that with regard to the laicization of priests the stipulation of canon 6 §1.4° is not fulfilled. And it is hard to take action against this procedure, since the autonomy of the supreme authority in the church allows them to add any conditions they want. It does not seem to create a problem for them that there is some inconsequence in the fact of promulgating a new Codex which the legislator himself does not consider to be rigorous enough and which he supplements then with additional rules. Some canonists, and not only progressive ones, have some questions on this point. But in the church there is no separation of powers, so that there is no legal defence against the continuation of the old rulings after the promulgation of the new Codex.

According to canon 290 a cleric can loose his clerical state by a rescript of the Holy See, which can be given to deacons only for serious reasons and to priests only for very serious reasons(!)[3]. However, such

---

[3] There seem to be serious reasons that are not very serious.

a rescript does not entail a dispensation from the obligation of celibacy, which can only be accorded by the pope (can. 291). This shows how keen the hierarchy is on this obligation, which is not one obligation among others but a superobligation. Canon 292 literally rules that "A cleric who loses the clerical state in accord with the norm of law also loses with it the rights which pertain to the clerical state; nor is he bound by any of the obligations of the clerical state, with due regard for the prescription of canon 291 (celibacy!); he is prohibited from exercising the power of orders with due regard for the prescription of canon 976; and by the very fact he is deprived of all offices, functions and any delegated power"[4]. The rights of the clerical status which the person concerned loses certainly imply the title to remuneration and social assistance, as provided by canon 281.

The prohibition from exercising the power of orders is clear. But the deprivation of *all* offices and functions is a far-reaching rule. According to canon 145 §1, an ecclesiastical office is any function, stably or indefinitely constituted in virtue of either a divine or an ecclesiastical regulation, and to be exercised for a spiritual purpose. According to Torfs, this is not limited to offices connected with the power of orders, such as that of a parish priest (*parochus*) or a dean. Offices which can be exercised by the laity are also not open to dispensed priests. This includes, of course, offices which are determined by universal law, such as those of ecclesiastical judge or administrator of church property, but also offices which are created by particular law, such as those of diocesan official responsible for a pastoral sector, e.g. youth care or similar sectorial pastoral offices[5]. In other words, the legal status of a married priest is less favourable than that of a layman.

But that is not all. The married priest also loses all functions (*munera*). And since according to canon 145 §1 an office is a *munus* with a permanent quality, one could conclude that a *munus* is an assignment or task that lacks the permanent quality of an office[6]. That would mean that a dispensed priest is deprived of all functions that are practised in an ecclesiastical context, even the most simple ones. In agreement with Torfs, I think that it is impossible to give a more restrictive interpretation of a *munus*, as suggested by Heimerl, who defines it as a

---

[4] The English version of the canons is taken from J.A. CORIDEN, e.a. (eds.), *The Code of Canon Law* (cf. note 2).

[5] Cf. also can.194 §1: "One is removed from an ecclesiastical office by the law itself: 1° who has lost the clerical state."

[6] Thus J.E. LYNCH, "Loss of the Clerical State," in J.A. CORIDEN, e.a. (eds.), *The Code of Canon Law*, p.236.

non-permanent task given by the church authorities in connection with ordination. His example is that of temporary pastoral guidance of a group of persons[7].

Anyway, the question whether canon 292, as it stands, abolishes the former rules, is practically irrelevant. The Roman administration continues applying the old rules. It is clear that the Roman Catholic Church consists of three classes: the clergy, the lay people and last *and* least the laicized priests. In fact, the juridical position of priests who are married only civilly without dispensation, is better. In the new CIC they are no longer automatically excommunicated but only automatically (*latae sententiae*) suspended from their ministry (can. 1394 §1). But canon 1335 rules that, if such a suspension has not been declared, the priest can administer sacraments or perform administrative acts whenever a member of the faithful requests them, and "this request can be made for any just cause whatsoever". It means that priests who never obtained a dispensation and have contracted a civil marriage, can continue their pastoral work if the faithful request them to do so. The Roman Catholic Church may be a perfect society, but the logic of its Codex is not quite so perfect.

Whereas in the Code of Canon Law the freedom in choosing one's state of life is stated, we must conclude that this freedom is hardly recognized for priests[8]. The importance of obligatory celibacy for priests and bishops is sufficient reason for the church administrators to exclude the application of this freedom from the hierarchical structure. Canon 219 is not respected and we can question whether the reasons of this restriction are really sufficient.

2. The Real Situation

Of course, everybody knows that the real situation is somewhat more complicated and often more humane than these stringent canonical rules. Depending on the countries and dioceses, many dispensed priests are active in catechesis, in the catholic press and radio, in pastoral work, including preaching and other liturgical functions, in parochial and even in diocesan pastoral councils. Sometimes they are even members of important church committees, such as the National Catholic Committee for Ecumenical Relations, and thus represent in some way the Catholic

---

[7] H. HEIMERL, *Der Zölibat. Recht und Gerechtigkeit,* Wien, 1985, p.77.

[8] We didn't speak of married deacons who lack the right to remarry after the decease of their wife.

Church *ad extra*. Whether a laicized priest can in fact exercise such functions or not depends on the good will or, in juridical terms, on the arbitrariness of the local church leaders. And on this point the Vatican authorities are pressing hard on them to apply all the limitations and interdictions rigorously. We have seen in recent years how, for instance in Holland, the newly appointed bishops have no longer tolerated that married priests teach in theological institutions and faculties, and they have endeavoured by all sorts of juridical tricks to oust those who were still in their positions. The local bishops are also forbidden to be in contact with representative organisations of married priests. There are many examples of dioceses and religious orders or congregations that help their laicized priests to get started in their new life, but there are as many, if not more, examples of dioceses that abandon them and even refuse to give them, for instance, a certificate that they have been working for X years in a diocesan school, a certificate which they need in order to obtain the pension they are entitled to. A number of bishops panic when they have to consider a petition for dispensation. They suggest, for instance, that the priest remain in function and take his partner into his house as a housekeeper. They also try by all means to prevent a priest who has fathered a child from marrying the mother, thus preventing him from taking the responsibility for both mother and child.

But even though there appears to be a certain hardening in the official attitude of the church towards the problem, there is no doubt a perceptible evolution in the mentality of the faithful. There are, of course, the many who don't care. But among those who are concerned, lay people as well as priests, there is a growing incomprehension of and opposition to the obligation of celibacy for priests. And this feeling is not limited to querulous or reformist groups in the Catholic Church; on the contrary, rather conservative church members, who regret most of the post-conciliary evolutions, also often find that the obligatory bond between celibacy and priesthood is nonsense. This very day I have just read in a column in the leading Flemish newspaper: "Priestly celibacy should be free or reserved for monks. What Rome teaches on sexuality and the situation of women in the Church presumably will not survive the present pope for long"[9]. I know of more than one parish, rural as well as urban, where the average churchgoers have no problems with married priests

---

[9] M. RUYS in *De Standaard* (Friday, July 6, 1993) p.6: "Het priestercelibaat zou iets vrijwilligs moeten zijn of gereserveerd worden voor kloosterlingen. Wat Rome leert over seksualiteit of de plaats van de vrouw in de Kerk, zal vermoedelijk de huidige paus niet lang overleven."

officiating and do not understand why a married priest should not celebrate the Eucharist. In my own parish some good traditional believers tell the parish priest that he should not worry about his retirement, since I am there to succeed him.

This *sensus fidelium* is sound and might become important for further developments in this matter. People instinctively feel that this heavy emphasis on celibacy is unnatural and even contrary to nature. The way of life of people, not only priests, who dedicate themselves completely to their life-work and therefore sometimes prefer not to marry, commands respect. But the legal imposition of an obligatory celibacy on those who direct the church communities today injures the credibility of the church leadership. For, next to the natural feeling of people in general, educated church members now often have a better knowledge of the historical developments of the church and of the mechanisms and processes that have led to today's structure of the hierarchy and that have governed church policy in different domains, including that of celibacy. It is clear that the emphasis on and the high regard for celibacy and, in general, the almost morbid interest of those celibate hierarchs in sexual matters have their roots in encratic movements in the early church. They are not biblical but rather dualistic and gnostic; in sum, they are not christian but pagan.

3. Deeper Motives of Obligatory Celibacy

A couple of years ago many Catholic believers were shocked by the announcement that the Roman authorities had allowed the ordination of two older married men in Brazil on the condition that they should observe some sort of separation from bed, but not from board. This clearly showed that in this respect the ultimate concern of the church leadership is sex. A priest is allowed to enter into all kinds of relationships, he can engage in many time-consuming worldly matters, such as university teaching, trade-unions or hobby-clubs, and in the case of the two men he may even be married, provided no sex is involved.

This attitude is completely in harmony with the deeper motives for the introduction of the obligatory bond between celibacy and priesthood. The priest as sacrificer had to be pure and sex renders him impure. The ecclesiastical decrees from the time when most of the priests were still married bulge with prescriptions about sexual continence of the priest, for instance before celebrating the Eucharist. Officially other motives have now come to the fore: the priest should be unmarried in order to be completely available for the church or for the Lord. But for those who can read between the lines of history, that is only a sublimation of the sexual taboo. And, moreover, it is an error. God does not compete with humans. What a priest gives to his partner is not taken away from God or Jesus Christ. And as far as ecclesiastical commitment is concerned, it depends on what one means by that. A priest who is a teacher and spends most of his time in the classroom, who prepares classes and corrects homework: what an amount of energy and time that is not spent on pastoral work! Family life as such leaves more room for pastoral duties than the office of a teacher or an administrator of a welfare organisation. Why can in the church the latter be combined with priesthood and not the former? That has nothing to do with being available for pastoral work but everything to do with sexual taboo.

It is often said that the unmarried priest has a special bond of friendship with Christ. All right, but this is true of the married priest as well. The relation between a disciple and Christ has nothing to do with his being married or not. It is not the part of Christ to replace the spouse or husband. Otherwise it would mean that married people are christians of a lesser quality. And in fact they are so in the eyes of church leaders, in spite of all high-sounding words about the sublime state of holy matrimony. For that matter, the canon of the Council of Trent, which states that "it is better and more blessed to remain in a state of virginity or celibacy than to marry"[10], has never been retracted.

As I have just said, if somebody renounces marriage because of his commitment to a cause, this can be meaningful and it *can* be a sign of the Kingdom of God in our midst. But there is no instrinsic bond between any pastoral function and celibacy. The commitment of married people is, in a different form, as meaningful and as much a sign of the Kingdom of God. Moreover, in many instances celibacy is obviously a burden which does not benefit pastoral work. The law of celibacy has been transgressed massively through the ages, including by those who imposed it. And today the many requests for dispensation, the bewildering number of secret and, in some countries non-secret, liaisons of priests and the escape of many priests into compensations that are sometimes hardly evangelical, are as many telling symptoms that should warn the leaders of the church. A good family life is a stabilizing factor in the development of personality and thus a support in pastoral work. I am convinced that married priests have a better chance of being less autoritarian or meddlesome, and in other case less unwordly or shy.

---

[10] Sess. XXIV, can.10: "Si quis dixerit... non esse melius ac beatius, manere in virginitate aut coelibatu, quam iungi matrimonio, anathema sit".

The compulsory bond between celibacy and priesthood has no biblical foundation. In the course of history arguments in favour of celibacy have been advanced, arguments in the domain of spirituality and mysticism. No doubt, the concern about the possible alienation of church property by the family of the priest has also played a part in the development of ecclesiastical legislation in this matter. Also the lust for power of church leaders has played a part: unmarried priests can more easily be manipulated like pawns at chess. But the deeper motive is an antisexual attitude with some Old Testament antecedents (purity laws) and a manicheistic anticorporeal strain. Yet christian orthodoxy has always condemned manicheism: the defenders of imposed celibacy for priests are closer to heresy than the opponents. The question can rightly be asked where church leaders think they have the right to impose such ethically unjustified demands on their pastors.

Meanwhile the number of priests has dropped dramatically in recent decades. Many church leaders continue telling us that celibacy is not the reason for this situation. They are lying and they know it. Otherwise one would have to suppose that they are stupid, and they are not. Of course, today's materialistic style of living is not very conducive to priestly vocations. But this materialistic lifestyle was already there one or two generations ago, when candidates for the priesthood were still counted in the hundreds per year for Belgium and in the thousands per year for Europe. Everybody involved knows that there are many young people, male and female, who are studying theology, are committed to all sorts of social and pastoral work and choose for a pastoral career. Many of them would accept a priestly mission, if they were admitted to the priesthood, but they are not. And a lot of dispensed priests would continue doing pastoral work, if they were allowed to.

Of course, many of those young people and many of these laicized priests would no longer accept a priestly function immediately, because the traditional image of the priest as an unworldly man, an administrator of a mighty organisation or a dispenser of sacraments has lost much of its appeal. And this is not a bad thing. It forces us to rethink the function of a priest in the christian community: more from below than from above, more in terms of community than of hierarchy, more in line with the New Testament image of the *episkopos, presbyter(os)* and *diakonos* than of the Old Testament *kohen* and the pagan *sacerdos, minister sacer, pontifex, hiereus* or *arkhiereus*[11]. The official conception of the priestly

---

[11] Greek *episkopos* means "overseer", *presbyteros* "elder", *diakonos* "servant" or "attendant", *hiereus*, like Hebrew *kohen* and Latin *sacerdos* means "priest, sacrificer" and *arkhiereus* like Latin *pontifex*, means "arch-priest, chief-priest".

function is too static and ontological, not sufficiently dynamic and functional. In this conception the priest is an ecclesiastical functionary not because of his special bond with a community. He is it in himself, because of an indelible mark which remains ontologically impressed on his person. Therefore the world is full of priests without a community and there are quite a number of bishops without a diocese[12], whereas on the other hand there are many more communities without a priest.

4. What Can Be Done?

This consideration leads us to the question what we can do about this problem of celibacy and the large group of laicized priests. There is no easy or straight answer to this question. As long as the present juridical system in the church is operative, laicized priests should form unions in order to help each other and to defend their human rights to follow their conscience and to a decent living, if necessary with the help of civil law. This is what they are already doing worldwide[13]. In this action cooperation is needed with all sorts of organizations which devote themselves to the promotion of human rights and to the development of a more open management within the church. This is not an easy struggle, for the real social and political power of the church as an institution is still very strong in a number of European countries and civil law mostly tends to consider these problems as belonging to the sphere of the 'right of association' or 'freedom of religion'. As for the fundamental problem itself, it would be solved by the abolition of the obligation of celibacy for priests. On this point one might consider entering into a dialogue with the ecclesiastical hierarchy about the desirability of such an abolition. But many of us have experienced that such a dialogue is simply impossible. The best illustration is the 1990 Synod of Bishops in Rome on education to the priesthood, where the question of celibacy was not on the agenda and was even forbidden as a subject of discussion. Another token of this unwillingness to dialogue is the prohition for bishops to make contact with the associations of married priests.

---

[12] Let us be serious and pass over the farce of the titular sees.

[13] There is an International Federation of Married Catholic Priests, which has its secretariat in Spain, Pasco de la bastellana 159/10c, 28046 Madrid. The president is Julio Perez Penillos from Spain. There are affiliated unions in Argentina, Austria, Belgium, Brasil, Canada, Czechia, England, France, Germany, Ireland, Italy, Malta, the Netherlands, Paraguay, the Philippines, Portugal, Spain, and the US. The federation has also contacts with groups in Chile, Ecuador, Haiti, Hungary, India, Madagascar, Mexico, South Africa, Sri Lanka and Switzerland. The federation publishes a half-yearly bulletin and organizes an international congress each second or third year.

In the long run it might be more useful to further develop the feeling among the faithful that obligatory celibacy is wrong and that the hierarchy has no right to impose it. It is high time to return to the sound principle the apostle James expounded at the Council of Jerusalem with respect to circumcision: "that we should impose no irksome restrictions" (Acts 15:19). It is also important to set the problem in a broader context. There are obvious connections with the question of the admission of women to the priesthood, and the struggle for the abolition of compulsory celibacy should go hand in hand with that for full equality of the sexes in the pastoral administration of the church. And finally it seems necessary to deal with these problems in the framework of a more evangelical concept of pastoral leadership in the church. The church as the community of the disciples of Christ needs a structure for the pastoral office. The christian life of the individual as well as of the community needs guidance, encouragement, inspiration, nourishment. That is precisely the function of the pastor, the shepherd who offers these services to his community. According to the needs of the congregation or parish, pastors should be elected from, or at least by, that congregation and then inducted. Thus we do not mean here men who first are 'elevated' to a priestly class and for whom then only a congregation is chosen. The pastors should be chosen in function of the congregation and not in a vacuum in order to be sent afterwards to some congregation or other. They should be men and women, married and unmarried. And according to their talents and possibilities they should be inducted to their office on a part-time or a full-time basis, temporarily or for life. Why should somebody stay lifelong in a pastoral office, even if s/he is not or no longer fit for it? Some might have a restricted mission, because they are better, say, in teaching than in organizing. But the full-time pastors preferably are those who by their life in the congregation are able to lead this congregation in preaching, communion, prayer and sacrament. There should not be two classes of pastors, viz. the so-called lay pastors and the ordained priests. In principle, each pastor should be able to lead in the celebration of the Eucharist and the sacraments for the community of which s/he has the pastoral care. Of course this pastoral leadership needs a hierarchical structure. The local pastors must be recognized by the broader church community. This is true also of a bishop who is elected by a diocese. But the community should come first and the hierarchical leadership develop from it.

It is a fundamentalistic argument to object against this design for a pastoral church structure that Jesus wanted the present hierarchical structure. If Jesus wanted a church, then he also wanted a pastoral office for it. But the present form of it has been developed *completely* in the course of later history. And if this development has led to deformation, then the church in our day has the charge to reform its own official structure on the basis of its evangelical inspiration. Let the church take the courage to build a functional and diversified pastoral office. I have witnessed church communities praying in their liturgy for such a reformed leadership.

CONFIRMING ELECTED BISHOPS

PETER HEBBLETHWAITE

Dysfunctional, untraditional, counter-productive, the result of a partial and unilateral theology, the present system of appointing bishops cannot endure. According to Peter Hebblethwaite there is nothing sacrosanct about it. The fact that 'the church is not a democracy,' so often repeated, does not mean that it is a tyranny. Moreover, in the Code of Canon Law there are already instruments which could involve the diocese in an episcopal election.

In December 1991, Norbert Werbs, auxiliary bishop of Schwerin, laid six questions before the European Synod of Bishops meeting in Rome. The first two concern us particularly:

1) The peoples of Europe think and feel in an increasingly democratic way. Yet our church is hierarchically structured. We are convinced that this cannot be given up. Yet we must ask ourselves whether the hierarchical set-up of the church makes possible participation and co-responsibility of all the members of the church. The consultation process begun by Vatican II seems to many Catholics insufficient. Are they wrong? How could this be improved?

2) In stressing the priesthood of all believers Vatican II brought out their responsibility for the life of the church. But many Catholics feel that they are denied any influence in the important process by which bishops are named. They well understand that the bishop must be in communion with the pope. But they cannot understand many recent episcopal appointments. Does this have to be so? How could it be improved? [1]

Two external factors make this statement highly significant. First it comes not from some dissident group or left-wing publication, but from a bishop. Admittedly he is only an auxiliary bishop – and after this will no doubt remain so – but he is a product of the system he deplores. Such men have a special witness to bear.

---

[1] H. FRIES, *Das neue Europa und die Christlichen Kirchen*, in *Stimmen der Zeit*, November 1992, p.744.

1. Yearning for Freedom

Again, Bishop Werbs comes not from the 'West' which in current mythology is deeply sunk in the morass of secularization, and therefore unreliable, but from the East, the former DDR, where the church is believed to have been 'purified' by persecution from such 'secularizing' importations.

The great motive for the overthrowing of Communism was a *yearning for freedom* from totalitarian oppression. If the church, in her own inner life, shows that she does not share in this yearning and wishes to *restore* her own authoritarian control over society, then the 'decade of evangelization' in Europe will be delivered a blow from which it cannot be expected to recover. The church is weakened wherever she gives the impression that she is concerned primarily or only with her own institutional freedom.

This is indeed the criterion for distinguishing between pre-conciliar and post-conciliar attitudes. In the pre-conciliar period the church (= the hierarchy) measured freedom in terms of its own freedoms supposedly guaranteed by Concordats. If in the post-conciliar setting the church is seen as "the sacrament of salvation," then the church (= the people of God) shares in all the aspirations and hopes of humanity and articulates them, including the yearning for freedom.

The problem posed by the appointment of bishops is a particular instance of a general problem posed inevitably in the post-conciliar period: Vatican II asserted strongly certain theological principles which also contained *values*; but these values cannot take effect unless they are embodied in a praxis, entrenched in canon law, which expresses them as adequately as possible. To borrow a distinction from Ladislas Orsy, the church is both contemplative and active: as a contemplative body it is *quaerens intellectum fidei* (searching the understanding of faith); as an active body it is *quaerens aedificationem regni* (searching the edification of the Kingdom).[2]

Any gap that opens up between the contemplative vision and its translation into action, any contradiction between theology and corresponding praxis, creates the sense of frustration and malaise referred to by Orsy. His comment is highly pertinent to our question: "A good deal of what is usually described as post-conciliar restlessness is really nothing else than grace-filled vision postulating action. The energy contained in

---

[2] L. ORSY, *How to Relate Theology and Canon Law,* in *Origins* 22 (January 21, 1993) no. 32, p.549. This was an address given at the Pontifical Oriental Institute, Rome, December 10, 1992.

the word received is seeking corresponding action. Thus, our laity have heard that they were the people of God no less than the clergy, and now – no wonder! – they are asking for a more intense sharing in the sacred mission of the Church. Never again will they be satisfied with being told – as they often are – that their vocation is to sanctify secular realities."[3]

2. Episcopal Appointments

I want, in this chapter, to test that hypothesis by suggesting that just such a gap between theological vision and canonical praxis exists in the case of the appointment of bishops.

The episcopal appointment that caused the greatest *furore* was that of Joachim Meisner, transferred from East Berlin to Cologne in December 1989. The fact that none of the 815 priests of the diocese of Cologne was deemed capable of becoming bishop and none of the existing West German bishops was deemed worthy of promotion seemed like a judgement on the local church. It required an 'outsider' with no experience of life in the West to rule the richest and most prestigious diocese in the country. Moreover, the provisions of the Concordat were arbitrarily set aside. In the papal mind, there must have been very grave reasons to justify taking the risk of appointing an unpopular bishop.

What those reasons are can be illustrated by considering the appointment of Johannes ter Schure to the diocese of Den Bosch in October 1984. Ter Schure was a religious who had lived outside the country for twenty years, and was therefore 'untainted' by what had been happening there. Ter Schure has one remarkable distinction: he is the only bishop whose appointment was defended in his own cathedral by Pope John Paul. On May 11 1985 Pope John Paul was driven through the deserted streets of Den Bosch alongside Ter Schure. With no one to wave to, he resorted to prayer. In the newly restored cathedral, and with Ter Schure sitting sheepishly just a few feet away, he explained: "I know that you have been going through a difficult time in recent weeks. The recent appointments of bishops have deeply offended some of you who are wondering about the reasons for these tensions. I should like to say in all sincerity that the Pope attempts to understand the life of the local Church in the appointment of every bishop. He gathers information in accordance with ecclesiastical law and custom. You will understand that opinions are sometimes divided. In the last analysis, the Pope has to take the

---

[3] *Ibid.*, p.550.

decisions.[Must he explain his choice? Discretion does not enable him to do so.] Believe me brothers and sisters this suffering on account of the Church grieves me. But be convinced that I have truly listened, considered carefully and prayed. And I appointed the person whom I thought before God the most suitable for this office."[4]

The two sentences in square brackets were in the text prepared in Rome but omitted on delivery. That was a pity. Moreover, the argument that "discretion" demanded secrecy was not convincing. Deprived of the 'real reasons' for the appointment, the Dutch could only speculate about what they were: and the simplest and most likely explanation was that the entire course on which the Netherlands Province of the church had embarked since the Council under the leadership of its bishops, was being repudiated. The papal defence of Ter Schure amounted to saying that the pope knew better than the local church what it required.

Moreover, it was difficult to believe that the pope had the time to take such an intensely personal interest in the dossier of every individual candidate in every diocese of the world. The "listening" and "careful consideration" said to have gone on cannot have involved the clergy or laity of the local church involved or the conclusion would never have been reached that Ter Schure was "the most suitable candidate" for his office.

However, Ter Schure remains an *unicum*. Subsequent appointments were not even given a cursory defence. Georg Eder was appointed bishop of Salzburg in January 1989. Very little was known about him, except that he wrote letters to newspapers criticizing alleged "novelties" and "laxism" in the Austrian church. He turns his back to the people during Pontifical High Mass, refuses to give Communion in the hand, and was described as "somewhat to the right of the excommunicated Archbishop Marcel Lefebvre". Eder's 'theological' opinions came out in various *obiter dicta*. In his first New Year sermon he stressed the importance of Fatima with its "condemnation of atheistic bolshevism". He declared that "he who recites the rosary does more for peace than any pacifist demonstration". And of course he knew that AIDS was a "punishment inflicted by God". It would be truer to say that Eder was a punishment for the Salzburg cathedral chapter for turning down the other candidates, Klaus Küng, head of Opus Dei in Austria, and Andreas Laun, a Vienna Salesian.

Central Europe was the last place where the cathedral chapter played a significant role in the nomination of bishops. This made the appointment of Wolfgang Haas as Bishop of Chur, Switzerland, not only

---

[4] P. HEBBLETHWAITE, *Synod Extraordinary,* London, 1986, p.44.

unpopular but juridically doubtful[5]. In March 1987 his predecessor, Bishop Johannes Vonderach, privately consulted with some 180 people over the choice of an auxiliary bishop. What he got, just over a year later was not an auxiliary but a "coadjutor with right of succession". No sooner was Haas ordained bishop on May 22, 1990 – the guests had to tread nimbly over the prostrate bodies of protesters – than he announced to general astonishment that Vonderach had resigned "on grounds of health," and that he therefore was now bishop of Chur.

At no point had the diocesan chapter been consulted. This made the election irregular according to the Bishops-treaty (*Bistumsvertrag*) of 1823 which had been renewed in the decree *Etsi Salva* of 1948. Mayhem followed. Haas removed the Vicar General, Gebhard Matt, replaced the St Luzi seminary rector, Franz Annen, with an Opus Dei priest, Peter Rutz, and prompted the canton of Zürich to contemplate breaking away to form a diocese of its own. The Council of Priests of the diocese voted against their bishop by 33 to 11 (who included five members nominated by the bishop and three members of his advisory board).

Attempts at mediation failed. November 26, 1991, Cardinal Bernardin Gantin, Prefect of the Congregation of Bishops, and Cardinal Angelo Sodano, Secretary of State, replied curtly that "Wolfgang Haas is and remains bishop of Chur". Pope John Paul promised to busy himself with the question, but still nothing happened. At Pentecost the Zürich pastoral council issued a letter stating: "We cannot go on as at present. None of us want to split the Church. We would all like to see a Bishop in whom we can have confidence, and episcopal leadership that unites rather than divides, that opens up rather than closes down, which takes people seriously instead of trampling on them."[6] This statement from the Zürich pastoral council was fully in accord with the vision of the Council; the Roman reply showed no understanding of it.

The Haas case represents both an impasse and a *reductio ad absurdum*: the irresistable force of public opinion seems to have met an immoveable obstacle — the papal determination to impose this wholly unsuitable man on Chur.

3. Vision and Praxis

Now though the picture I have drawn stresses the satirical aspect of these unpopular bishops, it is not a caricature. Yet the imposition of

---

[5] What follows is based on *Bischofswählen in der Schweiz. Expertenbericht im Auftrag der Romisch-Katholischen Zentralkonferenz der Schweiz*, 1992.

[6] *Ibid.*, p.161.

unpopular bishops is not, seen from the point of view of Rome, wholly irrational. On his papal journeys Pope John Paul has repeatedly said what he expects of Bishops and suggested that he has not found it. The classic statement was found in the Special Synod of the Dutch church in 1980 which set down a marker for other churches. "A bishop," the Dutch were reminded,"is the true teacher of the faith" and not just the interpreter of some vaguely perceived *sensus fidelium* (censensus of the faithful). This was designed to forestall bishops appealing to their people to legitimate a particular approach. They are not to think of themselves as somehow 'delegates' of their churches. They have to teach and lead from the front.

Unfortunately, even in its own terms the theory does not work. For a bishop cannot achieve anything without the cooperation, willing or reluctant, of his clergy and people. The only effect of such quixotic appointments is to leave the bishop brooding on his misfortune, alone in his palace, contemplating "the folly of the cross". I suggest that it is the theory (or ideology) that results in such disastrous appointments, not the system by which they are appointed.

The evidence is that Pope Paul VI used substantially the same system for very different ends. His appointments had a wholly different purpose. In consultation with the local churches he sought men who were in the spirit of Vatican II and understood its pastoral purpose. Finding conciliar bishops was the chief task of the papal diplomatic service. By discreet listening and extensive consultation the nuncio would be able to serve the local church by helping provide it with the bishops it needed.

Two particular comments on Paul VI's appointments. When Jean Jadot was made Apostolic delegate to the United States (it became a pronunciature only under his successor, Pio Laghi), his specific brief was to renew the episcopacy. The organization men, typically builders and administrators like CEOs (Chief Executive Officers) in a large company, were to give way to pastorally-minded men at ease with the consultation and due process the new situation required. Jadot's success can be measured by the extent to which his successor, now Cardinal Pio Laghi, tried to "remedy" his "mistakes" by naming authoritarian "hard men" to keep them in control. Thus Cardinals Bernard Law in Boston and John J. O'Connor in New York were set against Cardinal Joseph Bernardin who had arrived in Chicago only because someone of great conciliatory power was needed to clear up the mess in Chicago caused by the public scandal that was the ministry of Cardinal John J. Cody.

A second comment on Paul VI's appointments. Two Benedictines whom he appointed – Basil Hume to Westminster and Rembert Weakland to Milwaukee – both quote him as making the same remark: "The best preparation for being a bishop is to have been a Benedictine abbot." Everything that the Rule of St Benedict says about the office of abbot applies to the bishop, such that it can be considered a treatise on authority in the church. Its purpose is the service of unity. Its method is to listen (the first word of the Rule is *audite*). The art of government is so to arrange things that "while the strong have something to strive for, the weak are not crushed". It is also relevant that Benedictine abbots are *elected* without anyone complaining of democracy invading the church. It is no accident that Hume and Weakland have both been well-received, confirming the wisdom of St Benedict's Rule.

It is important to recall the successful episcopal appointments under Paul VI because they indicate that the present system has been made to work, provided that all concerned share the same aim.

4. Objections Against the Current Practice

Of course it is unlikely to work so well again in the immediate future, as pre-conciliar habit and routine set in once more. The momentum of the Council has been lost. The confidence and lightness of step it brought to everyone in the church is no more. Ichabod, the vision is departed. At this point that one feels the lack of those canonical checks needed to balance a unilateral view of the church.

So the first objection against the current procedure is that it is *dysfunctional,* that is, it does not achieve the ends the appointment of bishops should serve. The purpose of authority in the church is to ensure that "all who are of the people of God, and therefore enjoy a true Christian dignity, can work towards a common goal, freely, and in an orderly way"[7]. The present praxis results in disunity. It produces the *malaise* referred to by Bishop Werbs.

The second objection is that it is *untraditional.* In the first millennium bishops were elected by the people or nominated by a lay patron (emperor or king, and eventually feudal lord). Elections by the people sometimes led to unseemly tumults, so election by the cathedral chapter tended to replace them. The most authoritative canonical statement on the question was canon 28 of Lateran II which states very firmly that bishops shall be elected by cathedral chapters.

---

[7] *Lumen Gentium,* no. 18.

The two systems – capitular election and royal or imperial patronage – were still in vogue as late as 1829 when the papal power to appoint bishops extended to a mere twenty-four dioceses outside the Papal States; but since the pope was sovereign within his own states, he was in the same position as the King of France or the Emperor of Austria. It was as temporal ruler, not as bishop of Rome, that he was appointing them. The first bishop of of the United States, John Carroll, was elected in 1789 by the twenty-six priests then active in the new republic[8].

The present centralized system of appointing bishops is a product of the nineteenth century. The Vatican takeover was justified on the grounds that it was the only way to assert 'the freedom of the Church' against interfering governments. France with its Gallican tradition was a particular target. The argument that papal patronage was better than state patronage carried the day. Even so by 1917, when the first Code of Canon Law was promulgated, the pope appointed only 700 or about half of the world's bishops. Though Gallican and Josephinist threats had receded if not disappeared altogether, the centralizing tendency continued until by 1980 out of the 2,456 dioceses of the Catholic Church, only twenty-four still had chapter elections. Yet the 1983 Code of Canon Law keeps open the traditional possibility of election to the office: "The Supreme Pontiff freely appoints Bishops or confirms those lawfully elected."[9] The whittling away of these last remaining exceptions to centralization has been the story of this pontificate.

Dysfunctional and untraditional, the present method of appointing bishops is unfaithful to the theology of Vatican II. It acknowledges neither the reality of the church as the People of God nor the reality of the local church, described by Vatican II as embodying all the attributes of the church, "for in their own locality, these are the new people called by God, in the Holy Spirit and in much fulness"[10].

5. Papal Absolutism and the Local Church

Now it is never easy to translate theological principles into canonical norms. It would be hasty to conclude, for example, that common baptism implies that a bishop should be elected by all the baptized. But

[8] Cf. L. SWIDLER, *People, Priests and Bishops in U.S. Catholic History*, in L. and A. SWIDLER (eds.), *Bishops and People*, Philadelphia, 1970, pp.113-135. This is a translation and expansion of *Theologische Quartalschrift* 2(1969), published by the Tübingen Theological Faculty.

[9] CIC, can. 275 §1.

[10] *Lumen Gentium*, no. 26.

some things can be said negatively: if there is no role whatsoever for anyone in the local church, if no consultation takes place, if cathedral chapters are ignored, if the baptized are reduced to total passivity and their 'reception' of the bishop is dismissed as irrelevant, then we are in the presence of a monarchical conception of the papacy that is at odds with the theology of Vatican II.

The debate – or battle — about the appointment of bishops is therefore only one aspect of a broader discussion about the relationship of the local church to what is usually called the universal church. In this debate, the Congregation for the Doctrine of the Faith has been neither dispassionate nor neutral.

The document still in preparation on episcopal conferences, the principal means of expression of the local church, denies them any theological status or mandate to teach. They are a merely practical arrangement with no theological implications. *The Catechism of the Catholic Church* reverses the clear statement of the *General Catechetical Directory* that a universal catechism was impossible and that "it will be for episcopal conferences to issue more precise directives and to apply them in catechetical directories, catechisms geared to different age-groups and cultural levels..."[11].

These are but two examples of the emasculation of the local church. But the most sustained assault on the local church is found in the *Letter on Some Aspects of the Church understood as Communion*. It caricatures even as it denounces "ecclesiological unilateralism" which allegedly asserts that "every particular local Church is a subject complete in itself, and that the universal church is the result of recognition on the part of particular Churches"[12]. The universal church is said to be "ontologically and temporally prior" to every local church, and so "the universal Church cannot be conceived as the sum or as the federation of particular Churches"[13].

True though these propositions may be, it is an abuse of *koinonia*-theology to use them to legitimate papal absolutism. And it is a form of theological bullying to treat questions addressed to this absolutism as an act of disloyalty. A new form of 'ecclesiological unilateralism' occurs when the local churches lose all their autonomy, and it "does not follow that the exercise of universal jurisdiction serves the good of the Church in all

---

[11] General Catechetical Directory, 46. Text in A. FLANNERY (ed.), *Vatican Council II. More Post-conciliar Documents*, vol.2, p.555.
[12] *Letter on Some Aspects of the Church understood as Communion*, no. 8.
[13] *Ibid.*, no. 9.

circumstances. Orsy gives as example the different forms of episcopal appointment in history and in different regions." [14]

While retaining the right of any Catholic to make a suggestion as to the next bishop, the main burden in the selection procedure must surely fall on the diocesan pastoral council and council of priests. These two bodies are not exposed to the objection that "they do not know enough about the possible candidates," and indeed they are at a considerable advantage compared with the Congregation of Bishops which has only paper-knowledge. There should no doubt also be a screening role for the conference of bishops and, of course, confirmation by the pope in accordance with canon 376: "Episcopos libere Summus Pontifex nominat, aut *legitime electos confirmat.*"

One can allow that it takes time for canonical structures to catch up with theological realities. But as Orsy warns, "when energies do not have an outlet, they become restless, and in danger of going in the wrong direction" [15].

---

[14] H.J. POTTMEYER, *Kirche als Communio,* in *Stimmen der Zeit,* September 1992, p.586. Quoting L. ORSY, *The Conversion of Churches: Condition of Unity,* in *America* 166(1992)479-487.

[15] *How to Relate Theology and Canon Law,* p.550.

LEGAL PROTECTION

KLAUS LÜDICKE

Since the promulgation of the Code of Canon Law on January 25th, 1983, legal protection against ecclesiastical administration, no longer seems a burning issue. German canonist Klaus Lüdicke investigates the history preceding this promulgation and discusses concrete experiments and proposals. Finally, he takes a look at the current situation and makes some suggestions for the future.

In an article[1] about this legal protection in the Roman Catholic Church, I worried like Heinrich Flatten in 1975 in an address to the deans of the archdiocese of Cologne that the material to be exposed would not please the readers[2]. The question of legal protection for the faithful against actions of the ecclesiastical administration arose in the sixties when the Second Section of the Apostolic Signatura was created. This Section was intended to clarify in judicial procedure disputes regarding administration[3]. A little while later the principles of the revision of the Code of Canon Law, issued by the Synod of Bischops in 1967 explained the objective. Principle 7 stated: "It is not sufficient for our law to offer legal protection. The recognition of real and proper subjective rights is necessary. Without this the juridical organization of the community is hardly imaginable. There should be a proclamation in canon law that the principle of legal protection can be invoked for superiors and subordinates so that any suspicion of arbitrariness in ecclesiastical administration will completely disappear. This aim can only be reached by forms of appeal, wisely organized by law. They can restore in a higher authority the right that is claimed to be violated by a lower authority. (...) There is a need to establish administrative tribunals of

---

[1] This article was initially published in the book edited by H. WARNINK, *Rechtsbescherming in de kerk,* Leuven, 1991, pp.37-50. It was the result of the scientific meeting of the working group of Dutch speaking canonists / werkgroep nederlandstalige canonisten in Vught (NL), 1990.

[2] H. FLATTEN, *Kirchliche Verwaltungsgerichtsbarkeit. Address at the seminar of the deans of the Archdiocese of Köln,* April 2nd, 1975 , Bad Honnef.

[3] This Section was created by the apostolic constitution *Regimini Ecclesiae Universae,* August 15th, 1987 (art. 106-107).

various degrees and kinds, to determine which actions can be brought before such tribunals and to clarify the rules of administrative procedure." There was indeed sufficient reason to consider ecclesiastical administration as too powerful. Flatten stated: "Many of our faithful feel themselves completely at the mercy of the anonymous apparatus of ecclesiastical administration. They are not opposed to law in the church but to the power of the administration."[4]

1. Legal Situation

The cause of the uncontrolled functioning of the ecclesiastical administration can be found in canon 1601 of the 1917 Code of Canon Law. This canon stated that grievances against decrees of ordinaries (like bishops) were to be handled exclusively by the congregations of the Roman Curia and that an appeal to the Sacra Romana Rota was not possible here. This same principle was extended to all lower administrative bodies by a decision of the pontifical commission on the interpretation of the Code in 1923: there could be no judicial appeal against decisions of the executive power / potestas executiva, and so one could only turn to higher administrative authorities[5]. The people concerned did not have much confidence of finding justice in a church where there were clerics in authority on the one hand and the simple faithful considered as unemancipated sheep on the other. With article 106 of the apostolic constitution Regimini Ecclesiae Universae (REU), the Second Section of the Apostolic Signatura opened the possibility of bringing decisions of highest administrative bodies, the Roman Congregations, before a tribunal. The only argument in a complaint could be the violation of a law. The procedure demanded an advocate. In actual fact, in a worldwide church access to this procedure was too difficult to be considered as real legal protection.

2. Projects for Judicial Procedures

Among all the proposals presented to the consultation committees of the commission of revision of the code, the proposal procedura admin-

---

[4] H. FLATTEN, *Kirchliche Verwaltungsgerichtsbarkeit*, p.18.
[5] PCI, May 23rd, 1923 to canon 1601 (code 1917): no judicial objections are possible "contra ordinariorium decreta, actus, dispositiones, quae ad regimen seu administrationem dioecesis spectent" in *Acta Apostolicae Sedis*, 16(1924) p.251.

istrativa was the first[6]. The preliminary remarks start with the statement: "Many who stand for the abolition or the reduction of law in the
church feel the need to have better protection of physical and juridical
persons against decrees issued by those who possess executive power in
the church". The objective of the proposal was the following. Because
of the lack of norms concerning administrative actions in the Code of
1917, the proposal provides prescriptions to be respected when administrative actions are issued (can. 4-7). The episcopal conference will create
one or more administrative tribunals of first instance (can. 19). The conference can also create a tribunal of second instance (can. 20). These tribunals are competent when decrees of bishops or their subordinates are
involved (can. 19). The Apostolic Signatura, however, will decide on
decrees of episcopal conferences or their institutions, particular councils,
dicasteries of the Holy See and all administrators directly subordinate to
the pope (can. 21). In addition, the Signatura will decide on appeals
against judgements of the first or second instance tribunals of the episcopal conference.

The procedure of administrative tribunals should respect the norms of
ordinary judicial procedure (can. 25 §5). Any attempt at reconciliation
should precede the judicial procedure (can. 9). This attempt consists of a
request addressed to the person taking the administrative action to withdraw or change his decision (can. 10). Such a demand is not prescribed
when the decision being challenged has already been confirmed by a
first instance (can. 10 §5) The request will be adjourned only if the hierarchical appeal were to have this effect as well (can. 12 §1). The procedures of hierarchical appeal and of administrative tribunals have the
same value. One is free to choose either of them (can. 8). After a hierarchical appeal against an administrative decree, one still can call upon the
administrative tribunal. But after a decision of the Holy See in an appeal,
one can only call upon the Apostolic Signatura (can. 21). This means
that the decision of a bishop confirming a decree of a parish priest can
be challenged by an appeal to Rome or a complaint in a administrative
tribunal of the first instance.

The administrative tribunal will have a wider competence than the
Second Section of the Apostolic Signatura by virtue of art.106 of REU.
The tribunal is not only competent where the violation of laws is concerned but also in cases of the violation of general canonical principles,
e.g. *equitas*. Moreover, the tribunal can judge whether the reasons for an

---

[6] *Schema canonum de procedura administrativa*, Rome, 1972.

administrative decision were correct (can. 17 §1). Unlike a hierarchical
superior (can. 16), the tribunal cannot change or replace an administrative action; he can only confirm or cancel a decree (can. 26 §1). The
right or even the obligation to issue a new administrative action remains
with the holder of executive power. The tribunal can however decide
about possible damages (can. 18 and 26 §2). The tribunal of first
instance will judge with a court of three judges, the second instance with
a court of three or five. If there is a shortage of persons, a single judge
can be sufficient in the first instance (can. 22 §1-2). In a collegiate tribunal, as a rule consisting of priests, a layperson or a deacon can be
involved if necessary on condition that the procedure is not concerned
with a decree of the bishop (can. 22 §4).

Several bodies consulted reacted to this fifth version of the proposals[7],
but the results of the debate within the commission itself were no longer
published. In the proposal of procedural law of 1976[8], 39 canons were
reserved for adminstrative procedures without giving the text which had
already been sent out in 1972. In the sixth version new modifications
were proposed:
- the episcopal conferences should create norms for the promulgation
  of decrees, for the trial of requests to change decrees addressed to
  the proponent and also for the qualification of the persons involved
  in the procedure (can. 3);
- as a rule there will be a diocesan tribunal, created by the bishop and
  competent over those decrees issued by lower authorities (can. 9
  §1);
- a tribunal of first instance at the level of the episcopal conference
  will judge decisions of bishops and institutions of the conference
  (can. 10 §1); there can be a second instance as a tribunal of appeal
  (can. 11 §1);
- the episcopal conference can allow two deacons or laymen (not
  women) in a college of three judges if the complaint is not directed
  towards an episcopal decree (can. 13 §2);
- the episcopal conference can establish permanent places of judgement and issue norms for these (can. 5 §2).

The essentials of these proposals were included in the 1980 draft of
the Code of Canon Law as canons 1688-1715[9]. A few prescriptions

---

[7] Cf. the article of P. CIPRIOTTI in *Communicationes* 5(1973) pp.235-243.
[8] *Schema canonum de modo procedendi pro tutela iurium seu de processibus*, Rome,
1976.
[9] *Schema codicis iuris canonici*, Rome, 1980.

about the administrative procedure disappeared because they had already been provided in the context of General Norms[10]. There were some modifications: where administrative acts of authorities subordinated to the bishop are concerned, a complaint has to be addressed to the bishop (can. 1704) and only priests can become judges (can. 1692).

The 1980 draft of the code was sent to all members of the commission for the revision of the code, which had to prepare the plenary sessions of 1981.

One of the reactions criticized the possibility of administrative procedures because it would hinder the life of the church. The clear answer of the secretary of the commission of revision was as follows: "Any hindrance that might occur will be caused by abuse, not by the norms. The divine law on bishops is not jeopardized, but this law must always be based on justice and be prepared to bring about justice."[11] A cardinal sent an alternative of 16 canons, which was rejected by the commission because it declared that it was tied to its own work which was the result of the coorporation of many scholars from various countries. The commission even had some substantial objections[12].

Cardinal König's proposal to make the creation of an administrative tribunal an obligation and not just an option, received the following reaction: "Although the creation of administrative tribunals is desirable for episcopal conferences in order to protect the rights of subjects and the justice of administration, an obligation by a general law would not be timely. There are already many difficulties in creating ordinary tribunals because of the shortage of doctors and masters in canon law competent in law. The creation of an administrative tribunal demands a very specific knowledge of law and statutes. And because those tribunals are new in the law of the church, it is better to introduce them step by step and voluntarily. Nevertheless there remains always the hierarchical appeal of last recourse to the Apostolic Signatura. The suggestion will however be discussed during the plenary meeting."[13]

Cardinal Bernardin proposed modifying the prescription that only priests be admitted as judges. He suggested also laypersons and deacons as a second judge in a collegiate tribunal. The secretariate of the commission answered: "That is not proper, because it concerns administrative acts of bishops. It would be opposed to 'canonical tradition'."[14] The

---

[10] Cf. the actual canons 35-58 in the code of 1983.
[11] Cf. *Communicationes* 16(1984) p.79.
[12] *Ibid.*, pp.79-85.
[13] *Ibid.*, pp.85-86.
[14] *Ibid.*, p.87. Cardinal Siri suggested only bishops as judges!

second suggestion of Cardinal Bernardin was also rejected, when he proposed a single judge in the first instance. To this the secretariate answered: "That is not proper because the matter is very delicate i.e. a judgement on decrees issued or confirmed by a bishop. Therefore it is necessary that a collegiate tribunal be available..." [15]

These arguments are interesting because they reveal the reasons that finally led to the disappearance of the norms from the code promulgated in 1983. Before this, a so-called *schema novissimum* was published [16] which still contained the canons on legal protection in administration. Only priests are allowed te become judges whereas the common procedural law allows laypersons as well (can. 1740 against can. 1421 §2); clearly the commission had also decided not to accept the suggestion to make the creation of administrative tribunals an obligation [17]. The nasty surprise occurred on January 1983. Many press people welcomed the promulgation of the new code because of the fact, among others, that it would finally introduce legal protection against administration. But when they got hold of one of the first copies, they discovered that these canons had been removed at the last minute. The reasons for this decision were never made public. One can suppose however, that there was a political argument and reasons on the theoretical constitutional level.

The political argument had already appeared in the suggestion of Cardinal König: the various situations in the universal church are so different, that the compulsory creation of an administrative tribunal was rejected. That would have led to different forms of legal protection in different parts of the universal church. This was not the intention, especially in the East European countries still under totalitarian domination. In these countries, judicial control of the ecclesiastical administration would be a foreign element. The theoretical and constitutional reasons could have been related to the fact that they did not want to submit the bishops to the jurisdiction of deacons and laypersons. The so-called 'undisputed canonical tradition' starts from the medieval notion of the unity of powers where the judge would be superior to the judged. The lawfulness of the actions of a superior could only be judged by a higher superior. This inaccurate notion determines the whole problem of lay-judges in the church [18]. Here it meant any possibility of a judgment over bishops, apart from those executed by the apostolic see, was withdrawn.

---

[15] Cf. *Communicationes* 16(1984) p.88.

[16] *Codex iuris canonici. Schema novissimum,* Rome, March 25th, 1982.

[17] Cf. canon 1767 §1, schema novissimum.

[18] K.LÜDICKE, "Laien als kirchliche Richter. Über den Inhalt des kirchlichen Richter-amtes," in *Österreiches Archiv für katholisches Kirchenrecht* 28(1977) pp.332-352.

3. Experiments and Proposals

Because the universal law of the Code of 1917 did not allow the creation of administrative tribunals in particular law, several dioceses took refuge in establishing so-called bodies of arbitration. Helmut Krätzl wrote[19] in 1974 about the "Ordnung für die pastoralen Schiedsgerichte in der Erzdiözese Wien"[20]. In 1978 I wrote about other experiments[21] e.g. in Graz-Seckau[22], Eisenstadt[23], Linz[24] and finally in Chur in Switzerland[25]. These institutions were not intended to be tribunals, but institutions of mediation with specific competence in individual cases. They had in common the charge to search for an amicable agreement. Their decision would be binding on both parties if they submitted themselves (Graz-Seckau, Linz, Chur) or if diocesan law attaches this binding character to a specific subject-matter (Graz-Seckau). In Eisenstadt, the consent of the bishop was needed, in Chur the bishop himself should decide, in Linz an appeal to the bishop was possible.

I have never heard what happened to these courts of arbitration or how many cases they had to handle. The diocese of St. Pölten created a court of arbitration in 1975[26], whose task it was to decide on questions of the lawfulness of decisions of ecclesiastical bodies and ministers. The consequences of the judgement for both parties to a conflict were not determined. In the official diocesan publication of Vienna the *Ordnung für die pastoralen Schiedsgerichte in der Erzdiözese Wien* was published once again[27]. For the Catholic Men's Movement a court of arbitration was created to decide in controversies between members or groups[28]. These are indications of the importance and activities of these courts of arbitration and for the positive effect they have.

---

[19] In *Theologisch-praktische Quartalschrift* 122(1974) pp.244-255.

[20] *Wiener Diözesanblatt* 110(1972) pp.136-140.

[21] K. LÜDICKE, "Auf dem Wege zu einer kirchlichen Verwaltungsgerichtbarkeit," in *Theologisch-praktische Quartalschrift* 126(1978) pp.352-354.

[22] "Diözesane Schlichtungs- und Schiedstelle Graz-Seckau" in *Kirchliche Verordnungsblatt für die Diözese Graz-Seckau*, 1974, pp.66-68.

[23] "Ordnung für pastorale Schiedsinstanzen in der Diözese Eisenstadt" in *Amtliche Mitteilungen der Diözese Eisenstadt*, 1974, pp.76-77.

[24] "Statut für die Schlichtungs- und Schiedstelle der Diözese Linz," in *Linzer Diözesanblatt*, 1974, pp.180-182.

[25] "Statut für die Verwaltungsrechtspflege in der Diözese Chur," in *Schweizerische Kirchenzeitung*, 143(1975) pp.268-269.

[26] "Errichtung und Statut der Schlichtungs- und Schiedstelle des Diözese St. Pölten," in *St. Pöltener Diözesanblatt*, 1975, pp.124-126.

[27] *Wiener Diözesanblatt*, 1987, pp.91-94.

[28] *Ibid.*, p.90.

The German dioceses have also created courts of arbitration in the area of ecclesiastical labour law. They handle conflicts concerning the regulations governing participation in ecclesiastical employments. These courts of arbitration are still in function and are demonstrating their effectiveness. They are very specific however; the ordinary faithful are not involved. During the seventies in West Germany, two attempts were made to create interdiocesan ecclesiastical administrative tribunals. In February 1971 the Bavarian bishops submitted to the prefect of the Apostolic Signatura a *Kirchliche Verwaltungsprozeß-ordnung der Kirchenprovinzen in Bayern (VPO Bayern)*[29] which was intended to be issued as a pontifical law specifically for this ecclesiastical province[30]. The Common Synod /*Gemeinsame Synode* of the dioceses in West Germany decided on November 19th, 1975 to establish a *Ordnung für Schiedsstellen und Verwaltungsgerichte der Bistümer in der Bundesrepublik Deutschland (Kirchliche Verwaltungsgerichtsordnung - KVGO)*[31]. This decision was formulated as a wish: "The Common Synod of the dioceses in the Federal Republic of Germany requests the Holy Father to issue a general regulation governing administrative tribunals or to concede the German Episcopal Conference the possibility of establishing ecclesiastical administrative courts. At the same time, the Common Synod of the dioceses in the Federal Republic of Germany requests the German Espicopal Conference to establish ecclesiastical administrative tribunals with the following regulations as soon as the general regulations or the possibility are issued."[32] These two regulations were oriented more or less towards German civil law, the *Verwaltungsgerichtsordnung* (VwGO).

In both proposals, parties aggrieved by an adminstrative action had first to address a complaint to the adminstration in order to obtain the withdrawal or modification of the administrative act. Only after the complaint had been rejected could the judicial procedure be initiated. The VPO Bayern proposed a judicial procedure in a regional tribunal, created in Munich for the two ecclesiastical provinces by the Apostolic Signatura. It would have jurisdiction over those administrative acts that violate a rule of law or administrative custom or that harm dutiful

---

[29] Published in *Archiv für katholisches Kirchenrecht* 140(1971) pp.59-73.

[30] Cf. also P. WIRTH, "Gerichtlicher Schutz gegenüber der kirchlichen Verwaltung. Modell eines kirchlichen Verwaltungsgerichtes," in *Archiv für katholisches Kirchenrecht* 140(1971) pp.29-59.

[31] *Gemeinsame Synode*, Freiburg i.Br., 1975, pp.734-763.

[32] *Ibid.*, p.735.

judgement[33]. It concerns the administrative decisions made by the bishop or the episcopal administration. The administrative acts of subordinate authorities must first be discussed at diocesan level[34]. The procedure starts with an attempt at reconciliation. If this attempt fails a judicial procedure will be initiated according to the principles of judicial arbitration. This means essentially an oral hearing. It will be concluded by a judgement of the tribunal that overturns the administrative decision which is considered to be in defiance of the law. The judgement cannot replace such an administrative decision. An appeal is possible to another chamber of this tribunal. A second appeal must be addressed to the Apostolic Signatura.

In contrast to this procedure which is very orientated towards German civil law, the ecclesiastical regulation for administrative tribunals of the Common Synod of German Dioceses (KVGO) provided a special feature concerning these instances. After the rejection of the complaint, it is submitted to a court of arbitration whose members are partly permanent and partly chosen by the parties from a list of names. This court of arbitration executes an ordinary procedure of arbitration in a tribunal of first instance. The procedure concludes not with a judgement but with an arbitral decision. This decision is not meant as a compromise but as explanation of the objective juridical situation. It is submitted for acceptance by both parties: if they agree, it will become a juridical judgement between them. If one of the parties refuse to accept it, a complaint can be made in an ecclesiastical administrative tribunal. The administrative tribunal settles the affair only so far as the proof of the arbitral procedure is being contested. So it judges in an authoritative way looking at the justification of the complaint. Administrative acts are not replaced, but their legitimacy is examined and decisons are sometimes cancelled. Appeal to a judgment of the administrative tribunal is to be addressed to a higher administrative tribunal; in the end the Apostolic Signatura can be invoked according to its own procedures.

According to the regulations of the KVGO, there has to be a chamber with a pastor and an expert in canon and civil law. At least one of the judges must be a priest or deacon. The courts of arbitration should be geographically very close by, the administrative tribunal should be diocesan, the higher administrative tribunal on the level of the German

---

[33] Administrative acts "die gegen eine Rechtsnorm oder Verwaltungsgewohnheit verstoßen oder das plichtmäßige Ermessen verletzen (art. 2 §1)".
[34] Cf. P. WIRTH, "Gerichtlicher Schutz," p.38 and 46.

Episcopal Conference. Both of these regulations have not been realized. The VPO Bayern was never issued as a pontifical law. The vote of the Common Synod to create the KVGO was not carried out. A special competence was not given in relation to the forthcoming revision of the code; the expected general law was removed from the Code of Canon Law, as we mentioned above.

4. Administrative Legal Protection

After the disappearance of the administrative tribunals from the Code of 1983, there was not much left. There are two places where the term administrative tribunal is used. In canon 149 §2 it states that a person can be deprived in some circumstances of an office by an administrative tribunal, if he lacks the qualities required. In canon 1400 §2 it says that controversies arising from an act of *potestas administrativa* can only be brought before the superior or administrative tribunal. This means that one cannot turn to an ordinary tribunal if he claims a violation of his rights in the church by an administrative action.

It is true that the secretariate of the commission for the revision of the code rightly indicated that according to the creation of the complaints procedure, the possibility remains for complaining to the Apostolic Signatura. Canon 1445 §2 describes its competence: "This tribunal deals with contentions legitimately referred to it which arise from an act of ecclesiastical administrative power, with other administrative controversies which are referred to it by the Pope or by the dicasteries of the Roman Curia, and with a conflict of competence among these dicasteries".

This norm is specified by art. 123 of *Pastor Bonus*. According to this, the Signatura will decide on appeals against individual administrative acts issued or confirmed by dicasteries of the Roman Curia. The text avoids the word 'complaint' but it speaks of "recursus". This is not a very good choice because the competence of the Signatura is explicitly limited to the control of legitimacy: one can only argue that the act being challenged violated a statute *in decernendo vel in procedendo,* and that the tribunal pronounce a *iudicium de illegitimitate*. The Signatura cannot issue administrative acts. The word "recursus", which is used for the procedure of complaints within the administration is not correct. The placatory reaction of the secretariate of the commission saying there still remains the appeal to the Apostolic Signatura as a last resort if administrative tribunals are not created is no real consolation.

It is impossible to maintain that the wish to protect the rights of the subject in the church has been complied with. In the preface to the code of 1983 the principles of the revision of the code are mentioned once again. One of them is the protection of the rights of the subject and the need for administrative legal protection. In the final version it says that there should be attention in the new law for administrative appeals and the administration of justice[35]. Although the German translation made by order of the bishops translates *administratio iustitiae* with "Rechts-sprechung", administrative tribunals no longer exist in the text. The preface does not admit that in this case the result of the revision did not attain its objective.

5. Future Possibilities

As I stated in the beginning, administrative legal protection is not a very popular theme. Are people no longer interested in such legal protection? Are there no longer any conflicts between the ecclesiastical administration and the faithful? Or has the new code improved the behavior of ecclesiastical authorities to such an extent that there is no more reason for complaining? That cannot be the case.

The Code of Canon Law of 1983 guarantees the faithful complete legal protection, as did the code of 1917. Canon 221 §1 protects subjective rights of the faithful against the relevant authority in the church. Canon 1491 states that all law is protected by the possibility to complain when there is not something explicitly prohibiting it. But: controversies arising from the execution of administrative power can only be brought about in a procedure before an administrative tribunal (can. 1400 §2). It is obvious that the universal legislator of the church did not want administrative jurisdiction. Clearly he abandoned the principles of the revision of the code and deliberately disappointed the expectations of the public.

But did he really intend to block the development of administrative legal protection by initiatives taken by local churches? This cannot be deduced from the events with any certainty. In canon 1733 §2 he opens the possibility that the episcopal conference, and thus each bishop, create a permanent office or council which can seek and propose fair solutions in controversies about administrative decrees. According to the current views, the particular legislator does not possess authority in the area of procedural law. Canon 87 concerning the episcopal authority to

---

[35] recursus administrativos et administrationem iustitiae

dispense, clearly states that the bishop cannot dispense from procedural legal norms. Does this mean that he cannot create a specific procedural law?

The opinion that procedural law can only be created by the Apostolic See dates from the preconciliar period. The legislative authority of bishops existed only on paper; it was effective only in order to push papal law. Since the rediscovery of the local church, since the statement of the conciliar decree *Christus Dominus* article 8 (integrated in canon 381 §1 of the code of 1983) an explicit norm is necessary prohibiting a bishop from issuing a law by which he – as legislator, administrator and judge in his diocese – creates a legal protection against some administrative action opposed to the law. If the bishop is head of the administration, he can submit his action to juridical control, of which he is also the head as judge in his diocese. To organise this is part of his competence as legislator.

The older view in the church says that in judicial judgements, the execution of authoritative power should remain superior to the parties. This excludes the bishop from submitting himself to a judgement of the court, from accepting the control of his own actions. There is, however, no constitutional reason to exclude the acts of the vicar general from such juridical control. Supposing administrative judicial control on a diocesan level were possible, the only question remaining is: why is it not put into reality? The answer is quite simple. Since the promulgation of the code of 1983 canonists have not been concerned with this problem. There does not seem to be ecclesiastical pressure, the impulse of the seventies has been lost, there are no longer identifiable groups struggling for this issue[36]. This indicates the importance of opening the debate on human rights in the catholic church with this article on legal protection.[*]

---

[36] In 1993 the German bishops decided to create tribunals for the matter of labour in the church. The *Zentralkomitee der deutschen Katholiken* took a new initiative to reanimate the above mentioned project of *Schiedsstellen und Verwaltungsgerichte...* in Germany.

[*] Translation by A. van der Helm.

FREEDOM OF CONSCIENCE AND RESEARCH

JAN JANS

It is no coincidence that the encyclical Veritatis Splendor explicitly refers back to Humanae Vitae. In a historical overview Flemish moral theologian Jan Jans demonstrates how the concepts of freedom of conscience and research as imposed after the Second Vatican Council imply a return to a nineteenth century pessimistic anthropology.

"The Congregation for the Doctrine of the Faith addresses an invitation with confidence and encouragement to theologians and above all to moralists, that they study more deeply and make even more accessible to the faithful the contents of the teaching of the Church's Magisterium. ... The precise indications which are offered in the present Instruction therefore are not meant to halt the effort of reflection but rather to give it a renewed impulse in unrenounceable fidelity to the teaching of the Church." [1]

1. Setting the Stage

This passage, as it turned out in the debate that took place after the publication of *Donum Vitae* in March 1987, gave birth to rather different interpretations. On the one hand, representatives of the Magisterium speaking about the *duty* of theologians to carry on their investigations and research stressed the "inrenounceable fidelity to the teaching of the Church". No less authority than cardinal Ratzinger, Prefect of the Congegration of the Doctrine of the Faith which issued the Instruction, spoke of the "urgent and necessary task to theologians" — adding however the important qualification that "this task of more fundamental anthropological and ethical reflection" has to be carried out "in fidelity to the Church's Magisterium" [2]. On the other hand, theologians claimed the *freedom* of research necessary to carry on "the effort of reflection",

---

[1] *Donum vitae. Instruction on Respect for Human Life in Its Origin and on the Dignity of Procreation,* Vatican City, 1987, p.38.

[2] Cf. "Cardinal Ratzinger presents new CDF Instruction to journalists," in *L'Osservatore Romano* (Weekly Edition in English) 16 March 1987, p.8.

even if this might lead to so-called dissent. The well known and highly
regarded American moral theologian, Richard McCormick, worded this
as follows: "I find the congregation's analysis and reasoning on the
'simple case' unpersuasive"[3].

Some will perhaps remember to what this difference of interpretation
lead, namely the — infamous — anonymous leading article in the Vatican newspaper *L'Osservatore Romano* on Christmas Eve 1988. Here,
every type of dissent, both in words and in practice, was condemned as
"gravissima ribellione" — grievous rebellion —, because public opposition to the Magisterium comes down to the elaboration of a moral doctrine which affirms as licit acts, which under the same conditions have
been declared illicit by the Magisterium[4]. Others will perhaps remember
the address that Pope John Paul II delivered about a year after *Donum
Vitae* to the participants of a congress in Rome on the occasion of the
twentieth anniversary of the encyclical *Humanae Vitae*. In this, the pope
reacted in very strong terms against those who maintain that concrete
norms proposed by the Magisterium are still open for theological discussion. According to him, this position of theologians is based on an
erroneous idea of the moral conscience, namely "l'idea di coscienza cre-
atrice della norma morale". The correct conception of the moral conscience, however, reveals according to the pope its inner relation to the
Magisterium: since the Magisterium has been established by Christ in
order to enlighten conscience, to appeal to conscience with the aim of
contesting the truth of what is being taught by the Magisterium is to
refuse both the catholic concept of Magisterium and of moral conscience[5].
And finally, probably even more will remember the so-called "Cologne
Declaration", in which theologians — with explicit reference to this
papal adress — protested against the presented concept of conscience:
"Conscience is not an aid to the implementation of papal teaching, as
might appear from such adresses. Rather, the conscience of the faithful
provide the point of reference for the teaching office in the exposition of
the truth"[6].

---

[3] R.A. McCORMICK, "Document is Unpersuasive," in *Health Progress* 68 (1987)
53-55, p.55.

[4] Cf. "Sull' autorità dottrinale della Istruzione 'Donum Vitae'," in *L'Osservatore
Romano*, 24 Dicembre 1988, pp.1-2, p.1.

[5] Cf. JOHN PAUL II, "Non si può parlare di diligente ricerca della Verità se non tiene
conto di ciò che il Magistero insegna," in *L'Osservatore Romano*, 13 Novembre 1988,
p.4.

[6] Cf. "Against incapacitation - for an open Catholicism" (The Cologne Declaration),
in *The Tablet*, 4 February 1989, pp.140-142, p.141.

As has become clear in the meantime, the final word from this last quotation became the central notion in the ongoing discussion and disagreement on freedom, conscience, law and moral acts: truth. The encyclical *Veritatis Splendor,* signed by Pope John Paul II on August 6, 1993 and made public on the 5th of October, gives the following summary of the present state of affairs: "In fact, a new situation has come about *within the Christian community itself,* which has experienced the spread of numerous doubts and objections of a human and psychological, social and cultural, religious and even properly theological nature with regard to the Church's moral teachings. It is no longer a matter of limited and occasional dissent, but of an overall and systematic calling into question of traditional moral doctrine, on the basis of certain anthropological and ethical presuppositions. At the root of these presuppositions is the more or less obvious influence of currents of thought which end by detaching human freedom from its essential and constitutive relationship to truth"[7].

Indeed, what needs to be scrutenized in order to understand *"what is certainly a genuine crisis"*[8] are these presuppositions. For my opinion, some insight can be gained by studying the reasons why the church in little more than a century's time changed its total condemnation of freedom of conscience — in the encyclical *Mirari Vos,* 1832 — towards a joyful acceptance of freedom of religion based on freedom of conscience — in the *Declaration on Religious Freedom,* 1965. In its turn, this will shed light on the events following the Second Vatican Council, events which to a large extent can be summarized under the heading of restauration.

2. Full Truth

In August 1832, Pope Gregory XVI published his first major encyclical under the dramatic title *Mirari Vos:* "We think that you wonder why, from the time of Our assuming the pontificate, We have not yet sent a letter to you. ... But you know what storms of evil and toil, at the beginning of Our Pontificate, drove Us suddenly into the depths of the sea"[9]. The gloomy tone of the encyclical and its theme as indicated by the subtitle, "On the Unrest in Church and State", becomes understandable if one takes into account the situation in which Gregory became pope.

---

[7] *Veritatis Splendor,* no.4.
[8] *Veritatis Splendor,* no.5.
[9] *Mirari Vos,* no.1.

Elected on the 2nd of February 1831 — to become the successor of Pius
VIII who died on the 30th of November 1830 — the new pope had to
postpone his solemn accession to office until the 15th of August 1832,
also the day his first encyclical is dated. The reason for this was the
ongoing difficulties in the relations between the church and the state.
With his encyclical, Gregory XVI took a firm stand against political liberalism, the ideas of which, through the influence of Lamennais, lead
towards a most serious division in the (French) church. In his reaction,
the Pope condemned the so-called "indifferentism" and labelled "freedom of conscience" to be madness. Yet, these clear-cut condemnations
do not stand on their own: underneath them is a certain concept of the
relation between salvation and truth, supported in the last analysis by
well defined anthropological presuppositions. Let me illustrate this by
some quotations from *Mirari Vos*.

The starting point — "an abundant source of evils" — is the so-called
indifferentism: "This perverse opinion is spread on all sides by the fraud
of the wicked who claim that it is possible to obtain the eternal salvation
of the soul by the profession of any kind of religion, as long as morality
is maintained" [10]. Next, those who accept indifferentism claim — in
order to practice it — freedom of conscience. For Gregory, this is also
obviously unacceptable: "This shameful font of indifferentism gives rise
to that absurd and erroneous proposition which claims that liberty of
conscience must be maintained for everyone. It spreads ruin in sacred
and civil affairs, though some repeat over and over again with the greatest imprudence that some advantage accruess to religion from it. 'But
the death of the soul is worse than freedom of error', as Augustine was
wont to say. When all restraints are removed by which men are kept on
the narrow path of truth, their nature, which is already inclined to evil,
propels them to ruin. Then truly 'the bottomless pit' is open from which
John saw smoke ascending which obscured the sun, and out of which
locusts flew forth to devastate the earth" [11].

What do we learn from this? First of all, over against indifferentism,
the pope holds that only the truth of the Catholic faith guarantees eternal
salvation. Second, given the anthropological presupposition that the
"nature of man is inclined towards evil", only clear guidance can keep
people on this necessary path of truth. Freedom, therefore, be it freedom
of conscience or freedom of thought, can only lead to misguidance,
resulting in the destruction of both church and state. Put in other words:

[10] *Mirari Vos,* no. 16.
[11] *Mirari Vos,* no. 15.

if the truth is contained in the teaching of the church, freedom which results in points of view at variance with this teaching can only be false and to the detriment of the common good. From what one could call a pessimist anthropology follows the suspicion that freedom equals arbitrariness. In the light of this, I would claim that the strong condemnations are not — so to speak — *intrinsically* oriented against freedom of conscience (and later on in the same encyclical against freedom of press) but against a concept of freedom as 'liberty from truth'.

Practically speaking this truth, in the form of the *depositum fideï* (deposit of the faith) guarded and authoritatively taught by the Magisterium, can only be harmed by such a freedom. From this then follows the famous dictum regarding the position civil governments should take over against the question of religious freedom and plurality, namely: "Only the truth has rights".

3. True Freedom

As I pointed out in the introduction, there is an obvious difference between the attitude just described and the teaching of the Second Vatican Council in its *Declaration on Religious Freedom*. Here I will not discuss the *Declaration* itself, but I will only focus on the very first preconciliar preparatory meeting of the appointed sub-commission, which took place at the end of December 1960 in Fribourg, Switzerland[12]. This commission found itself confronted with two drafts, the first entitled *On the Freedom of Conscience,* the second bearing the title *Religious Freedom.*

The first text contained what one could call an exposition of the classical doctrine: "Only the truth has rights". For its application in political reality, this doctrine used the distinction between the so-called 'thesis' and 'hypothesis'[13]. The point of departure was that the Catholic Church is the only true Church of Christ. Therefore, only she has the right to exist and to be recognized and protected by civil authorities. This means that the "Catholic State" must be maintained as the ideal, the 'thesis'. However, in states where Catholics are a minority and Catholicism is not institutionalized as the state religion, any constitu-

---

[12] For some information on this meeting, cf. J. HAMER, "Histoire du texte de la déclaration," in *La liberté religieuse* (Unam Sanctam, 60), Paris, 1967, pp.53-57.

[13] As will become clear, it is no coincidence that for the next lines, I am relying on an article by L. JANSSENS, "The Non-infallible Magisterium and Theologians," in *Louvain Studies* 14(1989)195-259, p.231.

tional situation deviating from the ideal can be only the object of tolerance — not of approval — a concession to the requirements of an
'hypothesis'. The whole argument comes down to a double standard:
although the church demands freedom for her own religion in countries
where Catholics constitute a minority, uniformity is imposed on all citizens in those countries where Catholics possess a political majority. In
this scheme, tolerance is nothing but a negative reality, regretfully necessary in case of the 'hypothesis'. The corollary of this is an equally
negative interpretation of freedom of conscience, something that would
be superfluous if the 'thesis' would reign supreme. Because of this negative approach, the text of this draft was rejected by the preparatory
commission.

The second text, which after being accepted became known as the
Document de Fribourg, was quite different from the outset. Its key-
phrase stated: "The intangible dignity of the human person determines
the positive content of tolerance"[14]. This elaboration of tolerance as a
virtue was based on a vision of interpersonal relations not as between
objects, means or things, but as between subjects, beings with a free and
conscious life, masters of their acts, sources of initiative and responsibility, called towards the conscious and free realization of their destiny
through the mediation of their judgments of conscience. The document
rejected the expression "freedom of conscience" if this means the freedom to form one's conscience according to what one sees fit but it
adapted the formula "conscientious freedom", to stress the dignity of
those honestly pursuing truth. During the Council, and manifestly so in
The Pastoral Constitution on the Church in the Modern World
(*Gaudium et Spes*) and of course in the *Declaration on Religious Freedom* (*Dignitatis Humanae Personae*) this approach came to be identified with the term 'personalism'.

Let me just quote from Louis Janssens, the author of the approved
text, to clarify what this means: "Being conscious and free, we are
equally responsible. We must answer personally for the conformity
of our free acts to the one truth, to our conviction, to our judgment of

---

[14] In a former publication, while claiming that the Louvain moral theologian Louis
Janssens was the author of the *Document de Fribourg*, I wrote that the original manu-
script of this second text was not yet located. In the meantime, the document was found
in the archives of the chairman of the sub-commission, Mgr. Emiel-Joseph De Smedt
(then bischop of Brugges, Belgium) and Janssens has confirmed that he is indeed its
author. Cf. J. JANS, "Some Remarks on the Work of Professor Emeritus Louis
Janssens," in J.A. SELLING (ed.), *Personalist Morals. Essays in Honor of Professor
Louis Janssens* (BETL, 83), Leuven, 1988, pp.319-328, p.324.

conscience. Conscience (in the psychological and moral sense), liberty and responsibility are the essential properties of our personal interiority. They bestow upon us the dignity of 'moral subject', responsible for the conformity of free activity to judgment of conscience. It is as moral subjects — conscious, free and responsible beings — that God calls us to the realization of His will or of moral exigencies and it is our duty to answer this call as conscious, free subjects who determine moral obligation" [15].

The same connection between freedom and responsibility marks the optimistic anthropology of Pope John XXIII. He was the first pope who, in his 1963 encyclical *Pacem in Terris,* welcomed the so-called *Universal Declaration of Human Rights* (1948). In this *Declaration*, the well-known article 19 goes as follows: "Everyone has the right to freedom of opinion and expression". The real significance, however, only comes to the fore if one adds to this the second paragraph of the preambula of the *Declaration*: "The advent of a world in which human beings shall enjoy freedom of speech and belief ... has been proclaimed as the highest aspiration of the common people." On the basis of this anthropology, the classical conflict between truth on the one hand and freedom on the other, where freedom is mainly conceived of as a threat for truth, is dissolved. Freedom becomes here — as already said — the call for responsibility. Or, freedom is accepted as the necessary medium in the dialectical unity of human *rights* on the one hand and human *duties* on the other. In this understanding of rights/duties, they refer to one another, and by doing so, to the human person which is the subject of both. This appeal to the subject is the core of the optimism in this anthropology, in principle open to "all people of good will". Freedom, be it freedom of conscience, of religion, of speech and press, of profession, of choice of partner, etc., is not arbitrariness, but the self-revelation of responsibility.

This said, it is of crucial importance to notice that the rejection of arbitrariness does not end in uniformity on the level of concrete decisions and acts. For the faithful, free conscience is not an empty barrel. In the words of John XXIII: "The world's Creator has stamped man's inmost being with an order revealed to man by his conscience; and his conscience insists on his preserving it" [16]. The significance of this text is highlighted by the often quoted passage from *Gaudium et Spes,* no. 16: "In the depths of his conscience, man detects a law which he does not

[15] L. JANSSENS, "The Foundation for Freedom of Conscience," in *American College Bulletin* (Louvain) 43(1964)16-21, p.19.
[16] *Pacem in Terris,* no. 5.

impose upon himself, but which holds him to obedience. Always summoning him to love good and avoid evil, the voice of conscience can when necessary speak to his heart more specifically: do this, shun that. ... Hence the more that a correct conscience holds sway, the more persons and groups turn aside from blind choice and strive to be guided by objective norms of morality". The "law" is first and most the absolute demand "to love good and avoid evil". Therefore, the real conflict is no longer between truth and freedom, but between conscientious responsibility and blind arbitrariness. In the realisation or the taking up of this responsibility, however, the concrete voice of conscience does not rule out legitimate diversity: "Often enough the Christian view of things will itself suggest some specific solution in certain circumstances. Yet it happens rather frequently, and legitimately so, that with equal sincerity some of the faithful will disagree with others on a given matter" [17].

4. Freedom and Truth

In the last part of this article, I will briefly indicate what happened to this "new edition of the Catholic tradition" [18]. Even at first glance, some recent documents from the Magisterium seem to resemble more the style and tone of the pre-Vatican II area, for instance the so-called *Oath of Fidelity* (1989) and the *Instruction on the Ecclesial Vocation of the Theologian* (1990). Yet, their content is simply presented as being in accordance with the whole of tradition in the *Catechism of the Catholic Church* (1992) and repeated with the authority associated with an encyclical in *Veritatis Splendor* (1993). I will return to this encyclical at the end, but want to devote this section mainly to the significance of another encyclical, published no more than three years after the closing of Vatican II. I am referring, of course, to Pope Paul VI's *On the Regulation of Fertility,* better known as *Humanae Vitae,* promulgated on the 25th of July, 1968. It was here indeed that the insights articulated during Vatican II were put to the test. And, sad but true (*sic*), they did not pass.

In order to avoid a possible misunderstanding, let me first point out that the authoritative teaching of the Catholic Church is not against the idea of 'responsible' or 'planned' parenthood. Married people are encouraged to reflect on their call to become parents. Practically

[17] *Gaudium et Spes,* no. 43.
[18] Cf. J. MAHONEY, *The Making of Moral Theology. A Study of the Roman Catholic Tradition,* Oxford, 1987, p.302: "Vatican II ... has produced a new edition of the Catholic Tradition".

speaking, this means they have to decide on the 'when' and the 'how many' of their children. Therefore, problems do not occur on the level of this principle, but on the level of the means to realize it. After the famous address delivered by Pope Pius XII on the 29th of October 1951 to the Italian Midwifes, there was no doubt any more on the licitness of the so-called periodic continence. But what about other means, especially the hormonal means to regulate female fertility, which became available by the end of the fifties? Did the general condemnation of contraception, issued by Pope Pius XI in his encyclical *Casti Connubii* (1930) still apply?

When this question, in the context of a broader theology of marriage, appeared during the thirteenth session of Vatican II in the autumn of 1964, it was promptly removed from the agenda of the Council. The reason for this was the existence of a — until then secret — commission installed since the spring of 1963 by Pope John XXIII, which continued its work under his successor Pope Paul VI[19]. This commission, in the meanwhile enlarged to about 60 members, finished its investigations by the end of June 1966. With regard to the question of the means to realize responsible parenthood, it came to an almost unanimous conclusion: given their duty to procreate in a responsible way, it also belongs to the conscience of the couple to decide on the proper means. It was only after long debates and intense exchange of arguments that this conclusion was reached, and still it was heavily contested by a minority of four members. But the interesting thing is — as becomes clear from the report of a participant and eyewitness — that because the members were given total freedom of research and speech, a learning process took place in which participants gained insight in the reasons for 'traditional teaching' and therefore in the possibility and even the need to change it![20] Under the influence of conciliar personalism, it became evident that those who bear the responsibility to decide on procreation are also capable in conscience to decide on the proper moral means to answer "the question of harmonizing conjugal love with the responsible transmission of life"[21].

---

[19] Cf. *Gaudium et Spes*, no.51, n.14: "Certain questions which need further and more careful investigation have been handed over, at the command of the Supreme Pontiff, to a commission for the study of population, family and births, in order that, after it fulfills its function, the Supreme Pontiff may pass judgment. With the doctrine of the magisterium in this state, this holy Synod does not intend to propose immediately concrete solutions."

[20] Cf. P. DE LOCHT, *Les couples et L'Eglise. Chronique d'un témoin*, Paris, 1979, 267 p.

[21] *Gaudium et Spes*, no. 51.

However, *Humanae Vitae,* both referring to the conclusions of the commission and rejecting them (no. 5-6), did not rely on the conscience of the couples concerned and consequently pointed out concrete norms regarding the means permissible to regulate fertility. My principle point in this whole story is that the rejection of the so-called artificial means is not only substantiated by claiming continuity with former teaching[22], but also by referring to the harmful consequences of the use of artificial means. From my own experience, many people are unaware of this consequentialism present in the teaching of *Humanae Vitae,* because they stop reading after no. 14 in which the unacceptable means are outlined and prohibited. In no. 17, however, two serious consequences are spelled out: infidelity of husbands towards their wives and pressure by immoral civil authorities on families. This first consequence is based on what I would call the return of a pessimist anthropology: instead of trusting the dialectic between a persons right to freedom and his/her corresponding duty towards moral truth, human frailty and egotism — especially of men — is stressed. I consider it worthwhile to quote the first paragraph of no. 17 in full: "Upright men can even better convince themselves of the solid grounds on which the teaching of the church in this field is based, if they care to reflect upon the consequences of methods of artificial birth control. Let them consider, first of all, how wide and easy a road would thus be opened up towards conjugal infidelity and the general lowering of morality. Not much experience is needed in order to know human weakness, and to understand that men — especially the young, who are so vulnerable on this point — have need of encouragement to be faithful to the moral law, so that they must not be offered some easy means of eluding its observance. It is also to be feared that man, growing used to the employment of anti-conceptive practices, may finally lose respect for the woman and, no longer caring for her physical and psychological equilibrium, may come to the point of considering her as a mere instrument of selfish enjoyment, and no longer as his respected and beloved companion".

In spite of the reference made in this passage — as in no. 12 — to the capacity of contemporary humans to grasp the inherent reasonableness of the teaching proposed, the encyclical qualifies in its pastoral guidelines the freedom of teaching and research by means of a theologically claimed obedience. *Humanae Vitae* no. 28 — addressed to priests and

---

[22] On the question of continuity and change, cf. the study by J.A. SELLING, "Magisterial Teaching on Marriage 1880-1968. Historical Constancy or Radical Development?" in *Studia Moralia* 28(1990)439-490.

especially those who teach moral theology — reads as follows: "Be the first to give, in the exercise of your ministry, the example of loyal internal and external obedience to the teaching authority of the Church. That obedience, as you know well, obliges not so much because of the reasons adduced, but rather because of the light of the Holy Spirit, which is given in a particular way to the pastors of the Church in order that they may illustrate the truth".

With this claim then, theological research possibly leading to conflict and even dissent based on an investigation and probable refutation of arguments used, becomes something marginal if not immediately unacceptable. The science of (moral) theology and its service to the church should be completely oriented towards affirmation of the existing teaching.

5. Conclusion

It is no coincidence that the encyclical *Veritatis Splendor,* in its section on the service of moral theologians, explicitly refers back to *Humanae vitae,* no. 28. And so it seems that the idea of 'thesis' — 'hypothesis' has returned under a new disguise. The 'thesis', being the ideal situation, does exist in the teaching of the Magisterium which "with the guarantee of assistance of the Spirit of truth"[23] presents and explains the demands of faith and morals. Since this teaching — also in the elaboration of concrete norms in the areas of human sexuality, the family, social, political and economic life — is representing truth itself, it is morally binding: "In proclaiming the commandments of God and the charity of Christ, the Church's Magisterium also teaches the faithful specific particular precepts and requires that they consider them in conscience as morally binding"[24]. The questioning of this by means of theological research might perhaps be tolerated — as happened in the years following *Humanae Vitae* — but under the restrictions of a 'hypothesis', given the danger of confusion in the life of the church and the faithful[25]. However, to bring into the open forum the results of this tolerated research — *public dissent* — is unacceptable, and makes it necessary for the Magisterium to lay bare the roots of the mistake made by these the-

[23] *Veritatis Splendor,* no. 4.
[24] *Veritatis Splendor,* no. 110.
[25] Cf. R. McCORMICK, "Dissent in the Church: Loyalty or Liability?" in Id., *The Critical Calling. Reflections on Moral Dilemmas Since Vatican II,* Washington, 1989, p.25-46.

ologians: they have given in to "modern" currents of thought, detaching human freedom from truth.

From the history of theology[26], we have learned that by means of a responsible freedom in research inspired by a equally responsible freedom of conscience, the splendour of truth that is present in all the works of the Creator becomes revealed to those who dare to stand in its light. All of us are granted the freedom to take this step, all of us share the responsibility to realize it. Will we?

---

[26] For an excellent example, cfr. the already mentioned article from Louis Janssens, note 13.

GERMAN KIRCHENSTEUER

KNUT WALF

The church tax (Kirchensteuer) is a speciality of the church system of finances in the Federal Republic of Germany. It is the church's main financial support. In a modified form it also exists in Denmark, several Swiss cantons, and more recently in Spain and Italy. It was not until the nineteenth century that it was introduced by the state (Prussia 1875, Württemberg 1887) as a source for the self-financing of churches and as an instrument of the separation of church and state. But today it is a guarantee of a close connection between the state and the churches, unknown in other countries. And that is also the reason for opposition against the church tax in Germany itself, professor Walf states.

In the context of modern economic and social conditions the church tax represents a compulsory monetary tax on church members, without a legal entitlement to receive anything in return.

1. Background Information

The legal basis for the tax is article 140 of the German Constitution (*Grundgesetz*) in conjunction with art. 137 par. 6 of the former German Weimar Constitution (1919)[1]. In accordance with these articles — as in the Weimar Constitution — 'denominations'[2] are recognized by the state as public corporations (*Körperschaften des öffentlichen Rechtes*). They receive the right "to levy taxes on the basis of the civil tax register". The church tax is protected by the constitution and can only be abolished by a two-thirds majority of the two chambers of the German Parliament[3]. Canon 1263 of the 1983 Code of Canon Law provides an added juridical basis for the bishop to impose, in the words of the canon, an extraordinary and moderate tax.

---

[1] The first constitution of the (East-)German Democratic Republic of 1949 had a comparable regulation (art.43 par.4) which disappeared with the second, the so-called socialist constitution of 1968.

[2] *Religionsgesellschaften*; today we speak about religious communities, or *Religionsgemeinschaften*.

[3] *Bundestag* and *Bundesrat*, art. 79 par. 2 of the Constitution.

With regard to the civil law, problems begin with the term "public corporations" (*Körperschaften des öffentlichen Rechtes*). This term is ambivalent and during the last decades it has fallen into disrepute in the Federal Republic. In Germany it means a very general legal form of an association. The public corporation is, to put it briefly, a juridical form in the so-called indirect civil administration; as a rule it is applied to administrative units which more or less depend on the state! Because of this, Rudolf Smendt, the German expert in constitutional law, two generations ago, referred to the application of this term to the churches and ecclesiastical denominations as "a mysterious honorary title". But the effects of this honorary title are very concrete: compulsory imposition of the church tax by the civil administration.

The revenue from the church tax in the Federal Republic of Germany amounted in 1988 to almost 13 billion marks[4]; from this amount the Catholic Church received more than half: 6.493 billion marks[5]. In 1989 it was more than 7 billion marks, in 1990 the amount sank to 6.771.000.000 marks. But then in 1991 the amount rose rapidly in the old *Länder* (Federal states) to 7.5 billion marks, and even for 1992, 8.2 billion marks are anticipated. Overall in the Federal Republic the 1990 revenue from the church tax came to 13.3 billion marks; more than half was for the Catholic Church (6.771 billion marks, as noted above); in 1991 it was 15.2 billion marks[6]. No doubt there have always been large fluctuations; for example the Catholic Church rate of increase went from 11.4% in 1985, to 1.6% in 1986 and 8.6% in 1987, to 3.2% in 1988; similar fluctuations can be seen in earlier years[7]. The share of the money in the churches' budgets derived from the church tax fluctuates at around 90%. The laws concerning the church tax of the various *Länder* allow different sorts of church taxes (additional charge on the income tax, wealth tax, or property tax); furthermore it is possible for the churches, independently of the church tax, to raise a so-called *Kirchgeld* (a parish tax). Both the church tax and parish tax can be deducted from income tax, as tax-deductible expenditures. The church is free to decide which variety or form of taxation it will apply. Various kinds of taxation can also be used cumulatively next to one another.

[4] 12.893 billion marks.

[5] 27 million Roman Catholics live in Germany.

[6] Respectively about half for each of the two major churches. Annual rate of increase was around 15 %.

[7] In the diocese of Rottenburg-Stuttgart the revenues of the church tax in January-September 1991 were raised by + 14,3 % in comparison with the previous year. The valuation was only + 7,3 %! Accordingly for the whole year 1991 a rate of increase of 12 % was expected. For 1992 an increase of not more that 8 % is expected.

The right to levy the church tax must be differentiated from the collection of the church tax by the government. This latter is not guarantied by the constitution. With the exception of Bavaria, where there is a distinct administration of the churches for the collection of the church tax, in general the churches make use of this right. But they have to pay for it with about 3.2% of the church tax revenue. This amount covers the costs of the civil tax authorities. Certainly it would be more expensive for the churches to establish and maintain their own offices for collecting the church tax than to pay for the services of the civil authorities.

Because the main part of the church tax comes from an additional charge (8-9%) on the income tax, the churches are dependent on the income tax policy of the government and also on declining or increasing economic trends. This fact explains the interest of the churches in maintaining the connection between the church tax and the income tax. Other kinds of taxes are more dependant on alterations or shifts, today partly influenced by the tax guidelines of the European Community (primarily the taxes concerning material objects; i.e., sales taxes).

2. Juridical Basis

Under the present German tax system only a quarter of church members must pay the church tax. This fact may seem astonishing, but it is a fact: citizens without their own income or with a small income are exempted from the church tax as well as certain others, for example, recipients of high state pensions (so far, these last mentioned are not subject to income tax in Germany). Because income tax is progressive, the burden of the church tax on top wage-earners is considerable and a cause for concern. So it is not true to say with regard to the present tax system that *all* church members contribute to the maintenance of the church and that the church does not depend on the wealthy or more well-to-do.

The juridical basis for the obligation to pay the church tax is a tax assessment. Those affected can refuse to comply with the demand, if necessary by a suit in the tax court. The church for its part must not go through the courts for bankruptcies. One can avoid payment of the church tax by leaving the church by a civil act, which is a declaration to the registry office or the district court. In Lower Saxony, for example, this is by a declaration to the registrar in accordance with the July 4, 1973 (civil) law on leaving the church, in conjunction with the amendment of April 20, 1978: "The announcement that one is leaving the

Church can be made orally or in writing. It is not allowed to declare reservations and conditions or to make additional clauses. Minutes must be taken of the oral declaration, which must be signed by the one who has declared it. The written announcement must be certified publicly" (sec. 2, par. 2). Leaving the church with civil effect in the Catholic Church leads to excommunication, but not to an exclusion from the church! In accordance with the doctrine of the Catholic Church this is not possible, any more than leaving the church.

To deal with leaving the church (with civil effects) for purely financial reasons the so-called "capping" of the church tax has been devised. This fixes an absolute or relative amount of the church tax; for example, a limitation of 2 or 4% of taxable income. In most of the German federal states capping has been declared legal, but it is not always practiced.

People who are committed to paying the church tax retain little influence on its distribution. Various church organs are competent to deal with this, with lay people well in the majority; but members who depend on or who are appointed by church authorities form an obstructive minority. The transition from the former system of the local church tax (parish tax) to the diocesan church tax or — in the Protestant Churches — to the Land church tax after the Second World War, has prompted persistent attempts at centralization by the church hierarchy.

As was said above, the revenues from the church tax make up the lion's share of church budgets in Germany. But one must not forget (in view of a longed-for reduction or even abolition of the church tax in its existing form) that the German churches have a variety of different kinds of income supplied partly by the government, where the money does not come from the church tax:

- Payments of the government on the basis of art. 140 of the Constitution in conjunction with art. 138 par. 1 of the Weimar Constitution. The legal titles which go with these are of various kinds. For the Catholic Church they go back to a large extent to art. 35 of the *Reichsdeputationshauptschluß* of 1803. From these revenues salaries, or at least a portion of salaries, are paid for bishops, canons, parish priests, sextons, organists, and even choirmasters. Revenues are also devoted to the training of the church staff (Faculties of Theology), to the construction and maintenance of church buildings, and so forth.
- Subsidies and exemptions from taxes by the government. Regularly the church receives various financial contributions from the government as a social welfare agency, for youth work, hospitals and old people's homes, but also for example as an entity responsible

for the preservation of historic monuments. These government contributions are not based on firm legal titles. So, they are revocable, must be used for a specified purpose, and are granted often only on a temporary basis. But undeniably, the annual renewal of such government subsidies develops into the character of permanent government contributions.

Then there are tax exemptions. For example, members of orders or other religious communities are exempted from the income tax. The *Bensberger Kreis,* an association of German left-wing Catholics, has listed more exemptions and favors in its memorandum "About Some Aspects of Church Financing" (1985; third edition, 1992). The subsidy report of the Federal Government reveals how much money was involved. The sixth report (1980) showed that the churches had received annually at least 31.7 billion marks; on the basis of changed criteria, the ninth subsidy report (1983) mentioned only a sum of 15.5 billion marks.

There is a serious purpose for mentioning here the rather general category of these various payments, subsidies, exemptions, or preferential treatments. Often the churches deliberately give the inappropriate impression to the public that their social efforts are financed by money coming from the church tax. But that is only partially true. If one looks at a budget which a German diocese presents to the public, one can calculate that social efforts today in general make up only 10% of the budget (for example, in the 1990 budget for the diocese of Rottenburg-Stuttgart[8]). Two points can be made about this. First, this item has been declining continuously for the last ten years (from nearly 14 to 10%). Second, one must realize that this item is not at all exclusively a matter of personnel or material costs; rather, this money is largely invested profitably, for example in buying property or for construction (or building maintenance, for example in public housing). But to what extent, these payments are made with money derived from the church tax or from goverment subsidies, is not clear. However, one can presume that government subsidies alloted for this specified purpose make up the lion's share. It must be mentioned explicitly that the diversification of the items of other church budgets, for example in parishes, can be different.

3. Discussions on the Church Tax

Allegedly the majority of the German population is well disposed toward the church tax. There is no doubt about this, but one might

[8] In the 1990 budget estimate of the Archdiocese of Munich and Freising 19,98 %!

wonder if it is because the people are not informed sufficiently, or even not informed at all, about the problematic nature of the church tax. Of course there is a popular disapproval of taxes, but it amounts to a kind of resignation.

Incidentally, a question from the group *Christenrechte in der Kirche* ("The Rights of Christians in the Church") in March and April of 1990 to all parties represented in the German parliament, resulted in the remarkable insight that all parties including the Greens take a skeptical or negative view of the repeal of the church tax, although for different reasons. It is also interesting that during the last election campaign in the federal state Schleswig-Holstein the chairman of the Christian Democratic Party (CDU) and candidate minister-president Ottfried Hennig called for a thorough rethinking of the church tax. According to *Der Spiegel* of March 2, 1992, the deputy of the German Social Democratic Party (SPD) Edith Niehuis wants to plug the sources of income for the clergy because of the unconstitutional discrimination against the women. Wolfgang Lüder of the Liberals (FDP) thinks that the German church tax conflicts with European Law. And Franz Romer (CDU) intends to replace the church tax by a general "culture and social tax". Of course the churches immediately opposed this.

For quite some time there has been a considerable literary debate in Germany about the church tax. Whereas in former times — approximately to the middle of the seventies — the dividing line was clear between non-ecclesiastical, possibly even anticlerical critics on the one side, and supporters who were involved in the churches on the other, since then a more subtly differentiated way of looking at things has been gaining ground.

Critics inside the church still remain a minority. Yet in 1973 the Common Synod of the Dioceses in the Federal Republic of Germany could not evade the task of at least reflecting on the church tax. But because of the personnel who made up the commission one could not expect an in-depth critique of the German church financial system. The result of the comparative study of church financial systems in the whole world presented by the Synod's Commission V in a paper titled "Tasks of the Church in State and Society" (part D: The Financing of the Church Tasks) culminated as expected in a favorable defense of the German system. Also in this paper the major argument was for the social and charitable component, which (it was thought) could hardly be objected to. But one can surely ask why they praised the German system so highly since it is not copied anywhere else in the world.

A critical contribution from inside the Catholic Church was the previously mentioned memorandum of the *Bensberger Kreis*. It met with critical approval in serious periodicals, but one must also recognize that the church media have kept silent about the memorandum. What is kept quiet eventually breaks out vehemently! It has been noticed generally that in the last few years several signs of rebellion against the church tax can be observed. In Kerpen, a small town in the Catholic Lower Rhine valley, an action group has formed against the church tax. In a grass roots community (*Basisgemeinde*) in Wuppertal a project has been developed about the problems of the church tax. This project is aimed especially at the redesignation of the church tax (for example, in favor of married priests); the idea of a "grass roots church tax association" is also being considered. Finally, in the last phase of the GDR there were discussions here and there as to whether the reunited Germany should return to the church tax system; especially the active church members thought that the GDR system of a voluntary parish tax ought to be retained because of the smaller influence of the civil government on the churches. Later, in the unification treaty — one might say, by a trick — the West German church tax system was introduced in the new federal states in the East; this is yet one more curiosity in the history of the German church tax[9]. As a result of the *Katholikentag von unten* in 1990 (an assembly of grass roots Catholics in competition with the official *Katholikentag*) an association was founded for the redesignation of the church tax.

All these initiatives have resulted in the bureaucracy of the so-called official church condescending to give more information about how the church tax money is used. This is done as an argument in favor of continuing the status quo. The archdiocese of Cologne, for example, the richest German diocese, perhaps the richest in the whole Catholic Church, especially stands out. Believe it or not, the budget of this diocese was balanced in 1991 with 1.140.259.239 marks. This is more than the budgets of most Black African countries. Again, only for comparison: in 1990 the Cologne budget was "only" 978 millions marks; thus between these two years there was a rate of increase of nearly 17%!

---

[9] The draft of a GDR-church tax law (without date!) from the time after the so-called *Wende* ('change') was not discussed in the *Volkskammer*, the East German parliament, and was not put to a vote. Later, however, it was decided this was a valid law in the new Federal States, although these States did not formally exist at that time, let alone that their elected parliaments could vote about this question (art. 9 par.5 chap.3 of the German unification treaty [EVertr]).

4. What Can Be Done?

The church tax in its present form is advantageous especially for dioceses and the Land Churches. In the short term one must try to return to the parish tax which existed in principle until the Nazi period. I should like to stress that even in the present system the Protestant Churches grant a far greater autonomy to their communities than Catholic dioceses to their parishes. That is evident from a very recent and thorough study at the University of Cologne's Institute of Public Finances.

The participation of church lay committees in the distribution of the church tax is absolutely insufficient. That is why a major effort must be made, especially in a more democratic manner, for more independent and competent lay people to be named to the diocesan advisory committees for the distribution of the church tax. Eventually this could lead to other priorities being adopted in church budgets; for example, more money could be given over for social purposes in Germany itself and — hopefully — for the so-called Third World countries. On the other hand, we may assume (or at least hope) that less would be invested in absurdly large church bureaucracies which are now out of all proportion to the real significance of the churches within our society.

Also, less money would flow from Germany to Rome, which would contribute to a speeding up of church reforms. For example, the Association of the German Dioceses (VDD, or *Verband der Diözesen Deutschlands*) which since 1968 has looked after the economic interests of the (West) German dioceses, has reserved in its 1990 budget nearly 160 million marks for the budgetary item "World Church and Mission"; that was more than 53% of its total budget! This money flows for the most part to Rome and at best from there to the so-called mission territories or countries. In 1990 and 1991 the Vatican was supported directly by the VDD to the sum of 10 million marks annually. Not included in this item are special gifts of dioceses or the so-called Peter's Pence, a special gift for the Holy See every year, which is collected by parish collections.

Because many church members are confronted with many and diverse problems associated with the church tax, one must look for solutions to escape from paying the church tax, without having to leave the church. Many German Catholics pay the church tax only because they are forced to do so. Many German Catholics pay the church tax only of necessity. The church tax is a relic from the times of the State church.

Implemented perhaps in stages, the church tax should be replaced by a system of voluntary contributions in keeping with various models in foreign churches. To finance itself in some other manner than it does today, the German church should learn from its own past and from the experience of its neighboring churches.

But there are also theological reasons for opposing the church tax:

- How is it possible that a church can not only defend such a system, but also legally and theologically justify a system which was originally forced on it by the anticlerical liberal state of the nineteenth century?

- Anyone who is no longer willing to pay the church tax is forced to leave the church (with civil legal consequences). But in accordance with the traditional doctrine of the Catholic Church, one cannot resign from the church.

Nevertheless such an act of legal significance in the civil law sphere is not accepted as a fact without any opposition within the Catholic Church. Whoever refuses to pay is automatically excommunicated. Probably many Germans take this step, for whatever reasons, and do not have any problem with the doctrine of the church. Or at any rate not so much so that they think they might have to leave the church on that account. The only reason they leave is to get free of the church tax (that is the case of the so-called modified departure from the church). Also in these cases there is no possibility to discuss the matter with relevant church authorities. It is claimed that those who take this step do not want to support the bishop and thereby separate themselves from the church community. Therefore they are to be considered schismatic. In the Archdiocese of Cologne and the Diocese of Trier this offence traditionally carries the heavy penalty of excommunication. Canon lawyers even suggest that "spiritual sanctions (for example, exclusion from the Eucharist, excommunication) challenge those who refuse to share the responsibility for meeting the Church's financial needs" [10].

In the meantime the consciences even of clerics in senior positions have been stirred. For example, according to the *Süddeutsche Zeitung* of January 14, 1992, the Benedictine Abbot Odilo Lechner of Munich made a statement about the possibility of a boycott of the church tax in extreme cases, as a legitimate kind of protest inside the church: "Where I notice a totally incorrect use of the money, possibly I can let my protest be seen through a tax strike without leaving the church community". As is obviously often the case in the Catholic Church, Lechner later said his remarks were "misunderstood," according to the left-leaning Catholic magazine *Publik-Forum* of February 28, 1992.

---

[10] K. MÖRSDORF, *Kirchenrecht II*, Paderborn, 1967, p.497.

Hopefully it is clearer how much financial power is concentrated in the hands of the church hierarchy in Germany. With money one can change the world. But also a church's image is formed by the wealth it possesses and how it manages this money. In modern democracies more and more precautions are taken institutionally so that the money of the taxpayers is used sensibly and is kept safe from arbitrariness, corruption and stubbornness of officials. One can read everyday in the newspapers that this objective is not always reached either in the state or in society. Having gained an insight into the church over a longer period, one knows that things are quite human there as well.

The German church is responsible for a lot of money. Those who allocate this money have an inadequate influence on its distribution or investment. The church in Germany is maintained with the church tax. It provides over 90% of church budgets. Something must be done to bring the management of this money under scrutiny. To demand this must be the prime concern for lay people in the church. In the meantime something has already been gained as a result of pressure from the popular church, pressure from the base. But much remains to be done.

HOMOSEXUALITY IN THE NETHERLANDS

JAN VAN HOOYDONK

This contribution by the Dutch journalist Jan van Hooydonk outlines the changes, from the turn of the century, in the position of gay men and lesbian women within Dutch society and church. Catholic intellectuals, pastors, and last but not least the gay and lesbian movement outside and within the church, actively contributed to this emancipation. Before describing this he offers, in the following section, a few general historical observations.

"Within our community of faith, there are men who love men and women who love women. Gay men and lesbian women, as they are usually referred to, make up part of the People of God. The place of many lesbian women and gay men within the church is still inconspicuous. They are silent, or worse yet, they are silenced. Their very existence, with all the joys and sorrows that are part of any life, is denied recognition and affirmation."

These are the opening lines of the *Pastoral Letter on Faith and Homosexuality,* published in 1989 by the *Werkverband van Katholieke Homo-Pastores* (Working Group of Catholic Gay Pastors) in The Netherlands. But, the letter continues, "more and more, we are made aware of another movement: gay and lesbian believers are acquiring a name and a face within the community. They are standing up and speaking out, often out of discontent, though also increasingly in witness to the fact that they are happy with who and what they are, and that they have chosen to embody their gay and lesbian existence in creative ways, in friendship and solidarity and, in particular, as people of faith"[1].

---

[1] Working Group of Catholic Gay Pastors, *Called to Blessing: A Pastoral Letter on Faith and Homosexuality,* Mt. Rainier, 1992, p.1. (Original: Werkverband van Katholieke Homo-Pastores, *Tot zegen geroepen: Pastorale brief over geloof en (homo)sexualiteit,* Amersfoort/Leuven, 1989. German translation: Arbeitsgruppe Katholischer homosexueller Seelsorger Niederlande, *Homosexualität und Glaube. Zum Segen berufen: Ein Pastoralbrief,* Neuss, 1989. For orders: Secretariaat WKHP, fr. Theo Koster O.P., Postbus 59, 6850 Huissen, Nederland.

1. The Fallacy of 'Unchangeable Church Doctrine'

"I wonder and cannot express my amazement
That my John has not hurried back to me,
Though he is forever promising that he will return.
Either the boy is sick, or he has forgotten me.
(...)
The boy is fickle, like everything young.
(...)
A man is never secure that it can never come fast enough."[2]

"People who are homosexually inclined should realize that there are more people, either homosexual or otherwise, who manage to be strong through grace; who unclamorously lead their lives in solitude or friendship."[3]

The authors of the above quotations are both archbishops. Frenchman Baudri of Bourgeuil lived from 1046 to 1130 and rose to be archbishop of Dol. Dutchman Adrianus Simonis, who wrote the second text, was born in 1931; in 1970 he became bishop of Rotterdam, in 1983 archbishop of Utrecht and primate of the Dutch Church Province; he was made a cardinal in 1985. In archbishop Baudri's time it was by no means uncommon for clergymen to put to paper frank homo-erotic poetry: "The single source of writing about romantic love during the first millennium of the Christian tradition is monastic literature. Monks fell in love with each other — often," American historian John Boswell says[4]. In Cardinal Simonis' days, however, statements by ecclesiastical authorities tend to actively stimulate hostility towards gay and lesbian people.

To the examples of Baudri and Simonis many others could be added. The study of history can lead to no other conclusion than that the assertion — nowadays subscribed to by both the hierarchy and some of its opponents — that regarding homosexuality there is an 'unchangeable church doctrine' is just not true. It goes without saying that those who, within the community of faith, work for gay and lesbian emancipation, find this a liberating view. Simultaneously the above examples raise the question where an explanation can be found for the homophobia that now characterizes so many deeds and words of christians and their

---

[2] J. BOSWELL, *Christianity, Social Tolerance, and Homosexuality. Gay people in Western Europe from the beginning of the Christian Era to the Fourteenth Century*, Chicago/London, 1980, pp.245-246.

[3] A. SIMONIS, circular letter of 10 June 1985; in the author's records.

[4] J. BOSWELL, *Rediscovering Gay History* (The Fifth Michael Harding Memorial Address), London, 1985, p.16.

leaders. There is no clear-cut answer, but research points out several factors:

* In his fundamental study of the history of social (in)tolerance regarding gay people within western christianity the aforementioned Boswell records an important turn in the thirteenth and fourteenth centuries. In his view the increase of intolerance is connected with the rise of 'absolutist' political structures which require submission to uniform systems. This forcing into line is not only realized through civil law, but also through moral-ecclesiastical regulations and theological underpinning.

* This same era shows us the first collective stigmatization and persecution of gay people. Often a link is forged between homosexuality and heresy or witchcraft. Boswell says there are striking parallels between the persecution of gays and Jews[5].

* An equally important factor is provided by the patriarchal division of power which extols men and 'the male' over women and 'the female'. German authors Monika Barz, Herta Leistner and Ute Wild show its consequences for lesbian women: their existence was, and still is, just denied. When women are supposed not to have any sexual feelings of their own, a thing like lesbian sexuality is outside the realm of imagination. Accordingly Barz c.s. define male homosexuality as 'love between people of the dominating sex', and lesbian sexuality as 'love of the dominated sex'[6].

* At the same time other authors stress the impact that the patriarchy has also with respect to gay men: sexual contacts of men having for ages been defined mainly in terms of anal intercourse, the 'passive partner' in this intercourse was especially despised. For "he debases the male nature into a female one"[7].

* Since the Middle Ages state and church have continuously grown more apart. During the 'bourgeois' era the church retired more and more to what might be the last stronghold left to her: the family. "Within this broader context ecclesiastical teaching approached the problem of homosexuality (...) not merely as a matter of sexuality,

---

[5] J. BOSWELL, *Rediscovering Gay History*, p.7.

[6] M. BARZ, H. LEISTNER, U. WILD, *Hättest du gedacht dass wir so viele sind?*, Stuttgart/Zürich, 1987. Dutch translation: *Wie had gedacht dat we met zovelen zijn?*, *Lesbische vrouwen in de kerk*, Baarn 1988, p.74. It may be useful to point out that the author of this article is a male, and that this may influence his way of thinking and writing.

[7] Th. BEEMER, "Sodomie in de geschiedenis van de kerkelijke zedenleer," in Th. BEEMER e.a., *Liefde, lust en leven. Een bijdrage aan het gesprek tussen katholieken en protestanten*, in: Tenminste, no. 4., Kampen, 1982, pp.41-56, p.44.

but also as connected with her own (19th century) identity," Dutch
moral theologian Rinus Houdijk says. "Because in modern times
she linked her doctrinal authority so strongly with a specific interpretation of sexual morality, today's Church is not only concerned
with arguments regarding homosexuality as such (on the basis of
Scripture and tradition), but equally with the fact that here her
absolute claim to possess the truth and the absolute legitimacy of
her authority (in the 'modern' formula of 'unchangeable church
doctrine') are at stake. The problem of homosexuality affects the
complete institutional identity of the Church in her 19th century
materialization."[8]

* Every gay or lesbian church member — but not only they — can
tell from experience that what within the church is presented as
'christian morality', is in many cases just another way of expressing disgust, aversion or resistance. With regard to homosexuality
this might be connected with the celibate-male set-up of the church
hierarchy. Within such a 'homosocial context' the overt presence
of homosexuality is threatening. For homosexuality is marked by a
certain 'power to disturb' as late Michel Foucault called it. In an
interview this French author of a number of studies on the history
of sexuality said: "I think that what makes homosexuality so
untransparent is its style of life rather than the sexual activity itself.
Fantasizing about sexual acts which do not conform to law or
nature is not what makes people uncertain. It is the fact that individuals start loving each other, that is the problem. The institutions
are turned upside down, are thwarted by affective powers, are confirmed and rocked at the same time: take for instance the army [or
the Roman Catholic clergy and hierarchy! JvH], where love
between men is constantly both conjured up and discredited. The
institutional codes cannot regulate these relationships in their ever
returning intensity, in their varied colours, in their invisible movements, just because they are always changing. In areas where law,
rule and custom are supposed to reign, such relationships cause
short-circuits and introduce love."[9]

In gay and lesbian circles it is supposed that this hostile attitude
shown by the Roman Catholic hierarchy and clergy, comes for an impor-

[8] R. HOUDIJK, "Kerk en homoseksualiteit: Veranderende opvattingen en de aard
van kerkelijke reacties," in *Tijdschrift voor Theologie* 26(1986) pp.259-281, p.265.

[9] D.J. BOS (ed.), *Michel Foucault in gesprek. Seks, macht en vriendschap,* Amsterdam, 1985, p.26. (Original: R. DE CECCATTY e.a., "De l'amitié comme mode de vie,"
in *Le Gay Pied,* April 1981, pp.38-39.)

tant part from 'secret' homosexuals who hold power and authority in the church. "In the Church repressed homosexuality is an important source of sexual power games," says American theologian John J. McNeill, himself expelled from the Jesuit Order because he is gay[10].

Let us now see how, in the Catholic community of the 20th century Netherlands, the irrepressible longing we call homosexuality is both opposed and gainig ground.

2. A Moral Nation[11]

Thanks to the liberal constitution of 1848 the Dutch Catholics got the same legal status and rights their Protestant countrymen already enjoyed. This constitution ended a situation that had existed since national independence was won (1568): Catholics had been treated as second-class citizens. Legal equality having been established, the struggle for political, economical, cultural and social emancipation of Catholics could start. It led to the development of what the Dutch call Catholic denominationalism: Catholics of all walks of life were brought together in a closely knit framework of Catholic institutions operating in every area of personal and social life. And, of course, under the strict supervision of bishops and clergy.

The most important Dutch Catholic historian of this century, Louis Rogier, sketched this denominational climate: "Whenever half a dozen Catholics joined forces in a club or company, even with no loftier aim than to play cards or bingo, the bishops appointed a priest as spiritual director with the right of veto. In the long run a Roman Catholic couldn't take one little step without priestly guidance. He travelled, played football, swam or danced accompanied by a priest; and a priest of the Haarlem diocese, later to become its bishop, even had the nerve to

[10] J. VAN HOOYDONK, "Belichaamde spiritualiteit. An interview with John McNeill," in *De Bazuin* 72(1989) no.9, pp.3-5.

[11] References for this section: E. BORGMAN e.a., "Van Pastoraal Concilie tot Acht Mei Beweging," in E. BORGMAN a.o., *De vernieuwingen in katholiek Nederland. Van Vaticanum II tot Acht Mei Beweging*, Amersfoort/Leuven, 1988, pp.13-30; P. LUYKX, "De veranderende houding van de Nederlandse katholieken inzake homoseksualiteit, 1930-1980," in *Groniek* 12 (1980) no.66, pp.69-75; H. OOSTERHUIS, *Homoseksualiteit in katholiek Nederland. Een sociale geschiedenis 1900-1970*, Amsterdam, 1992; R. TIELMAN, *Homoseksualiteit in Nederland. Studie van een emancipatiebeweging*, Amsterdam, 1982; H. WANSINK, "Verzuiling en homo-emancipatie," in J. SCHUYF e.a.(ed.), *Homojaarboek 3. Artikelen over emancipatie en homoseksualiteit*, Amsterdam, 1985, pp.176-193.

write to a newspaper complaining there weren't enough priests to offer daily spiritual guidance to 'each Roman Catholic family'"[12].

Between roughly 1880 and 1920 this denominationalism profoundly changed the character of Dutch society. The rise of Catholic and Protestant political parties — for the Protestants developed an analogous denominational system — turned the liberal state into what is sometimes defined as a 'moral nation'. In this split-up and 'confessionalized' society civil authorities acted as the guardians of both public and private morality. From 1811 onwards homosexual behaviour had not been punishable, but exactly one century later Catholic Minister of Justice E.H.R. Regout managed to have an anti-homosexual article inserted in the penal code: "An adult who sexually abuses minors of the same sex, will be punished by confinement not exceeding four years" (art. 248 bis). Thus the state tried to keep in check the "adult lecher" who "prefers to look for his victims among youngsters that are insufficiently experienced to see straightaway what his evil game is".

This article 248 bis elicited the formation of the *Nederlandsch Wetenschappelijk Humanitair Komitee* (Dutch Scholarly Humanitarian Committee) led enthousiastically by lawyer esquire J.A. Schorer (1866-1975). This committee, which can be seen as the Dutch section of the German *Wissenschaftlich-Humanitäres Komitee,* founded in Berlin in 1897, by physician and sexuologist Magnus Hirschfeld, advocated the abolition of article 248 bis; its main activity was in the field of publicity. The NWHK's opponents were mainly to be found among catholics. Dominican priest dr. L. Bender published a counter-attack: *Verderfelijke propaganda* (Poisonous Propaganda). In this booklet he distinguished between homosexuality as an inclination and an act — a distinction, Bender says, the NWHK neglects to make. It is exactly the act which is "a serious offence against the natural order instituted by God, the Creator of nature". For the homosexual act lacks the finality of sexuality which consists in procreation. For the benefit of those who cannot immediately see that homosexual intercourse is sinful, the Dominican compares the homosexual act with "eating tainted meat".

Catholic physicians, too, gladly endorsed ecclesiastical ethics. In 1930 the *R.K. Artsenvereniging* (Society of Roman Catholic Doctors) convened to discuss 'the problem of homosexuality'. In his introduction to the report of this congress, published as late as 1941, secretary J.B.V.M. Veraart is outspoken: "In our modern time there is certainly no room for societies such as the Nederlandsch Wetenschappelijk Humanitair Komitee".

[12] L.J. ROGIER, *Vandaag en morgen,* Bilthoven, 1974, pp.140-141.

When "the modern time" had already gone for five years — after the German occupiers had killed an unknown number of homosexual Dutch people, amongst them resistance fighter Willem Arondeus — the study centre of the *Katholieke Volkspartij* (Catholic People's Party), the largest party in Dutch parliament, issued a suggestion that any form of homosexual contact — also between adults — should be made punishable. Incurable and recalcitrant homosexuals should be given obligatory treatment in mental hospitals. But about 1950 the Catholic denominational set-up and its political party had lost so much of their strength that the proposal died peacefully in the mothballs.

3. An Anthropocentric Turn

The distinction between homosexuality as an 'inclination' (personal characteristic) and an 'act' (behaviour) is rather new. The term homosexual first occurs in a brochure published in 1869 by German writer Karl Maria Benkert[13]. This new approach, symbolized by the gradually established word 'homosexuality', was mainly brought about by physicians and psychologists. It testifies to the increasing social importance of medicine and psychology, and relativizes the old moral-theological approach which was only interested in the 'act' as such (called 'sodomy') and did not reflect on the personality of those who did it. Doctors and therapists took up responsibility for human well-being. From now on the consulting room was visited more often than the confessional. Historian Harry Oosterhuis, who wrote an important work on the attitude of Dutch Catholics towards homosexuality in the present century[14], refers to this phenomenon as the dominance of the 'psy-complex'. It is against this background that one should interpret the developments that took place, from the fifties onwards, in Catholic thinking about homosexuality — and sexuality in general. Although this development took place nearly everywhere in the western world, it may have been quicker in The Netherlands than elsewhere. Catholic intellectuals smartly employed the extensive structures of Catholic denominationalism to spread their ideas quickly and efficiently.

Regarding morality in the post-war period The Netherlands experienced an 'anthropocentric turn', according to researchers Ed Simons and Lodewijk Winkeler. "This meant that the primary concern now is the

---

[13] G. HEKMA, *Homoseksualiteit, een medische reputatie. De uitdoktering van de homoseksueel in negentiende-eeuws Nederland,* Amsterdam, 1987, p.13.

[14] See note 11.

happiness of modern man, which is an internal matter, a matter of well-being. Moreover, there was a belief that man himself could shape both personal life and society. The inferences as to man's spiritual life — faith and morality — are obvious: the criterium was no longer pre-established and objective doctrine, but personal awareness and authentic experience."[15] From the fifties onwards traditional sexual ethics were increasingly criticized as 'inhumane'. Things that moralists characterized as morally correct could, according to the practitioners of the new discipline of mental health, be disastrous for personal happiness. Rigid sexual ethics they saw as a source of neuroses and personal misery. This criticism led to a new pastoral approach.

From now on it was not 'sin', but '(mental) health' that took pride of place in deciding what was good or bad in the field of sexuality. The 'objective doctrine' of the 'teaching authority' faded into the background, making room for the personal and informed judgement of the faithful, for their individual consciences, as the guidelines for decisions concerning sexuality. This applied not only to family size and birth control, but also to homosexuality. In the sixties, during and immediately after the Second Vatican Council, the Dutch bishops wholeheartedly supported this development.

As to homosexuality, the criticism of traditional ethical thinking led to the growing acceptance of homosexuality not only as an inclination but also as behaviour. Two phases can be distinguished here. First of all the thesis was that the homosexual inclination as such is an unchangeable, not personally chosen, and accordingly a 'morally neutral' condition. The way in which this 'fact' is established characterizes the period in which authors gave their opinions. In 1961, psychiatrist C.J.B.J. Trimbos, talking on the Catholic Broadcast Corporation, said "it is absolutely unjust to hold a homosexual responsible for his being a homosexual. He has not assumed this condition himself"[16]. Sixteen years later, in a pastoral study entitled *A Person Does Not Have To Be Alone*, homosexuality was presented as a "chosen way of life"[17].

The second step in accepting homosexuality was both crucial and delicate: the dualism of mind and body was rejected, and the distinction between inclination and act was branded untenable. Accordingly sexual

---

[15] E. SIMONS; L. WINKELER, *Het verraad der clercken. Intellectuelen en hun rol in de ontwikkelingen van het Nederlands katholicisme na 1945*, Baarn, 1987, p.215.

[16] C.J.B.J. TRIMBOS, *Gehuwd en ongehuwd*, Hilversum, 1961, p.157.

[17] C.O. HELLEMA, "Homosexualiteit als gekozen bestaansvorm," in A.J.R. BRUS-SAARD e.a., *Een mens hoeft niet alleen te blijven. Een evangelische visie op homofilie*, Baarn, 1977, pp.71-89.

abstinence was no longer seen as something that goes without saying. "The pastor should realize that the homosexual inclination is no ground for imposing an abstinent life. Abstinence is only humane if freely and consciously chosen." [18]

New insights in the field of mental health not only influenced pastors and public opinion. In 1958 a special pastoral centre for gay and lesbian people was opened in Amsterdam. In de mid-sixties it was followed by a *Werkgroep Pastorale Hulp aan Homofielen* (Working Group for Pastoral Help to Gays and Lesbians). In this Working Group pastors from various christian denominations cooperated harmoniously. In 1971, after sixty years of (gay)struggle, the Second Chamber of the Dutch Parliament abolished the objectionable article 248 bis. Catholic intellectuals and pastors were among the advocates of this decision. Two years later, and with the support of these same people, the national gay and lesbian movement COC — successor to the NWHK which was stopped in 1940 — got legal recognition.

Both facts point to a growing acceptance of gay men and lesbian women in Dutch society. Catholics do not lag behind, as is shown by many opinion polls. A significant example is found in the results of a representative enquiry among Roman Catholic women, published in 1987. It shows that only 11% of the people questioned endorse the official church stand with regard to homosexuality; 64% do not support it. Homosexuality is accepted more widely than abortion and divorce, we find: the church's stand on abortion is subscribed to by 29% of the women, and rejected by 18%; the ecclesiastical position on divorce is shared by 14% and dismissed by 30% [19]. Opinion researchers remind us that, within Dutch society, the religious factor is on the decline. This means that the differences between the view of the faithful (among them the Catholics) and those who do not believe, are disappearing: the dying-out of denominationalism goes together with an ever diminishing specific Catholic code of behaviour.

4. Treated With Understanding

Since 1975 the Vatican has published three important statements in which homosexuality is discussed: in 1975, 1986 and 1992. These reac-

---

[18] A. VAN HEUSDEN, "Pastorale benadering," in A.J.R. BRUSSAARD, *Een mens hoeft niet alleen te blijven*, pp.145-158, p.157.
[19] M.J. ANGENENT-VOGT e.a., *Vrouw en Kerk. Een onderzoek naar de relatie van Nederlandse katholieke vrouwen met de kerk* (KASKI-rapport, 392), Amersfoort, 1987, p.67.

tions have an unmistakably reactionary stamp: the Vatican takes position against the prevailing trend that more and more members of the
People of God defend the right to a gay or lesbian way of life, and that
a number of Catholics also practise this. As the voice of gay men and
lesbian women, and of their supporters, is gaining strength, the voice of
the teaching authorities is becoming gruffer.

The first document to be mentioned here is the Declaration on Certain
Questions Concerning Sexual Ethics, usually referred to as *Persona
Humana* by its first words in Latin. It was published, on Pope Paul VI's
order, by the Sacred Congregation for the Doctrine of the Faith on 29
December 1975[20].

"In the present period, the corruption of morals has increased, and
one of the most serious indications of this corruption is the unbridled
exaltation of sex," the authors of *Persona Humana* say. In this situation
the Congregation considers it its duty to offer a new enunciation of the
church's doctrine, and of course according to the "fundamental principles" which the Second Vatican Council declared to be contained in
"the divine law — eternal, objective and universal — whereby God
orders, directs, and governs the entire universe and all the ways of the
human community, by a plan conceived in wisdom and love. Man has
been made by God to participate in this law, with the result that, under
the gentle disposition of divine Providence, he can come to perceive
even increasingly the unchanging truth." The Congregation is of the
opinion that this divine law is accessible to human minds. To which it
adds: "Furthermore, Christ instituted his Church as 'the pillar and bul-
wark of truth' (I Tim. 3:15). With the Holy Spirit's assistance, she
ceaselessly preserves and transmits without error the truths of the moral
order (...)".

The central and apriori principle *Persona Humana* starts from is, that
"every genital act must be within the framework of marriage". That is
why premarital sex, onanism and homosexual relationships are rejected.
It should be noticed that the 1975 declaration introduces a moral nov-
elty, no doubt derived from modern life sciences. For there is a carefully
worded statement that some people seem to have an unchangeable and
'incurable' homosexual inclination. "A distinction is drawn, and it
seems with some reason, between homosexuals whose tendency comes
from a false education, from a lack of normal sexual development, from
habit, from bad example, or from other similar causes, and is transitory

[20] Original text in *Osservatore Romano* (16 January 1976); translation in *Origins*
5(1975-1976) pp.485 ff.

or at least not incurable; and homosexuals who are definitively such because of some kind of innate instinct or a pathological constitution judged to be incurable." Concerning the latter group, the 'incurables', the text says they "must certainly be treated with understanding and sustained in the hope of overcoming their personal difficulties and unability to fit into society". The road to an active experience of sexuality remains, however, closed for them. For "according to the objective moral order, homosexual relations are acts which lack an essential and indispensable finality" — with regard to procreation, that is. Moreover: "In Sacred Scripture they are condemned as a serious depravity and even presented as the sad consequence of rejecting God (Rom. 1:14-27)".

After its publication the Dutch bishops called this declaration a "signpost and an appeal". In their view "presentday society tends to disconnect human sexuality from procreation, and often also from the love between man and woman. That causes the problems". An opposite stand was taken in a text published in 1977 under the aegis of the Council of Churches in The Netherlands, of which the Roman Catholic Church is a full member. This text, A Person Does Not Have To Be Alone[21], defends the legitimacy of life as a gay or lesbian. Among its eleven authors we find five catholics (three of them priests).

In 1978 the Congregation for the Doctrine of the Faith informed the bishops that this publication was "clearly at variance with catholic doctrine". This was one of the reasons why the bishop of Roermond, dr. Johannes Gijsen, withdrew his subsidies for the Council of Churches. He also made it known that he would refuse Holy Communion to homosexuals living together, and accused those who asked the church to accept gay and lesbian people as full church members, of being intolerant. His colleague Adrianus Simonis, at the time still bishop of Rotterdam, took a similar position, albeit in 'milder' words. He exhorted homosexuals to lead a chaste life. These statements by the conservative bishops raised amazement and disapproval everywhere. Both of them became the target of a demonstration — the first demonstration ever in The Netherlands against pronouncements by ecclesiastical authorities — organized in Roermond by the gay and lesbian movement, on Easter Saturday of 1979 ('Pink Saturday')[22]. Reacting to the statement of their colleagues

---

[21] See note 17.

[22] By now Bishop Simonis has moved up and is archbishop of Utrecht. In January 1993, after the Dutch bishops' ad limina visit to Rome, his colleague Gijsen suddenly resigned, allegedly for health reasons; he was appointed chaplain to a convent of women religious in the Austrian diocese of Sankt Pölten, administered by his soul mate dr. Kurt Krenn.

Gijsen and Simonis a few other Dutch bishops informed the press that they held different views on homosexuality. Johannes Bluyssen, then bishop of 's-Hertogenbosch, said he wanted to work for a recognized position of homosexuals in the church.

The episcopal appointments by pope Paul VI of conservative priests Simonis (1970) and Gijsen (1972) led to a deep-going polarization in the Dutch bishops' conference. Homosexuality turned out to be only one of the many points of disagreement. In order to restore 'communio' in 1980 the bishops were summoned to Rome to participate in an Extraordinary Synod presided over by Pope John Paul II. But the synod's list of resolutions does not mention homosexuality at all.

5. Objective Disorder

The 1975 Vatican declaration was followed, on 1 October 1986, by a Letter to the bishops of the Catholic Church on the Pastoral Care of Homosexual Persons[23]. Signed by the prefect of the Sacred Congregation for the Doctrine of the Faith, Cardinal Joseph Ratzinger, this letter accentuates the 1975 Declaration. "In the discussion which followed the publication of the Declaration (...) an overly benign interpretation was given to the homosexual condition itself, some going so far as to call it neutral, or even good. Although the particular inclination of the homosexual person is not a sin, it is a more or less strong tendency ordered towards an intrinsic moral evil; and thus the inclination itself must be seen as an objective disorder." The letter says that the choice for an active experience of homosexuality goes against God's creation order. Hence homosexual persons are "called to enact the will of God in their life by joining whatever sufferings and difficulties they experience in virtue of their condition, to the sacrifice of the Lord's Cross".

The bishops get a special advice to offer adequate pastoral services to homosexuals prepared to take this course. And there are emphatical and repeated warnings against pressure groups which bring "together under the aegis of Catholicism homosexual persons who have not the intention of abandoning their homosexual behaviour. One tactic used is to protest that any and all criticism of or reservations about homosexual people, their activity and lifestyle, are simply diverse forms of unjust discrimination". Groups of this kind (insiders say the American Dignity move-

[23] Original text in *Osservatore Romano* (31 October 1986); translation in *Origins* 16(1986-1987) pp.377 ff.

ment is first of all alluded to here) should on no account be allowed to use churches or the premises of Catholic educational institutes, Ratzinger says. Clearly referring to the AIDS epidemic — which, as is generally known, in the western world mainly affects male homosexuals — the cardinal adds: "Even when the practice of homosexuality may seriously threaten the lives and well-being of a large number of people, its advocates remain undeterred and refuse to consider the magnitude of the risks involved".

Among other things because of this letter, in January 1987 the *Humanistisch Verbond* (the Dutch section of the International Humanist and Ethical Union) invited Cardinal Simonis to take part in a radio programme and give his views on homosexuality. In this interview he said he could understand a lodging-house keeper who, on grounds of conscience rejecting homosexual relations, would refuse to let rooms to homosexuals, fearing a bad influence on the development of his or her children. In the eyes of the national gay and lesbian movement COC this utterance was offensive and discriminating, and it took legal action. The court, however, was of the opinion that the cardinal had not been "unnecessarily offensive," although, the verdict in appeal said, the wording could have been less unfortunate.

On 25 June 1992 the Vatican Congregation for the Doctrine of the Faith sent a letter to the Catholic bishops of the United States. After parts of this letter had been leaked to the American press, the Vatican felt forced to publish the full text, in a slightly altered version, in the *Osservatore Romano*. It is entitled: "Some considerations concerning the response to legislative proposals on the non-discrimination of homosexual persons"[24]. The publication was accompanied by a note saying that the observations "were not intended to be an official and public instruction on the matter from the Congregation, but a background resource offering discrete assistance to those who may be confronted with the task of evaluating draft legislation regarding non-discrimination on the basis of sexual orientation". In spite of this — later added? — 'elucidation' on the document's status, its contents caused quite a stir, not only in the United States, but also in The Netherlands.

About half of the Considerations consists of quotes from the 1986 letter, and to these concrete moral applications are added for the legal and social sphere. Sexual orientation, the document states, is not a characteristic like e.g. race, sex, or age. Therefore sexual orientation is not a ground for claiming non-discrimination. The rights of homosexuals can,

---

[24] Original text in *Osservatore Romano*, 24 July 1992.

indeed must be limited in certain circumstances, because homosexuality just happens to be an "objective disorder" and cannot possibly be a "positive source of human rights". The limitation of the rights of homosexuals can validly be founded on the public interest, on a par with the state's competence to curtail the rights of contagious or mentally ill persons. "There are areas in which it is not unjust discrimination to take sexual orientation into account" the Congregation says, "for example, in the placement of children for adoption or foster care, in employment of teachers or athletic coaches, and in military recruitment". For that matter, the Congregation observes, homosexually oriented persons "who seek to lead chaste lives," need not be afraid of much discrimination. In general they do not show up their sexual orientation. To which the Congregation adds: "In addition, there is a danger that legislation which would make homosexuality a basis for entitlements could actually encourage a person with a homosexual orientation to declare his homosexuality or even to seek a partner in order to exploit the provisions of the law".

The bishops are exhorted to completely oppose anti-discrimination legislation. Exceptional provisions for churches are not sufficient, the guideline is. For: "The Church has the responsibility to promote family life and the public morality of the entire civil society on the basis of fundamental moral values, not simply to protect herself from the application of harmful laws".

6. Troubles of the Dutch Episcopate

For several months the Dutch bishops refused to give public comment on this new document. After the bishops' conference met in september 1992, however, a press statement was issued. It says the bishops "feel no need to change their position, given the fact that the document is not presented as an official instruction, and addresses itself specially to the American bishops". This refusal to speak out evoked a reprimand by five gay and lesbian organisations as well as by the *Federatie VPW's* (the federation of the professional organisations of catholic pastors). In a collective statement they qualified the bishops' stand as "too formalistic, and pastorally inadequate". Too formalistic, because "in the new Vatican text the social consequences of the official catholic position are formulated much more explicitly than ever before". And pastorally inadequate, because the bishops clearly show no concern for those who are emotionally hurt by this view.

Regarding the matter of non-discrimination and 'equal treatment' it should be added that in the past decade the Dutch bishops again and again opposed political proposals for establishing a legal prohibition of discrimination. After a ten years' agony, in 1993, Dutch Parliament — its Second Chamber — finally agreed on a Law Concerning Equal Treatment which, among other things, forbids discrimination on the 'sole ground' of a person's homosexuality. The law applies not only to public institutions — such as schools and hospitals —, but also to institutes based on religious principles. During the parliamentary debate the Minister of the Interior stressed that the law not only forbids discrimination because of a person's gay or lesbian inclination, but also as to the ensuing lifestyle or behaviour.

The bill was proposed by a government formed by the CDA (the christian democrats) — the largest party in Dutch Parliament, formed in the seventies as a merger of the aforementioned Catholic People's Party with two protestant parties — and the PvdA (the social democrats). The Catholic members of the Second Chamber, most of them belonging to the CDA, unanimously voted in favour. Neither the bishops' objections nor the recent Vatican document were apparently able to make them change their minds.

The moral authority of the Dutch episcopate is (also) regarding homosexuality not very great. One can assume it even decreased after the sensational way in which, in the spring of 1993, one member of this college felt obliged to hand in his resignation. Bishop Ronald Philippe Bär O.S.B. (1928) of Rotterdam, also bishop to the Forces, resigned on 13 March 1993, having left shortly before (on 17 February) and to the utmost surprise of his staff, to his abbey in Belgian Chevetogne for 'a period of rest'.

The offical statement was that he resigned 'for health reasons', but a few days later Bär admitted to a journalist of De Volkskrant he had also retired because of 'unpleasant rumours'. These rumours concern the bishop's alleged homosexuality. On 20 March at a press conference Cardinal Simonis and Bishop Hubertus Ernst confirmed their existence and their "origin in the circles of the army chaplains"; but they refused to discuss their content as they "had no evidence". According to the cardinal, these rumours had made impossible the continuation of Bär's work. During this press conference neither Cardinal Simonis nor Bishop Ernst contradicted their colleague was a homosexual, and the cardinal also spoke of "certain imprudent actions" the bishop might have put his foot in. Two days later the staff of the Army Ordinariate published the name of the army chaplain who had approached Simonis concerning the 'Bär rumours'. Soon afterwards a number of Dutch newspapers referred to files that were supposed to contain evidence of the bishop's homosexual contacts. They were said to have been collected bij traditionalist Catholics who didn't like the bishop because of his moderate position concerning church discipline, and who, it was suggested, might have blackmailed him. Cardinal Simonis was given those files by the afore-mentioned army chaplain.

After his departure the Catholic community sent Bishop Bär many tokens of sympathy. But from various sides cardinal Simonis was chided for — as he himself confirmed at the 20 March press conference — not having taken steps to retain bishop Bär for the diocese of Rotterdam and the church province. The bishop himself, for that matter, has not made any statement as to the veracity of the 'rumours'[25].

7. Called to Blessing

"The homophobia of the church's leaders is bigger than ever." This comment on what happened around the resignation of bishop Bär was noted down by journalist Henk Müller for *De Volkskrant* of 27 April 1993. It was given by one of the leading moral theologians in The Netherlands, Theo Beemer, retired professor at the Catholic University of Nijmegen and member of the Working Group of Catholic Gay Pastors. At this moment, Beemer said, in the eyes of the hierarchy homosexuality has "stopped being an outright sin", but it now "officially considers gays and lesbians as poor souls suffering from something". Such an approach, this theologian added, testifies to "an incomprehensible kind of gay-hatred", and he pointed out that at the 'basis' of the church — among pastors and the 'common flock' — an exactly opposite development was taking place: towards acceptance and emancipation.

The coming into existence of groups and organisations of gay and lesbian Catholics — in addition to the already mentioned COC with its

---

[25] For the 'Bär affair' see : "Plotseling vertrek bisschop Bär roept veel vragen op," in *1-2-1* (the official informationbulletin of the secretariate of the Roman Catholic Church), 21(1993) pp.161-163; Statement by Adrianus kardinaal Simonis, 20 March 1993 (not published); Bisschoppen probeerden niet Bär aan te laten blijven / Kwestie-Bär heeft Nederlandse kerk zwaar beschadigd / Vragen over aftreden Bär blijven / Verdriet en boosheid in bisdom Rotterdam na aftreden Bär / Kardinaal Simonis raakte in paniek door geruchten over Bär / Bisschoppen: stop met beschuldigingen en verdachtmaking (press service of ANP-Geestelijk leven, 22 March 1993, pp.1-8); Limburgse aalmoezenier informeerde Simonis over geruchten rond Bär (idem, 23 March 1993); H. MEIJER, "Roomse mores," in *NRC Handelsblad,* 10 July 1993.

about 9000 members — is a contribution towards the acceptance and emancipation of the homosexual longing, and at the same time one of its consequences. Most of these groups were set up after 1980. In the area of Catholicism there are, among others, gay and lesbian groups of priests[26] and lay pastors, women religious, theology students and teachers. There is also, modelled after the American example, a Dutch branch of the Dignity movement. Its members convene for a monthly eucharist, celebrated in the chapel of the Ignatiushuis in Amsterdam, a centre for spirituality organized by the Jesuits.

Most Catholic gay and lesbian groups have joined the *Acht Mei Beweging* (Eighth of May Movement). In this movement more than a hundred Catholic organisations and groups (religious, laity, pastors, pastoral centres, peace movement, missionary groups, 'Women and Faith' movement etc.) come together, working for what they call the 'renewal of church and society'. The movement grew out of a manifestation entitled *The Other Face of the Church,* held on 8 May 1985 in The Hague, on the occasion of Pope John Paul II's visit to The Netherlands. In August 1988 the Dutch bishops suspended their talks with the leaders of the *Acht Mei Beweging,* saying in their written explanation that the borderlines of the church were unacceptably blurred by the admission of member groups that "reject well-defined catholic points of ethics". The presence of such groups was one of the reasons why the bishops considered further dialogue "at this moment unprofitable".

Most Catholic gay and lesbian groups are also connected with the *Landelijk Koördinatie Punt Groepen Kerk en Homosexualiteit* (National Coordination for Groups on Church and Homosexuality), a federation, founded in 1987, comprising about thirty larger or smaller organisations of Protestant, Catholic or ecumenical hue. This LKP publishes a bimonthly magazine *Vroom en Vrolijk* (Pious and Gay); with varying success it tries to persuade parishes to pay attention, in the context of the annual International Lesbian and Gay Pride Day, to homosexual and lesbian emancipation (the Pink Sunday project). Several Catholic gay and lesbian groups also participate in the European Forum of Lesbian and Gay Christian Groups. More than thirty groups, representing thirteen European countries, cooperate in this Forum, which was founded in Paris in 1982[27].

---

[26] On gay priests, see my contribution "Kerk van de verkeerde kant. Priesters, hun homoseksualiteit, hun relaties," in W. BERGER e.a., *Priesters en relaties — ontkende werkelijkheid,* Amersfoort, 1980, pp.80-92.

[27] The members of this Forum come from Austria, Belgium (Flanders and Wallonia), Denmark, France, Germany, Great Britain, Ireland, Italy, The Netherlands, Norway, Spain, Sweden and Switzerland. There are contacts with gay and lesbian christians in the Czech Republic, Slowakia and Romania. The secretariate is at: Ungerplein 16b, 3033 BV Rotterdam, the Netherlands.

The activities carried out by christian gay and lesbian groups range from offering meeting facilities to (theological) study (the development of a specific 'gay and lesbian liberation theology'), the protection and promotion of group interests (the Law on Equal Treatment, already mentioned; a non-discriminatory personel policy with regard to people whose appointments are subjected to episcopal or ecclesiastical agreement), information, actions, (pastoral) assistance (including, and not in the last place, AIDS victims).

A common feature of these groups seems to be the tendency to address the grass roots christian communities rather than the ecclesiastical authorities (this certainly holds good for the Catholic Church). Similarly, more attention is paid to helping lesbian and gay fellow christians to come to grips with their situation, than to 'converting' heterosexual co-religionists.

A good example of how homosexual Catholics in The Netherlands see their faith, their calling, and their position in the church, can be found in the Pastoral Letter on Faith and Homosexuality, published under the title *Called to Blessing* by the Working Group of Catholic Gay Pastors[28]. This group, founded in 1980, has a membership of over a hundred, mostly male, both priests and lay people with a special commitment — through ministry, vocation or study — to the Catholic Church.

"As christians we are convinced that sexuality is something beautiful and good, a gift from the Creator. Therefore, we consider it to be neither shameful nor disturbing when gay or lesbian people make the nature of their longings known in the Church. As members of the Working Group, we also strive for this openness ourselves. We invite others in the Church, whether they be bishops, priests or religious, to be open in this way too. We consider it unacceptable that someone who is called to any form of service in the Church should be disqualified or frustrated in his or her vocation merely because the person has publicly disclosed a sexual preference," this Pastoral Letter declares[29].

The gay pastors are convinced, like many gay believers, that "homosexual people can give expression to their longings in ways that are good, ways that make them whole and which affirm them in their faith in God's love for them and for the world"[30]. Thus homosexual friendships and loving partnerships deserve everybody's respect and, if they

---

[28] See note 1. The title refers to I Peter 3:9, where the faithful are called upon to bless each other "so that they might obtain the blessing to which they have been called".

[29] *Called to Blessing*, 1992, pp.29-30.

[30] *Ibid.*, p.12.

develop into gay or lesbian life-bonds, can claim a blessing by the church[31].

First of all, however, the Pastoral Letter calls for a public discussion in the church about humane and dignified sexuality. In this context the gay pastors address the hierarchy as follows: "in this whole process of listening to God's Word, assimilating the past and wisely applying it with an eye for the good and humane future for all people, we expect help and direction from the Church leadership. The Church has the competence and the task to teach. But all of us, each in accordance with his or her manner and within each one's experience, are involved in this process of searching for truth. Only when an official statement is accepted and supported by the community of faith does it have true authority"[32].

And indeed: within the global Roman Catholic Church there is an increasing disagreement concerning the religious assessment of homosexuality. At least in The Netherlands gay and lesbian church members have reasons for some hope that the gap is going to be narrowed between official and public morality, between the views of the hierarchy and those of the People of God at large. The Dutch experience teaches us: also within the community of the faithful the promotion of the human and christian rights of gay and lesbian people includes well-considered objection and a both frank and believing witnessing about the 'alternative way of life' that is revealed in homosexuality.[*]

[31] *Ibid.*, p.28.
[32] *Ibid.*, p.14.
[*] Translation by R. Bunnik

CHURCH AND STATE IN ITALY

LUCIANO ZANNOTTI

*According to Italian civil law specialist, Luciano Zannotti, the prob-
lem of the organization of the Catholic Church with regard to the phase
of democratic development which Italy is going through is, in general,
causing a reaction of irritation and embarrassment, even in the secular
world. The more or less genuine concern not to fall into forms of jurisdictionalism is preventing experimentation with new hypotheses regarding the relationship between the majority confession and the state.*

The difficulty of situating the church within the process of change
ends by suggesting that it is better to take up positions on the sure
ground of traditional formulas, returning to emphasize the difference of
religious experience from the other events of secular society; the difference in the interpretations and in the prospects advanced in the two
spheres; and the principle of non-interference and institutional autonomy. Instead, there is a high degree of interpenetration between religious
society and secular society and a very close link between the renewal of
the one and that of the other. For example it is quite obvious today that
the future of political integration is determined for the most part by the
religious element[1]. Excluding the confessional organizations from the
development of the social model designed by the Constitution means
limiting this development. It means conditioning its results, circumscrib-
ing it within an area which does not then have any correspondence, not
even in reality. But it is precisely in this area that, in the past twenty to
thirty years, the transformation of the legal system has occurred.
This legal system has been characterized by the search for a greater integration with society, by the overcoming of separateness and by the
attempt to represent the unitary expression of the social sub-division. No
longer, therefore, the traditional absenteism of the liberal state, to which

---

[1] The religious factor is an all-important element in the political unification process of
the European Community, maintains F. MARGIOTTA BROGLIO, "Integrazione politica
e fattore religioso," in *Rivista di Studi Politici Internazionali* (1991) no. 229, p.31 ff.
According to him there is a risk that Europe would transform into a federation of societies
founded on religious membership. In a short time this could lead to the conflicts becoming acute once more and could dissolve the unitary cultural identity of the West.

corresponded a privatistic construction of the various associative realities, but an attitude of a decidedly interventionist nature for the legal system which interacts with society and, in certain ways, guides it.

1. Secularism

The problem of secularism should be seen in this framework. The
principle of secularism seems to be verified only in democratic development: it is in fact the process of democratic development that gives
meaning to 'secularism' as, moreover, it does to all the other constitutional values. It is the process of democratic development which shapes
the identity of the entire judicial system and together guarantees the integration of its fundamental principles.

In short, we should not be surprised if, in the face of such a rapidly
changing reality in secular and in religious society, the need is felt for a
strategy of ecclesiastical policy which definitively abandones not only
every form of sectarian interference in politics, but also every feature
that discriminates and divides religious experience from all the other
social phenomena, taking into account the loss of significance of general
theories and systematizations that by now are restrictive and unsatisfac-
tory.

The consequence of this change in view is therefore a different hierarchy of values in the relations between the secular legal system and the
religious groups. If we look at the direction of reform in Italian ecclesiastical law, the design for a recomposition of ecclesiastical legislation is
emerging within the perspective of a equal condition of religious groups.
With the revision of the Italian Concordat of 1929, a unitary process of
convergence was begun of the entire discipline in the direction of the
enforcement of this principle of equality which had never til now been
realized in this sector in Italy[2].

One of the novelties, perhaps the most significant one, of the reform
of the Concordat consists of the explicit and definitive abandonment of
the principle of a state religion, which provided authoritative control of
the main mechanisms of formation and the maintenance of consensus
and which, in fact, fascism had made its own, thus confirming its totalitarian choice also in the field of relations with organized religion. The

---

[2] On this point, see C. CARDIA, "Ruolo e prospettive della 'legislazione contrattata'
in rapporti tra Stato e Chiesa," in *Nuovi studi di diritto canonico ed ecclesiastico,*
Salerno, 1990, p.200 ff.; M. C. FOLLIERO, *Giurisdizioni in materia matrimoniale e
diritti confessionali,* Salerno, 1992, pp.20-21.

formula was proof of the association of the socially more significant confession with the political project of the regime. In exchange, the church was offered a juridical and economic condition privileged much more than every other social group, which stifled in a very serious way ideological pluralism and conditioned it in practice up to the present[3].

As is well known, not even the transition to a constitutional government has sufficed to announce the abandonment of 'confessionalism'. This concept of the relation between the secular legal system and organized religion has continued to dominate public life, the choices of ecclesiastical policy and the discipline of the subject. This domination continued even if the privileged condition of the church was no longer justified on the basis of the principle of a state religion, but by that of majority reason, that is, by the criterion of the will of the Italian people who by a great majority are presumed to be of the traditional Catholic faith[4]. Only with the new Agreement was the principle of state religion abandoned from the formal point of view[5]. In the additional protocol it is expressly stated that it is no longer in force (point 1, in relation to Art. 1 of the Agreement). In confirmation of this very relevant aspect contained in the reform, Art. 9 in fact defines the religious culture and the principles of Catholicism only as an integral part of the historic patrimony of the Italian people (point 2, section 1). The Catholic religion, therefore, no longer occupies an exclusive and predominant place in the legal system of the state, but is combined indistinctly with all the expressions of the cultural patrimony of the country. It is the recognition of the important role that the Catholic experience had assumed in Italian history. This is however no more and no less than the other values that contribute to the spiritual and material development of society.

An epoch is over, the historic cycle of state religion has ended — the Constitutional Court affirmed in its judgement N° 203 of 12 April 1989[6]. The confessionalist choice of the Albertine Statute, confirmed in the Lateran Treaty of 1929, was thus formally and definitively abandoned in the

---

[3] See C. CARDIA, entry "Pluralism" (diritto ecclesiastico), in *Enciclopedia del diritto*, vol. XXXIII, Milano, 1983, p.983 ff.

[4] On the subject, see A. VITALE, "La fine della 'religione di Stato'," in *Il diritto ecclesiastico*, 1979, I, p.78 ff.

[5] See on this point S. LARICCIA, *Diritto ecclesiastico*, Padova, 1986, p. 157; G. LEZIROLI, "Fine di un confessionismo" (regarding point 1 of the additional protocol to the consensual modifications of the Lateran Concordat), in *Il diritto ecclesiastico*, 1984, I, p.495 ff.

[6] The judgement with the note by N. COLAIANNI, "Il principio supremo di laicità dello Stato e l'insegnamento della religione cattolica" is published in *Il Foro italiano*, 1989, I, p.1333 ff.

the Revision Agreement of 1985, giving rise to the possibility of finally affirming the quality of the secular state for the Italian legal system. Again the Court, further on in Judgement 203, was in fact able to maintain that the supreme principle of secularism constituted "one of the profiles of the form of government delineated in the Constitution Charter of the Republic," which is substantiated in the first place in the abandonment of the choice of confessionalism, but not in the indifference of the secular legal system towards organized religion and then, above all, in the guarantee of the protection of the freedom of religion within the wider sphere of the general regime regarding confessional and cultural pluralism. The truth is that many regulations[7] and particularly administrative practice[8], which is linked to the principle of a state religion, have remained unchanged. Nevertheless, on the theoretical level, there is no doubt that the judgement of the Court introduced an element of strong discontinuity as regards the past: pluralism really created in this reconstruction of secularism its "fundamental axis", its cornerstone and its form[9]. In brief, it is no accident that in the search for a definition of the concept of secularism, pluralism was considered as the "most contiguous". This confirms the opinion for which the radical, historical and theoretical antithesis of the confessionalist state could not be other than the secular state, when it presupposes a "confessional and ideological pluralism made legitimate prescriptively and intimately conflictual"[10].

This concept of secularism became the criterion of evaluation and the exegetic parameter for all law in force and of ecclesiastical law in particular[11]. Secularism characterizes the entire state legal system, from both the juridical and the ideological points of view, having repercussions on the totality of the institutional components and setting itself as a directive principle of their action[12]. It is the result of an historic process which has led the state to emancipate itself from all ideology and, moreover, to favour its more extensive confrontation, because only

[7] See L. MUSSELLI, entry "Religione" (reati contro la), in *Enciclopedia del diritto,* vol. XLI, Milano, 1989, p.729 ff.

[8] For a significant example of this practice, see L. ZANNOTTI, "Il crocifisso nelle aule scolastiche," in *Il diritto ecclesiastico,* 1990, I, p.324 ff.

[9] Cf. L. GUERZONI, "Considerazioni critiche sul 'principio supremo' di laicità dello Stato all luce dell'esperienza giuridica contemporanea," in *Il diritto ecclesiastico,* 1992, I, p.86 ff.

[10] Cf. C. CARDIA, entry "Stato laico," in *Enciclopedia del diritto,* vol. XLIII, Milano, p. 876.

[11] See again L. GUERZONI, "Considerazioni" p. 92.

[12] See G. DALLA TORRE, *Il primato della coscienza. Laicità e libertà nell'esperienza giuridica contemporanea,* Roma, 1992, p.36ff.

in this way can truly correct political choices emerge. Secularism is seen as a method that enters into a dialectic relationship with secularism as a value[13].

The principle of secularism is connected, therefore, with the development of the conditions for effective functioning of the democratic system and with the capacity of the legal system to absorb and to put to good use — in a circular process with social life — the variety of ideological convictions present in it, producing a political synthesis of it in its own legislation and in its own administrative activity. In this way, the pluralist principle and the democratic principle converge with reference to a society that is recognized in its own complexity and is expressed in a state which is the both neutral and continually changing product of the social elaboration of the interests and measures for satisfying them[14].

In line with this form of government which has gradually emerged in time and which has only recently been recognized, even Italian ecclesiastical legislation has been transformed by the reform of the Lateran Pacts. The new body of legislation sanctioned the break with the confessional regime. The legal system established relations with a plurality of religious phenomena. Ecclesiastical law no longer coincides with the law that governs the relations between the state and the Catholic Church. Since 1984, agreements have been realized with the Waldensian Assembly (Law N° 449 of 11 August 1984), with the Italian Union of Adventist Churches (Law N°516 of 22 November 1988), with the Assemblies of God in Italy (Law N°517 of 22 November 1988), with the Italian Israelite Communities (Law N°101 of 8 March 1989), to which must be added the agreements underwritten with the Evangelical Lutheran Church and the Christian Evangelical Baptist Union of Italy, while others — it seems — are in preparation. A process of subdivision of the subject has been set in motion which nevertheless presents new problems: e.g. that of rebalancing an unbalanced system in favour of the confessions that stipulated the agreement and, above all, of preventing phenomena of desintegretion of the discipline in which the demands of one religious group or other prevail over the general interest. Excessive recourse to the contractual procedure can, in fact, lead to favouritism and centrifugal tendencies[15]. It risks reproducing for a major number of confessions those advantages and that type of 'free zone' that up until now

---

[13] See P. ONORATO, "Laicità e democrazia," in *Democrazia e diritto*, 4/1992, p. 85 ff.

[14] See P. BARCELLONA, "Stato di diritto e principio democratico," in *Democrazia e diritto*, 2/1990, p. 260 ff.

[15] The birth of microsystems, as N. IRTI defines them, in *L'età della decodificazione*, Milano, 1989, p.22 ff.

had been reserved only for the Catholic Church [16]. and ends up by emphasizing not only the inequalities already existing in this area, but also the diversity of treatment of the religious groups compared with all the other social groups.

2. A Complex Transition

In short, on the one hand the realization of the agreements constitutes an important moment for ecclesiastical law because with it, the end of a monopoly has been arrived at, leading to a realignment — even if a very partial one — of the religious groups. On the other hand, it has been necessary to pass from this phase in order to finally put into effect Art. 8 of the Constitution which had remained a dead letter for far too long. The impression we are now getting, however, is that of a widespread dissatisfaction with a mechanism that, once set in motion, seems uncontrollable. We are living through a complex transitional phase, in which demands of secularism and remnants of confessionalism, elements of pluralism and phenomena of fragmentation are found side by side [17]. In this phase — which is precisely due to these contradictions and to the acceleration imposed on everything in our time — we can even glimpse the necessity for a rethinking of the present constitutional order of relations between church and state, which in the end not only might lead to the creation of a common law for religious denominations, but more generally to the regaining of a law that is equal for all social groups [18].

The realization of the agreements seems to be a phase which is probably not destined to last for long, if it is inserted in the process of approach of ecclesiastical law to common law and in the evolutionary process of the system. The abandonment of confessionalism and the relationship of the state with a plurality of religious groups are essential conditions, but are not however the only conditions for realizing a consistent advancement of democratic development. For this to occur, it is necessary that the institutions and every associative phenomenon,

[16] See S. FERRARI, "Pagine introduttive: appunti su una riforma incompiuta," in *Quaderni di diritto e politica ecclesiastica,* (1993) no. 1 p. 8.

[17] On this see G. CASUSCELLI, *Post-confessionismo e transizione,* Milano, 1984.

[18] See S. FERRARI, "Tra uguaglianza e libertà: funzione attuale del principio separatistico," in *Il diritto ecclesiastico,* 1987, I, p.409 ff.; F. MARGIOTTA BROGLIO, "Stato e Chiesa. Enigmi dimenticati dalla Costituzione," in *Corriere della sera* (6 febbraio 1988). On this point, see also F. ONIDA, "Considerazioni sul sistema pattizio alla luce dell'esperienza comparatistica," in *Anuario de Derecho eclesiastico del Estado,* vol. IV, 1988, p.47 ff., which moreover has always taken sides in favour of the separatist system.

without any exceptions, participate in this process of development, and be involved in the dialectics and in the democratic procedure. A democratic state does not exist without a democratic society; there is no political democracy if social democracy is lacking, Bobbio writes[19].

Within the sphere of the socialization of all the experiences of collective life, it does not appear at all contradictory to ask of the representative bodies of the religious interests, particularly those with a greater importance, to face up to the complex reality of contemporary society, leaving aside the precondition — of a secularist nature — for which, in principle, they refuse the possibility of communication, and of integration with the religious positions which are considered irremovable and relentlessly on the side of, and in defence of, tradition. The necessary extraneousness of the state in ecclesial transformations does not prevent it from being able to look for or take opportunities for relations with religious groups in order to introduce and extend the democratic principle which characterizes the legal system in such a decisive way. If it did not do this, it would be as though the state were hiding its own identity and delegating ecclesiastical policy to others. In order to give some significance to the reforms in ecclesiastical law — and also to the principle of collaboration — there is in fact no doubt that first of all the State must "proceed on the theoretical level to identifying the chosen values, the interests protected and the basic aims pursued by the governmental and confessional regulations"[20]. This was a necessary operation of recognition that serves to point out the limits of movement for each proposal and the evaluation criteria for each request, as was also finally done in the revision of the Concordat, because "the evolution of the times" and "the development of democratic life" had to be the two directives on which to conduct the entire negotiations[21].

Frankly, it seems to me that the concept of jurisdictionalism should be placed in quite a different context. Democratic development certainly does not constitute the objective of some enlightened oligarchies. It is an exigency which comes from below and finds an outlet in the institutions, enjoying a by-now general consensus. It also concerns the churches, and inevitably conditions them[22]. In this different perspective unfolds the

---

[19] *Il futuro della democrazia,* Torino, 1984, p.44 ff.

[20] V. TOZZI, *Gli edifici di culto nel sistema italiano,* Salerno, 1990, p.279.

[21] S. LARICCIA, *Stato e Chiesa in Italia 1948-1980,* Brescia, 1981, p.232.

[22] S. FERRARI, entry "Organizzazione ecclesiastica," in *Enciclopedia giuridica,* vol. XXII, Roma, 1990, observes that "the structures, processes and behaviour of the ecclesiastical organizations are often conditioned by a series of factors external to them and to a great extent not controllable by them". On this point see also M. COTTA, entry "Democrazia," in *Enciclopedia giuridica,* vol. X, Roma, 1988, p.1.

current reflection on the function of ecclesiastical law and on the systems of church/state relations, in order to verify whether conventional-type legislation can also perform the role "of having the confessional regulations evolve in a liberal direction, while respecting their independence"[23]. The purpose is to contribute to that enforcement procedure of secularism which "interacts in different ways in the relations between secular community and confessional community, to the point that it can constitute a dynamic element for the same ecclesial renewal"[24].

In Italy there is more often argument about the integralistic attempts of the church, the plans for spiritual reconquest of the present pontificate, and the hesitations of the lay conscience in the face of this phenomenon[25]. Certain attitudes of ideological intolerance of religions, which are probably by now the last groups to describe themselves in this way[26], and the very worrying consequences of this religious integralism[27], are subjects for reflection. The Catholic inside world, is questioning itself with greater insistence on the contradictions that exist between the claim for human rights in the states[28] and the measures, that are still so repressive, taken by the ecclesiastical authorities with regard to every form of dissent[29]. The reduction of canon law to a regulative system that is mainly concerned with the organizational structures of the Catholic institution, to the detriment of the recognition and protection of the subjective positions in the organization of the ecclesial community[30] is a subject for debate.

[23] G. CASUSCELLI, "Libertà religiosa e fonti bilaterali," in *Anuario de Derecho Eclesiastico del Estado,* 1987, vol. III, p.99.

[24] C. CARDIA, "Laicità dello Stato e nuova legislazione ecclesiastica," in *Il nuovo accordo tra Italia e Santa Sede,* Milano, 1987, p.159.

[25] Just think of the success which the book by P. FLORES D'ARCAIS, *Etica senza fede* (Torino, 1992) has recently had in Italy.

[26] Every religion tends to consider the others as superstitions, maintains N. COLA-IANNI, *Confessioni religiose e intese. Contributo all'interpretazione dell'art. 8 della Costituzione,* Bari, 1990, pp.54-55. "Every church is orthodox for itself and erroneous or heretical for the others" observes V. ZANONE recalling Locke (entry "Laicismo," in *Dizionario di politica,* Torino, 1983, p. 575). The organic vocation of every religion is to affirm how unique its own truth is and for this to make itself a State, as M. PROSPERO says in "Contro l'eutanasia del cittadino," in *Democrazia e Diritto,* 1992, 2, p.59.

[27] "There is no world peace without religious peace", affirms H. KUNG, in *Cristianesimo e religioni universali,* Milano, 1986, p.521 ff.: who could deny the fact — asks the well-known theologian — that it is precisely the important religions which are corresponsible for the hotbeds of tension in world politics?

[28] On this point see the collection of documents edited by G. BARBERINI, *Chiese e diritti umani,* Napoli, 1991.

[29] See in this regard the considerations made by H. KUNG, *Perché sono ancora cristiano,* Milano, 1991, p. 67 ff.

[30] In this regard see L. GUERZONI, "Grandezza e miseria del diritto," in A. and G. ALBERIGO (eds.), *Con tutte le mie forze. I nodi della fede cristiana oggi,* Genova, 1993, p. 311.

3. Towards Democratization

The central problem posed by the Second Vatican Council is that of a profound renewal of the institutions of the church, of a search for possible relations between ecclesial dynamism and democratic dynamism[31]. The development of the ecclesiastical structure in a democratic sense is the real question which lies in the background of every recent conflict within the Catholic confession[32]. As is well-known, the reform of the Code of Canon Law has put into effect in a very limited manner the theoretical revision initiated by the Council[33]. The fact that no single centre of power and decision is assigned in the church does not correspond, in short, to a juridically-recognized principle, but is certainly a verification of the dynamics in progress inside the church and of the by-now widespread exigencies within the ecclesial body[34].

It is therefore not a matter of conditioning the ecclesiastical organization, but of sustaining a process of comparison and of democratic development which corresponds to a general exigency and which would have positive effects for everyone. It is a matter of qualifying a line of ecclesiastical policy, so that not even a regime of separation would prevent the church from continuing to influence the state. Any sort of negotiation tends, moreover, by its very nature to realize a compromise between the parties who decide to choose this form of relationship. The point of mediation reached in an agreement never corresponds to the positions expressed at the beginning of the negotiations. Stressing, often in a frankly excessive way, the principle of confessional autonomy should, in my opinion, be accompanied by the reflection that, when all is said and done, it always comes about within the unitary framework of the state. That autonomy is the recognition of the power to give oneself rules, but is grafted on to the structural unity of the legal system; it is led back to the values of the juridical system.

[31] On the subject see G. ALBERIGO, "Ecclesiologia e democrazia," in *Concilium*, 1992, 5.

[32] See L. ZANNOTTI, *Stato sociale, edilizia di culto e pluralismo religioso. Contributo allo studio della problematica del dissenso religioso,* Milano, 1990, pp.5-16; p.254 ff., especially note 76 pp.266-267.

[33] See N. COLAIANNI, "Le strutture ecclesiali di partecipazione nel nuovo codice di diritto canonico," in R. COPPOLA and G. DAMMACCO (eds.), *Struttura e dinamicita del nuovo codice di diritto canonico,* Bari, 1985, p.229 ff.

[34] On the subject see W. AYMANS, *Diritto canonico e comunione ecclesiale,* Torino, 1993; G. FELICIANI, "Corresponsabilità ecclesiale nella struttura gerarchica della Chiesa," in *Comunione ecclesiale e strutture di responsabilità,* Roma, 1990; C. RIVA, *La partecipazione nella Chiesa,* Roma, 1970."Even if the years pass — Cardinal C.M. MARTINI recently maintained — the Council remains always and ever before us. It is not just the memory of yesterday, it is the hope of tomorrow" ("Il Concilio è sempre e ancora davanti a noi," in *Jesus,* 1993, 2, p.11).

Religious society with the confessions, the groups, as in general the whole of secular society, is never "either against or outside the State"[35]. The legal system can never completely disregard the social system. It cannot allow itself to underestimate the ties that derive from it. On the other hand, the autonomy of the social system does not mean that society can do without the legal system, without its binding decisions and its function as the distributor of resources. In short, there is an autonomy of the secular sphere and of the religious sphere — after all perhaps more correctly definable as the relation of 'otherness' between "ontologically different" orders[36] — which nevertheless presupposes a communication of experiences, of consensus and of values between the institutions of the state and confessional groups. Moreover, the significance of all law is that of summarizing social exigencies and at the same time, of also orienting them, of establishing new standards of behaviour[37], starting from the postulation of historicity and mobility of all forms of relationship[38].

In short, it can certainly be said that in every case, the laws "represent the structural and organizational level by means of which social pluralism is destined to be proposed in political unity, according to the procedures of progressive integration (...), guaranteeing the actuation of a process of composition of the social interests that oblige the numerous parties to prepare themselves and their own petitions, which are different and conflicting, according to the rule of confrontation"[39]. The principle of autonomy must therefore be reconcilable with the search for meeting points between secular institutions and society with a view to collective progress. For the state such a collective progress has mainly the significance of a development of the democratic dialectic and basically, the church has shown itself to be favourable to it when it declared its full availability to collaborate with the state "for the promotion of man and the good of the country" (Art. 1 of the new Concordat)[40].

---

[35] The expression is from N. IRTI, *Società civile*, Milano, 1992, p. 156.

[36] See L. GUERZONI, "Considerazioni critiche," p.98 ff. On the concept of the autonomy of the Church, see F. FINOCCHIARO, "Il diritto ecclesiastico e la teoria generale del diritto," in *Il diritto ecclesiastico*, 1987, I, p. 441 ff.

[37] On this subject see R. DWORKIN, *I diritti presi sul serio*, Bologna, 1982, p. 78 ff.

[38] See G. VACCA, "Sulla eticità della politica," in *Religioni e società*, 1991, 11, p. 42.

[39] Cf. I. VECCHIO CAIRONE, *Legalità democratica, diritto negoziale e misure fiscali agevolative*, Salerno, 1990, p. 54.

[40] On this point see G. CATALANO, "Interessi confessionali e società contemporanea," in *Il diritto ecclesiastico*, 1987, I, p.239; V. TOZZI, "La cooperazione per mezzo di accordi fra Stato e confessioni religiose ed i principi di specialità ed uguaglianza," in *Il diritto ecclesiastico*, I, 1990, p. 122 ff.

An example of this choice of ecclesiastical policy, which for me is extremely significant, has been the contractual discipline regarding the Institute for the Maintenance of the Clergy. Law N° 222 of 20 May 1985 provides, in fact, that the Board of Directors of the central Institute be made up, "for at least one third of its members, of representatives of the clergy according to procedures which will be established by the Italian Episcopal Conference" (CEI) (Art. 39, first sub-section). Even more incisively, the same Law establishes that the Board of Directors of the diocesan Institutes, "in every case" and for "at least one third", be "composed of representatives designated by the diocesan clergy on an elective basis" (Art. 23, second sub-section)[41].

In accordance with the law deriving from the Concordat, the church authorities then decided autonomously that the Board of Directors of the central Institute would be "composed of nine members, clergy or laymen, including a president and a vice president, nominated by the CEI. Three of these are designated by the Italian clergy, according to procedures established by the same CEI which take into account the different geographical areas"[42]. Correspondingly, it was arranged that the Board of Directors of the diocesan Institutes be "composed of five to nine members, clergy or laymen, including a president and a vice president, nominated by the diocesan clergy on an elective basis, according to procedures established by the Bishop in conformity with the provisions issued by the CEI"[43]. In any case, before beginning to carry out their functions, the elected Directors must take an oath before the President of the CEI (or his delegate), swearing that they will honestly and faithfully perform their administrative assignment, according to the provisions of canon 1283[44].

---

[41] On the subject, in a critical sense, see S. BERLINGO', *Enti e beni religiosi in Italia,* Bologna, 1992, p. 118: he maintains that "the regime reserved by Law 222 to those Institutes has public-law connotations with a vaguely 'giurisdizionalista' tone". Correlated to these regulations is Art. 16 of D.P.R. N°33 of 13 February 1987 (approval of the executive order of Law N°222 of 20 May 1985, bearing provisions on Church bodies and property in Italy and for the maintenance of the Catholic clergy in service in the dioceses) which enforces on the Institutes the communication to the Minister of the Interior and to the Prefect in charge of the composition of the Board of Directors with the subsequent variations.

[42] See the first sub-section of Art. 6 of the statutes of the central Institute for maintenance of the clergy, published in *Quaderni di diritto e politica ecclesiastica,* 1985, pp. 413-414.

[43] See the first sub-section of Art. 7 of the model statutes regarding diocesan Institutes, published in the appendix of E. CAPPELLINI, A. NICORA, C. REDAELLI, *Norme per il sostentamento del clero,* Brescia, 1985, p.156.

[44] See the fourth sub-section of Articles 6 and 7, cited in the preceding footnote.

Regarding the regulations to be observed in the nomination of the persons making up the decision-making organs of these new ecclesiastical bodies, the CEI has also recently confirmed that "the three representatives of the clergy on the Board of Directors and the representative of the clergy on the Board of Auditors for the accounts of the central Institute for the Maintenance of the Clergy will be designated by an electoral college made up of members of the Board of Directors of the Federation among the Clergy in Italy (F.A.C.I.)," confirming in addition that "the representatives of the clergy on the Board of Directors of the diocesan Institutes for the maintenance of the clergy will be designated by the diocesan clerical Council" and that "in dioceses where there are no more than one hundred and fifty priests, the Bishop will have the faculty to establish that the designation is made by the assembly of all the clergy serving in the diocese"[45].

The concrete application of Law 222 of 1985 can be argued about[46]. The fact remains that the discipline recognizes on this point the subdivision and the complexity of the current state of Catholicism in this country, and that the Italian Episcopal Conference admits the necessity for a greater representativeness in the elections of the bodies[47], emphasizing that "the Church is being offered the opportunity to realize itself on the level of property as well as on the level of economic resources, as a communion, by activating and exploiting all the subdivisions of its community structure"[48].

Beyond the reservations that one may have regarding the system, which however still maintains public financing for the Catholic clergy, there is no doubt that, at least for this aspect, it appears more compatible with the principles and dynamics of the constitutional legal system. The realization of the principle of representativeness and the obligation for an annual accounting of the CEI to the Ministry for the Interior[49] consti-

[45] They are Articles 10 and 11, first and second sub-sections, of deliberation n° 58 of 1 August 1991 (Testo unico delle disposizioni di attuazione delle norme relative al sostentamento del clero che svolge servizio in favore delle diocesi) of the CEI, published in *Il diritto ecclesiastico,* 1991, II, p. 479.

[46] See on this point the observations of C. CARDIA, *Stato e confessioni religiose,* Bologna, 1988, p. 274; L. MUSSELLI, entry "Istituti per il sostentamento del clero," in *Enciclopedia giuridica,* vol. XVII, Roma, 1988, p.2.

[47] This is affirmed in circular n° 19 of 25 September 1990 of the CEI (Comitato per i problemi degli enti e dei beni ecclesiastici).

[48] Cf. CEI, "Lettera informativa" on the subject of the maintenance of the clergy, published in *Quaderni di diritto e politica ecclesiastica,* 1987, p. 380.

[49] This is provided for by Art. 44 of Law 222 of 1985. Articles 20 and 21 of D.P.R. n° 33 of 1987 respectively state that: "The accounting provided for by Art. 44 of the Law will be as transmitted by the Italian Episcopal Conference to the Ministry of the Interior by the end of July of the year subsequent to the fiscal year", and that "the Ministry of the

tute instruments by means of which the state guarantees a more correct administration of public contributions. These are the means with which the joint commission for ecclesiastical bodies has intended to guarantee the demands of transparency and openness for the new legal system[50].

Administrative correctness and participation are important conditions for the development of democratic life, principles which the state cannot forgo. From this point of view, the example referred to seems to me to be indicative of how a law regulated by the Concordat can also serve to "ferry" the discipline of relations between a secular legal system and organized religion towards a condition common to all the forms of society, contributing to the launching of a process of transformation that today seems as necessary for the whole of society as its results are unpredictable.

Interior, within thirty days of receiving the accounting as per the preceding Art. 20, will transmit a copy of it with its report to the Ministries of the Treasury and for Finance".

[50] In the "Report on Principles" the Commission in fact affirms that "the demands for transparency and openness of the system will be guaranteed: a) by the presence on the Board of Directors of the Institute for maintenance of the clergy and in the body which will operate on the level of the CEI of representatives of the clergy, designated according to the statutes, so as to guarantee an effective and adequate clerical participation; b) by the obligation imposed on the Institutes to send an annual final report to the CEI; c) by the commitment of the CEI to transmit annually to the competent State authorities the accounting relative to the effective utilization of the sums provided to it and to give adequate information about this accounting in the ecclesial seat". The report is published in *Il diritto ecclesiastico*, 1984, I, pp.724-737.

ANTHROPOCENTRISM AND FAITH

The church has changed her approach toward human rights in an way which she earlier did not hold to be possible. Nevertheless there remains an element of indecisiveness in the new friendship between the church and human rights. According to the German moral theologian Karl-Wilhelm Merks that which has not yet been decided can be clarified in two questions: How consistent is the church's "yes" to human rights (to all human rights, in all areas, also within the church)? And the second question: When the church says "yes" to human rights, does she also say "yes" to the spirit which inspires these rights (namely a spirit of freedom and self-determination), or does she only say "yes" to the (or worse yet, to some of the) normative contents which are expressed in human rights?

These questions are posed against the background of a long and tension filled history between the church and human rights, a history which needs not be repeated here[1]. Nevertheless we cannot overlook the fact that even within the preparations for the Second Vatican Council the severe rejection of the "modern freedoms" could still be seen[2].

1. A Real Change?

In view of this long-lasting disturbed relation, and the basic causes thereof, the question may be emphatically posed, to what extent the church could really effect a fundamental change in her position over against human rights; in other words, to what extent can we really speak here of a conversion (in the theological sense of the word)?

In this context one must consider that the self-opening of the church to the positive content of the philosophy of human rights must mean

---

[1] Cf., e.g., G. LINDGENS, *Freiheit, Demokratie und pluralistische Gesellschaft in der Sicht der katholischen Kirche. Dokumente aus Verlautbarungen der Päpste und des 2. Vatikanischen Konzils,* Stuttgart, 1985.

[2] Cf. *De ordine morali,* in which unequivocal texts are memorialized with full agreement in the notes; cf. K. GOLSER, *Gewissen und objektive Sittenordnung,* Wien 1975, p.23 with notes.

more than merely the taking over of modern theoretical terms and concepts. It is not merely a matter of the theological assimilation of modern
theories about rights and morality, but rather a "practical" recognition
of the sensibility for justice and the righteousness (*Rechtsbewusstsein*)
which are expressed in the demands of human rights, thus in their consequences (also) for the — one's own — *praxis*.

The acceptance of human rights means another, new sensibility for
questions of righteousness and justice, an altered view of public morality, a new frame of reference for the organization of the social order.
Human rights are theories with a practical intention. Thus their acceptance or rejection is not a question of an arbitrary, more or less uncom-
mitted attitude toward theoretical constructs, but rather an expression of
morality, of moral commitment.

When we speak of the "history of suffering of human rights" (Hans
Maier) in the church, we should be conscious that first and foremost we
are speaking of the history of suffering of real human beings. Ideas do
not suffer. Thus in the rejection of the human rights ethos or in the
defense of human rights, what is at stake is thus not the failure or the
success of an idea, but it is a matter finally of the fates and life possibilities of real human beings. Human rights derive from the immediate
experience of suffering and injustice, and their denial directly produces
suffering and injustice. This attributes the real weight to the church's
attitude to human rights.

How consistently does the church say "yes" to human rights? "That
the defense of human rights represents a central concern of the most
recent social-ethical teaching of the church, also and especially of the
recent popes, requires no special proof... No less clear than this unambiguous center of gravity in the present teaching, however, is also the
fact that, at the time of their written proclamation some 200 years ago,
these human rights met with a severe and at times very clear rejection by
the church authorities. Even when this is not officially acknowledged,
we nonetheless stand here before a far reaching shift in the teaching tradition of the church...."[3] In his article, "Die Kirche und die Werte der
französischen Revolution"[4], M. Chappin characterizes this shift with an
unambiguous, double "yes" to both the question: "Does the church
today call for the 'immortal principles' of 1789?" as well as to the question: "Did the church of the past herself condemn these very same
'immortal principles'?"

    [3] F. FURGER, C. STROBEL-NEPPLE, *Menschenrechte und katholische Soziallehre*
(Iustitia et Pax), Freiburg, 1985, p.9.
    [4] *Communio*, 1989, pp.477-490

For all too long human rights have been interpreted by the church exclusively in light of the traumatic experience of 1789, as the historical continuation of the then emerging spirit of rebellion and destruction. The encroachment upon the traditional ecclesiastical-political conception of the established order and the declaration of human rights were interpreted as one, wholly negative complex. Thus early in 1791 Pope Pius VI refused not only the "Civil Constitution of the Cleric," but took this opportunity "also for a strict condemnation of the declaration of human rights, since their principles stood in contradiction to the Catholic teaching about the origin of the authority of the state, religious freedom and social inequalities"[5].

The ideals of the French Revolution, liberty, equality, fraternity, and their development into various human rights, were interpreted exclusively as potential of spiritual and social subversions, and thus not understood in their own inner *moral* dynamic. In this way the church obstructed for a long time her own access to the fundamental moral experiences, to the ethical core of modern thought. This assessment of a deep alienation of church doctrine from the fundamental experiences of modernity — alienation which persisted until well into this century, if not until our present day — is not invalidated by a second course of action in the relationship of the church with human rights: the new activity of the church with regard to the "social question" linked to the name of Pope Leo XIII (1891: *Rerum Novarum*). Of course, in an evaluation of the relation between the church and human rights, one may not ignore this development, for a whole series of social problems constitutes the very subject matter of the so-called social human rights. Moreover, in the relationship of the church to human rights, it is striking that, side by side with the initial global rejection, eventually the different kinds of human rights called forth clearly differing reactions from the church. The example of Leo XIII, and the development of the social doctrine of the church, demonstrate clearly that the problem is not really couched in the question of social rights and in the recognition of the necessity of a far-reaching participatory solidarity among persons. The social commitment of the church, and the recent dynamic of this commitment, certainly belong to the most positive assets in recent church history; the problem is found in the so-called rights of civil and political freedom. This can be seen from the history of the church up until Vatican II and even beyond.

---

[5] R. AUBERT, in H. JEDIN (ed.), *Handbuch der Kirchengeschichte,* VI-1, Freiburg, 1971/1985, p.32.

The importance of the church's commitment to the social question for the gradual opening of the church to the philosophy of human rights should therefore not be underestimated. One might even be able to defend the thesis that, ultimately, it was the church's commitment to the social question which helped her to engage on the road toward a modern church. The theme of human rights, so central to modern thought, was in fact probably made accessible to the church by social rights. These were more easily found within her own tradition.

Nevertheless one may not simply identify commitment to the social question and the acceptance of a philosophy of human rights. This problematic is already demonstrated in the fact that the far-reaching social demands of Leo XIII, were, according to G. Luf, "not directed toward the guaranty of fundamental rights, but rather remained in the category of a social solicitude for the people, in service of a religiously founded *salus publica* ... The extensive social demands were therefore combined with the traditional condemnation of the liberal rights of freedom"[6]. According to Chappin, "the fear of revolution" determined "the extraordinary meritorious formulation of a social doctrine at the papal level," and in Leo XIII's vision of a renewed Christianity, "this should be more in the line of a paternalistic monarchy rather than a mature democracy"[7].

In summary, the real crux of the matter seems to lie in the first of the three demands of the French Revolution and its formulation in the form of various rights.

2. All Human Rights — Or None

With regard to this, we must insist that human rights, when cut off from the dimension of freedom, cannot be maintained. Human rights are a multi-faceted and also a dynamically growing organic whole (civil and political rights of freedom, social and cultural rights, rights to participation and solidarity). There exists a kind of inner logic between the different groups of human rights. The social and cultural rights follow from the serious acceptance of rights of freedom, and the rights to solidarity follow from the other two. The other human rights lose their soul when they are not tied to the idea of the original rights of freedom. Their sense and meaning is the equal and real unfolding of human freedom.

All human rights are derivations of the original inalienable dignity of human beings. Yet the core content of this dignity is (in modern times)

---

[6] G. LUF, "Menschenrechte," in *Staatslexikon* III, 1987 (7th ed.), c.1114.
[7] M. CHAPPIN, "Die Kirche," p.485 f.

"the freedom of every person, who is to be understood as standing under an unconditional claim to prove oneself to be a subject summoned to responsible self-determination in all practical concerns"[8]. From this perspective, and from the thereby implied accompanying "unconditional recognition of the other as a subject of equal freedom"[9], the whole development of human rights receives its normative binding force and its almost genetic particularity. The core of all human rights is accordingly the unfolding of human freedom, this being the right which is due above all and originally to human beings. The moral dignity of the claims of freedom can only be developed, however, with the freedom of conscience and of religion as the core of the human rights ethos, and not as the result of a "bourgeois" interpretation centered around the right to private property.

Apart from recognition of the original dignity and freedom of self-determination and without recognition of the equality of all humans with regard to it, an active participation in the philosophy of human rights is not possible. Precisely here is found the biggest problem for the church, in any case when one views its history. The church has come a long way from the condemnation of freedom of conscience as *pestilentissimus error*, the most pestiferous error (Gregory XVI: encyclical *Mirari Vos,* 1832) to the appreciation of the conscience "as the hidden center and sanctuary of the human person, where he is alone with God, whose voice is to be heard in this his most inner self" (Vatican II, *Gaudium et Spes,* no.16), as well as to the solemn declaration of Vatican II: "Haec Vaticana Synodus declarat personam humanam ius habere ad libertatem religiosam" (*Dignitatis Humanae,* no.2); it has come an even farther way from the rejection of the ideals of the French Revolution by Pope Pius VI to the proclamation of Pope John Paul II during his first visit to France, namely that the values of the French Revolution are "basically christian."[10]; previously Pope Paul VI had already said that the Revolution "had done nothing other ... than [appropriate] certain christian ideas: fraternity, freedom, equality, progress and the desire to raise up the lower classes. As such all this was actually christian and only took on an anti-christian, worldly, irreligious appearance, thereby contributing to the deformation of that part of the evangelical patrimony, whose purpose is the appreciation, the promotion and the ennobling of human life"[11].

Do human rights now finally belong to the church's own thought? *Materialiter* this can be said without further ado. We witness even an

---

[8] G. LUF, "Menschenrechte," c.1107.

[9] *Ibid.*

[10] *Herder Korrespondenz* 8(1989) p.347.

[11] Cited according to F. FURGER, C. STROBEL-NEPPLE, *Menschenrechte,* p.80.

expressly active roll of the church in the formulation of further rights, as in a charter of family rights[11] or of the rights of migrants[12]. Does this also apply *formaliter*, this means: does the church consider and understand human rights out of their original dignity, meaning out of the self-responsible freedom proper to human beings, or still in other words out of the inner interweaving of the three principles of the French revolution? That is, is this fundamental freedom, including the risks of this freedom, approved? Is this freedom even considered as foundation for the whole ethos of human rights, or are human rights considered rather as a limitation and correction of a fundamentally dangerous freedom?

3. The Problematic Core

"In the content" of the teaching on human rights of the current pope one finds, according to Luf in the already cited article, "above all traditional requirements of the catholic social doctrine in the foreground, especially the right to life, completed with a 'right to birth', as well as social claims. A further emphasis can also be found upon those freedoms which concern the prerequisites of church activity, especially the rights to freedom of thought, conscience, and religion"[13] — "An essential precondition for the reception of the idea of human rights," continues Luf, "is the acquisition of a theologically mediated access to the contemporary ethos of freedom which support these rights."[14]

I have the impression that this pre-condition can in no way be assumed to have been met. Certainly the matter here concerns the acquisition of a theological access to the ethos of freedom, but, more precisely, to this modern ethos of freedom. This seems to me to be not sufficiently accomplished with respect to three perspectives:

a) First of all, insofar as a genuinely *anthropocentric* character is to be found in this ethos of freedom: the contents of this ethos are acquired from the personal experience and reflection of a responsible freedom. We speak here of an autonomous morality or also of an ethics of responsibility in order to bring this to expression[15]. On

---

[11] *Ibid.*, p.94.
[12] Cf. K.-W. MERKS, "Migration als ethische Aufgabe," in K.-H. KLEBER (ed.), *Migration und Menschenwürde,* Passau, 1988, pp.35-69, here: 58 ff.
[13] G. LUF, "Menschenrechte," c.1115.
[14] *Ibid.,* c.1115.
[15] Cf. with respect to this K.-W. MERKS, "Autonomie," in J.-P. WILS, D. MIETH, *Grundbegriffe der christlichen Ethik,* Paderborn, 1992, pp. 254-281.

the other hand, theories of essential-natural law or positivistic models of thought based on tradition or the ecclesiastical teaching
office often still characterize church doctrine. Question: How can
this contemporary anthropocentrism, as normative mode of thought
starting from human personal experience, theologically be integrated?

b) The ethos of freedom has in its anthropocentric character as such
an essentially *secular* quality: the personal experience of freedom
has primarily a reasonable, and not a faith, character. Question:
How can one integrate theologically this (autonomous) reasonableness (ethical insights are subject-oriented)?

c) Finally, the ethos of freedom is, next to all attempts to arrive at
objective rules of behavior — the human rights themselves with
their universal claims are an expression of this —, at the same time
still sensitive to the inescapable rights of *subjects* and *cultures*
(problematic of democracy, inculturation and pluralism). Question:
How can one take these aspects into account theologically, especially against the background of a traditional, universal claim of
competency of ecclesiastical authority?

Again: To what extent thus has the church opened itself not only to
the contents of human rights, but also to the specific ethical model of
experience and thought which is found in human rights, and which is
concentrated on the unfolding of human freedom? This question is identical with that regarding the acceptance of the legitimate anthropocentrism of ethics.

There are good reasons for considering human rights not as a coincidental manifestation within our modern culture, but rather precisely as
the ethical components of this very culture. Human rights are, as it were,
the foundational theme of modernity transformed into ethical obligations, the ethical implications of this culture, which modernity has
brought forth. And if we could be allowed to understand the facets of the
culture of modernity as variations on a single theme, this analogy would
hold also for the ethos of human rights.

The one, common theme is called "anthropocentrism" and its ethical
pivotal point is "responsible freedom." The human person who is aware
of her central standpoint in the world, who experiences her freedom and
power in the arrangement of world, society and history, must at the same
time experience herself as inescapably responsible. Thus she experiences
ethics in an anthropocentric mode: as one's own responsibility in the
fullest sense of the term. But it should be well understood that it is precisely an anthropocentrism of ethics itself, not a dissolution of ethics —

indeed an ethics of the human person assenting to her own free responsibility.

It is not a matter of the dissolution of the dismissal of the doctrine of "good" and "evil," of responsibility and duty, but rather the attempt to formulate anew this very doctrine in an anthropocentric perspective.

4. The Human Person as the Measure of Things?

Is the human person thus a measure of the ethical ought? Indeed: the human person finds the measure of ethical obligation in a certain manner in himself: in the claim to responsibly use of his freedom, based on his own insight into what is good and just and meaningful.

In passing: an anthropocentric ethic is certainly not the consequence of modern thought, as if it were produced automatically, but when modern thought incorporates an ethic, it can only do so from a fundamentally anthropocentric point of departure.

Thus the problem of the church-human rights seems now to by sharply posed: A reception of human rights in the church means a reception of this fundamentally anthropological perspective. Of course this also entails a religious-theological integration of this perspective into believing existence and its interpretation in the light of faith; but to be sure the believing interpretation of an *anthropocentric* ethics. Has the church really accepted that 'anthropocentrism' in ethics, like 'anthropocentrism' in technology, is in no way in itself a sign of unbelief? Does the church see itself as capable of a believing interpretation of anthropocentrism, whether it be a stamping of its own image on this ethics or a new coining? Has the church let itself get fully involved in the ethical theory of human rights, has the church really ventured itself into a culture of human rights?

The idea of an "anthropocentric ethics" deserves a short explanation. "The human person as the measure of things," in many ways a suspect formula, is actually however not a bad formula for what ethics is all about. Already the formulation of every day language signifies that moral behavior aims at "humanity" and at being truly "human". The traditional doctrine of natural law, when it saw the norms for human behavior as grounded in the nature of the human person, can also be understood as an explication of the formula that "the human person is the measure". Because of this, that which is specific to contemporary ethics is not found in the human person being the measure as such, but rather in the manner and way in which this measure is understood: as a

measure already given in nature which is primarily to be receptively perceived, or as a measure, in the formulation of which, the human experience of meaning, and the "creation" of meaning, are constitutively co-
foundational?

The determination of "good" and "evil," the determination of that
which is normative and binding, no longer simply follows from a pre-
given nature, whatever type of nature this might be. It is much more
unavoidably bound to the moral personal experience of the subject. Values and value-related norms presume the existence of a subject with her
openness to the experience of values and the capacity to value (above all
in conflict situations). This means however that a normative potential
can no longer be attributed to nature apart from a dialectic further to be
specified with the valuing subject. The experience of nature is not of
itself, but only through integration in personal experience normatively
relevant.

This personal experience however is less an experience of the particular nature of humanity as a given, than, and much more so, the experience of the call to compose a meaningful life in responsible freedom.
The determination of "good" and "evil" is thereby a task of freedom
itself. It concerns the experience of one's own responsibility in view of
one's own power and freedom, to make human life, human society and
the world meaningful. This shift in point of view can be described as a
shift from "nature" to "person." [16] One is concerned here essentially
with the question, whether or not the human person in his experience of
himself as a being with value and freedom is the basis also for the determination of the content of ethical obligation. By means of an
"autonomous morality" in a theological context, moral theology seeks
to unfold this idea. Freedom experienced as responsibility is not only the
locus of the perception of ethical obligation as such, but at the same time
it is determinative for modern ethics, that the material norms of ethics
are now focused upon the realization, the protection and the stimulation
of freedom. Ethical insights are not gained according to the way of physical assessment. The human person is, for herself, as acting subject, not
merely an (already complete) physical or metaphysical object. The valuing subject necessarily appears as self-reflexive in the determination of
that which is to be done. That this ethics is thought of as expressible in

---

[16] Cf. K.-W. MERKS, "Naturrecht als Personrecht?," in M. HEIMBACH-STEINS
(ed.), *Das Naturrecht im ethischen Diskurs,* Münster, 1990, pp.28-46; Id., "Freiheit als
Grundlage der Moral, Naturrecht — unter dem Vorzeichen des modernen Freiheitsver-
ständnisses neu gelesen," in J. HOFFMANN (ed.), *Begründung von Menschenrechten
aus der Sicht unterschiedlicher Kulturen,* Frankfurt, 1991, pp.75-103.

the form of general, binding human rights which aim at universality, despite necessary culturally bound variability, is a sign that human freedom is not merely a locus of subjective decision making, but can also be seen as the material foundation for a common, human experience of being human.

Human rights came into existence and evolved in the context of the fundamental ideas and sensibilities of modern thought. The philosophy of human rights necessarily presumes the modern consciousness of freedom, as well as its implications and consequences: secularization, autonomy, democracy, plurality, as general thought patterns of our experiences. But the philosophy of human rights does not only presume these ideas, it is also the ethics appropriate to them. Human rights are, to be sure, the expression of modern thought and feelings, but at the same time they are also the ethical measure to which these thoughts and feelings are invited to subject themselves. They are the pre-conditions for assuring that the situation of modernity remains livable as modern culture of freedom.

5. Human Rights in the Church

"All ... are amazed at a contrast: that concerning the contradiction between the present engagement of the roman church for the respecting and stimulation of the freedoms and the rights of human persons in the state, social and political fields and the incapacity of the roman authorities to respect and stimulate christian freedom in the church itself." [17]

Therefore in the defense of human rights in the world the church must "begin with an act of self-examination, with a close look at how and how far these fundamental rights are safeguarded within its own organization and realized in the praxis" [18]. According to me, the go about with human rights within the church itself is the touchstone for the real acceptance of the philosophy of human rights; yet here are found the greatest reservations and fears on the part of the church.

This observation does not merely point out an inconsistency in the behavior of the church which employs human rights differently "within" and "without" the church. When the inner meaning of human rights is properly understood, such a differentiation is no longer possible. The

---

[17] B. QUELQUEJEU, "Aussöhnung mit den Menschenrechten, Missachtung der 'Christenrechte': Die römische Inkonsequenz," in *Concilium* 1/1989, p.78.

[18] "Die Kirche und die Menschenrechte." (Ein Arbeitspapier der Päpstlichen Kommission Justitia et Pax, no. 62).

rights of freedom of human persons, if they are truly human rights, cannot stop, not even partly, at the doors of the church; reference to the church as a community of a special kind with proper rights, when this is used to justify the invalidity of human rights, has no dogmatic value, but is rather an expression of such reservations and fears.

6. A Believing Ethics of Reason

At times one can come to the impression that human rights are certainly necessary, also for christians, but that they concern not really a christian ethics. Quite to the contrary, I would like to defend the thesis that an ethics of human rights is not only a secular ethics, but is at the same time the "ethics of faith" in modern form. The tradition itself offers sufficient starting points and bridges to recognize this as appropriate after an unprejudiced examination[19].

Here, we should not seek out in an anachronistic manner human rights as such in one's own tradition. Human rights are a product of modern times. They correspond to the contemporary experience and consciousness of freedom. They have been developed, not on account of, but in spite of the church and its tradition. Yet they are of course also specially rooted in Christianity itself. And in fact they should have evolved there a long time ago. Then, along with the doctrine of man being the image of God, of being God's children and of God's universal salvific will, the dignity and equality of all human persons could have been taught most vigorously. The conviction of the freedom of the act of faith could always have already been the basis for judging political authorities to be incompetent in matters of faith and this conviction could also have been interpreted as inalienable right and unconditional duty of personal conscience in the quest for God. Freedom of conscience and of religion belong to the essential core of the christian understanding of faith itself. Also the non-identity between this world and the Kingdom of God could have long ago rendered questionable a certain understanding of the relation between church and state. Even the problem of democratic "codetermination" (participation) in questions of the search for truth finds sufficient starting points in the tradition of the church. Finally, the connections between the Ten Commandments and human rights, between the biblical ethos and liberation, between christian faith and christian

---

[19] Cf. K.-W. MERKS, "Autonomie"; Id. "De Tien Woorden: een weg van vrijheid," in K.-W. MERKS, N. POULSSEN, W. WEREN, *Weg of wet? Over de Tien Woorden,* Boxtel-Brugge, 1989, pp.70-95.

freedom, need not have waited until the 20th century for their (re-) discovery (in the Romana). Yet if the church nonetheless closed itself off from such consequences of its own tradition, then this is not a question of faith and the protection of its purity. Rather it is more a question of a refused inculturation of the gospel in the thought and culture of modernity. The ethos of human rights, precisely in its secularity, is not contrary to the gospel, but rather a timely development of the universal humanity and solidarity required by the gospel also from the faithful.

7. Conclusion

The ideal of human rights, the inviolability of human dignity and freedom, both of the others and oneself, have become terminative for our judicial, political, social and cultural order (and will become as such on a global scale more and more a corresponding commitment). The philosophy of human rights shapes the life of the individual and of society. Human rights have become like the climate in which we live, the very air which we need in order to breathe. Therefore it is not unimportant whether or not we are able to encounter this climate in the church also. There exists a very close connection between the culture of human rights and the ability of people to feel at home in the church. Faith and church are part of one culture only when they really move into this culture. Otherwise they will not be experienced as part of and relevant. This is certainly germane in such a serious issue as human rights. Human rights are not at all a coincidental by-product of our culture, but rather the ethical quintessence of modernity. They are one of the most important elements which makes modernity worthwhile. They are so important that we do not want to dispense with them, even when so many other elements of modernity are not to be retained. They are morally indispensable, such that no post-modernity, whatever its form, can be considered defensible apart from them.

There exists an indivisible link between the culture of human rights in the church or the church's involvement in a culture of human rights, on the one hand, and the church as a home for contemporary people. The future of faith and the church is not only dependent upon whether or not it succeeds in expressing the faith in understandable symbols in today's secularized world; it is every bit as dependent, if not more so, upon whether or not we recognize our fundamental convictions and ideals of righteousness and justice in the faith and in the church.[*]

---

[*] Translation by R. Gilbert

CREATIVE CANON LAW DEVELOPMENT

RUUD G.W. HUYSMANS

The author intends to investigate how the power of governance, which is due to the leadership of this church, has been or can be regulated in such a way that it is used as an act of justice. Ruud Huysmans is a Dutch canon lawyer and an expert of the canonical or ecclesiastical law of the Roman-Catholic Church.

This contribution is based on two views regarding the Code of Canon Law, as it was promulgated by Pope John Paul II in 1983 for the Latin Roman-Catholic Church. Firstly: "This Code wished to maintain very general formulations in order to leave the ultimate determination of the law to the competent local authorities who know best the circumstances of the place, so that the law may be better suited to the requirements of direct and concrete pastoral action" [1]. The Code of Canon Law does not contain all laws governing the church, but only a part. It wants laws from others sources as its complement.

Secondly: "No one would pretend for a moment that the Code of Canon Law is the final word in the Church on matters that touch its life and mission as a society. (...) New situations will arise that will have to be addressed; new difficulties will have to be resolved; new developments will call for changes in structures" [2]. The Code of Canon Law is an unfinished collection of laws. It should be revised if need be. Its *Preface* states: "If, due to the dynamics which affect our human society, certain imperfections in the law arise which necessitate a new revision, the Church possesses such resources that, no less than in de past centuries, it will be able to undertake the mission of revising the laws of its life".

Both views make clear that the laws of the church are in a continuous process of development, supported by canonists' studies. Law is here

---

[1] R.I. CASTILLO LARA, "Some Reflections on the Proper Way to Approach the Code of Canon Law," in *Communicationes* 17(1985) p.284.

[2] F.G. MORRISEY, "Applying the 1983 Code of Canon Law: The Task of Canonists in the Years Ahead," in *Le Nouveau Code de Droit Canonique. Actes du Ve Congrès international du droit canonique,* Faculté de droit canonique, Université Saint-Paul, Ottawa, Ontario, Canada, Part II, 1986, p.1143.

understood to be a. the Code of Canon Law of 1983[3]; b. the Code of Canons of the Eastern Churches, promulgated by the same Pope in 1990 for the Oriental Churches in union with Rome; c. particular law as promulgated by diocesan bishops and; d. other supplementary rules.

This contribution intends to investigate how the power of governance, which is due to the leadership of this church, has been or can be regulated in such a way that it is used as an act of justice. By justice is meant that power is wielded for "the building up of the Body of Christ" (can. 208 and 275 §1). This is supported by an ancient tradition dating back to Paul, who in II Cor. 10:8 and 13:10 speaks about his authority "to build, not to destroy"[4]. This power takes into account "the participation of Christ's faithful in their own way in the priestly, prophetic and kingly office of Christ" (can. 204 §1). It is seen as just within the church, if it does not annihilate but confirms the "genuine equality of dignity and action among all of Christ's faithful" (can. 208). Canon 208 concludes that "because of this equality they all contribute, each according to his or her own condition and office, to the building up of the Body of Christ".

This description of a just use of power still lacks a sharp juridical definition. The canons quoted do not contain any laws clearly and immediately regulating any relationships. For that purpose their character is too general and too theological, not unlike some other important canons of the Code of Canon Law. They rather contain programmatical and constitutional law. This means that they contain a programme the church will work upon and is yet to realize. This can be done by concrete rules of law transferring this programme to *defining laws* and transforming it into laws that apply more directly to relationships.

Yet in this contribution justice of governance has been dealt with in this sense. If justice should be dealt with only in terms of the rights and duties of christians, including human rights, only personal and individual rights and duties are taken into account. But then the fact is concealed that not only individual, physical persons have rights and duties in the church. Communities within the church, like dioceses (can. 368-369), parishes (can. 515 §1), orders and congregations (can. 574-577), associations and movements (can. 215; 298 and 299) take a lawful share in the building up of the church. Many are juridical persons within the church in the sense of aggregates of persons (can. 115 §2). But their

---

[3] Unless stated otherwise *can.* in this essay always refers to a canon or law from the *Code of Canon Law* for the Latin Church.

[4] In Latin: "in aedificationem, non in destructionem".

rightful share in the building up of the church is still underdeveloped juridically; it is still in the programmatical stage of the law[5].

Individual rights and duties have found an initial concrete formula in the Code of Canon Law (can. 208-231) and in the Code of Canons of the Eastern Churches (can. 7-26 and 399-409). The statute for recognized communities within the church still lacks concrete legal elaboration. Collective rights have so far hardly been defined. The Code of Canons of the Eastern Churches has its own way of expressing justice of governance. "Whoever issues a decree wants to intend and aim at whatever is seen as most conducive to salvation of the souls and public welfare, in accordance with the laws and the lawful customs, with justice and equity" (can. 1519 §1). This canon is not included in the Code of Canon Law.

The theme of power and law has been chosen in order to find out how ecclesiastical power, particularly that of diocesan bishops, is, or could be, subjected to the law, and how it is regulated by it[6]. This study can also shed some more light upon the nature of governing power within the church. A study of this kind has an in-built limitation, rooted in the very nature of justice. Justice is not whatever someone may assume it is; is not what someone believes is, or should be, valid. Justice is whatever is accepted and agreed upon. To put it more succinctly: justice does not consist in claiming a just cause, but in the communally accepted claiming of it. Should a claim go unaccepted, then it is no more than a plea for a just cause. But a plea does not constitute justice. Justice is not constituted unless the claim of it is recognized, and so is active within a community. This is the consequence of the insight: "When the Church does not accept it, a proposed law has no effect"[7].

1. Protection Against Power

In 1967 the First Ordinary General Session of the Synod of Bishops, convened by Pope Paul VI after the Second Vatican Ecumenical Council (1962-1965), agreed upon *Ten Principles Which Govern the Revision of the Code of Canon Law*.

Principle no. 6 is headed *Safeguarding the Rights of Persons*: "A very important problem must be solved in the future Code of Canon Law,

---

[5] Cf. E. CAPPELLINI, "La tutela dei diritti delle comunità territoriali: diocesi e parrocchia," in *Monitor Ecclesiasticus* 113(1988)85-104.

[6] Cf. M.R. MOODIE, "The Administrator and the Law: Authority and its Exercise in the Code," in *The Jurist* 46(1986)43-69.

[7] Cf. J.A. CORIDEN, "Rules for Interpreters," in *The Jurist* 42(1982) p.288.

namely, how can the rights of persons be defined and safeguarded? It is clear that power is one and the same, whether it resides in the Supreme Authority or in a person of lesser authority, namely, in the Roman Pontiff or in the diocesan bishops within their respective sphere of jurisdiction. Each one is totally competent to exercise his juridic power for the service of the community to which he has been assigned. This strengthens and establishes the unity of his power, and no one will doubt that this is of great benefit for the pastoral care of one's subjects.

The use of this power in the church, however, must not become arbitrary, because natural law prohibits such arbitrary use of power, as do also positive divine law and the law of the church itself. The rights of each and every faithful must be acknowledged and safeguarded, both the rights which they have by natural law and the rights contained in divine positive law, as also the rights which are duly derived from these laws because of the social condition which the faithful acquire and possess in the Church"[8]. In these words the tension is felt between the full papal and episcopal competence to exercise its lawful power of governance on the one hand, and the rights of the faithful on the other. The idea of ecclesiastical power as ministry within the church also needs the intermediary of law to function adequately. The *Principle* outlines a few matters.

In order to protect the faithful against arbitrary use of ecclesiastical power the *Principle* first and foremost intends to recognize and safeguard the rights of the faithful, on the implied assumption that ecclesiastical authority wields its power in a just manner. That is why no extensive rules need be given, nor any special limitations fixed. It is in safe hands. Moreover, the faithful enjoy several rights ensuring their protection, in extreme cases, against abuse of ecclesiastical power. The *Principle* refrains from imposing a set of legal rules upon ecclesiastical authority itself. It does not want to channel it by means of ecclesiastical laws.

There is a wide-open stretch of ground between church authority, entrusted with ecclesiastical power, and the faithful with their guaranteed rights. According to *Principle* no. 6, this area, where policies are made and governance is exercised, needs no further structuring by lawgiving. In accordance with present law this is left to the free and discretionary exercise of authority. Lined up around this area are the individual faithful with their personal and private rights. Ecclesiastical

---

[8] In J.F. HITE, G.J. SESTO, D.J. WARD, *Readings, Cases, Materials in Canon Law. A Textbook for Ministerial Students*, Collegeville, Minnesota, 1980, pp.75-76. The Latin original is found in *Communicationes* 1(1969) p.82.

communities as such have no rights of sharing power of governance; nor can they lay claims to it. Nevertheless not every single misuse of power constitutes a breach of individual rights of others. Ecclesiastical power can also be wielded in an unjust manner if equality, dignity, the common mission of all are not recognized, and the contribution of all towards the building up of the Body of Christ is not encouraged. Then collective expectations are thwarted, and remain unhonoured. That is the reason why procedural rules are so important for the exercise of power. These rules provide some form, not only to the rights of individual catholics, but, at least as a first step, to the collective rights of communities within the church.

Procedural rules are those which, in concrete cases, determine how church authority is to produce a general decree — a law (can. 29), an executory decree (can. 32) or an instruction (can. 34) — or a singular administrative act (can. 35)[9]. This may be a singular decree (can. 48), a precept (can. 49), a rescript (can. 59), especially a dispensation (can. 85). These rules may deal with collecting factual information, balancing interests, questioning of the parties concerned, seeking advice or consent from councils or committees, being accessible to objections against an impending decree, producing arguments to substantiate a decree and the possibility of recourse or appeal against it[10]. In all these rules a contribution of communities or of persons out of them is acknowledged, and a reasonable balance of options and interests is obtained.

2. Free Exercise of Power[11]

The *Principle* does not primarily opt for increased procedural rules. This can be explained in two ways.

On the one hand, in both ordinary and extraordinary circumstances, the pope or a diocesan bishop must be able to take every decision his office requires for the benefit of the church. Power is attached to the office, which is its yardstick. "Ordinary power of governance is that which by virtue of the law itself is attached to a given office" (can. 131 §1). Power is generated by the office as widely and extensively as is

---

[9] Cf. J.P. BEAL, "Confining and Structuring Administrative Discretion," in *The Jurist* 46(1986)70-106.

[10] Cf. Th.J. PAPROCKI, "Rights of Christians in the Local Church: Canon Law Procedures in Light of Civil Law Principles of Administrative Justice," in *Studia Canonica* 24(1990)427-442.

[11] Cf. R. HUYSMANS, "Pouvoir et liberté: Du gouvernement dans l'église catholique romaine," in *Praxis Juridique et Religion* 8(1991)84-103.

required for the mission of the church. This is how the Code of Canon Law puts it. "By virtue of his office, the Roman Pontiff has supreme, full, immediate and universal ordinary power in the Church, and he can always freely exercise this power" (can. 331). Moreover, "in the diocese entrusted to his care, the diocesan Bishop has all the ordinary, proper and immediate power required for the exercise of his pastoral office (...)" (can. 381 §1).

That is the reason why power needs to be exercised as freely as possible, whereas it should be tied as little as possible procedurally to those who are subjects within the church. The office, and the power that goes with it, are meant to rescue the church in emergencies from unacceptable situations in which it finds itself by either internal or external (political) circumstances. Church authority must have a free hand to act and react. Yet it is bound by the Church's mission, for an office is meant "to further a spiritual purpose" (can. 145 §1). Thus not only the care but also the concrete interpretation according to place and time of "the mission which God entrusted to the Church to fulfil in the world" (can. 204 §1) are the hierarchy's due.

Although church authority often has a limited freedom whether to take a decision or not, it often has adequate room for freedom of judgment. This means that it is its exclusive right to assess facts, circumstances and conditions justifying its right and duty to act. It alone decides how a rule of law is applied in a particular case. Sometimes its power to act is given by the Code of Canon Law without further arguments. This is found in canon 515 §2: "The diocesan Bishop alone can establish, suppress or alter parishes". Sometimes the law states that an assessment of circumstances should precede the exercise of a certain faculty. This is found in canon 235 §1 "if in the judgment of the diocesan Bishop circumstances require it", or in canon 517 §1 "where circumstances so require". In canon 805 both types are found: "In his own diocese, the local Ordinary — Bishop — has the right to appoint or to approve teachers of religion and, if religious or moral considerations require it, the right to remove them or to demand that they be removed".

On the other hand, church law presupposes that a church authority may feel compelled to use its power against those persons within the church whom it has a duty to co-operate with. If it should have a procedural obligation to act according to their advice or consent, it could, if necessary, hardly reach a different administrative or judicial decision anymore. That is why, generally speaking, the Code of Canon Law confines the relationship between church authority and its subjects to the obligation to consult them before deciding, even if, according to the law, the bishop is to co-operate with them. "The diocesan Bishop is to have a special concern for the priests, to whom he is to listen as his helpers and counsellers" (can. 384). "He is to consult the council of priests in matters of more serious moment, but he requires its consent only in the cases expressly defined in the law" (can. 500 §2). This, however, is nowhere prescribed by the Code of Canon Law.

When promulgating the Code of Canon Law Pope John Paul II wrote in his *Apostolic Constitution*: "The Code rather looks towards the achievement of order in the ecclesial society, such that while attributing a primacy to love, grace and the charisms, it facilitates at the same time an orderly development in the life both of the ecclesial society and of the individual persons who belong to it". The Code of Canon Law wants to serve just relationships within the church. The church lives by the ordering principle of permission, not of prohibition: all that is not forbidden, is permitted[12]. This is found in the old adage: "Whatever is not excluded by law, should not be excluded by ourselves"[13]. The reverse statement: all that is not — expressly — permitted, is forbidden, is invalid. The Code of Canon Law does not forbid the extension of good procedural rules to other situations for which it prescribes none. Although a church subject has no right to claim it, a church authority can allow such an extension.

Since ecclesiastical power is, through the office, attached to a person (can. 131 §1), community can make certain demands. Every ecclesiastical office "is to further a spiritual purpose" (can. 145 §1). It is to be exercised for the benefit of the church and her mission. The office-holder is expected to provide good and adequate governance. So traditionally a person can be removed from office in case his "ministry has for some reason become harmful or at least ineffective" (can. 1740; cfr can. 401 §2 about diocesan Bishops). Someone's duties towards the community do not impair his power but strengthen it. Recognition of other people's rightful demands does not diminish any rights or duties of one's office. The Pope recognizes this for himself too. "By virtue of his office, the Roman Pontiff not only has power over the universal church, but also has pre-eminent ordinary power over all particular Churches and their groupings. This reinforces and defends the proper, ordinary and immediate power which the Bishops have in the particular Churches entrusted to their care" (can. 333 §1).

---

[12] Cf. W. STEINMÜLLER, "Der Entwurf der Lex Ecclesiae Fundamentalis — Ein Klerikerrecht der Laien?" in *Theologische Quartalschrift* 152(1972)326-330.

[13] In Latin: "Quod ius not excludit, neque nos excludere debemus."

The Code of Canon Law contains, in scattered places, several rules for good and proper governance. It mentions certain procedures of church authority action against the will of a subject. The Code of Canon of the Eastern Churches contains a special *Article: The procedure in Issuing Extra-judicial Decrees* in canons 1517-1520, some of which, but not all are found in the Code of Canon Law in the chapter *Singular Decrees and Precepts* (can. 48-58). In this context canon 19 of the Code of Canon Law is important: "If on a particular matter there is not an express provision of either universal or particular law, nor a custom, then (...) the question is to be decided by taking into account laws enacted in similar matters (...)". Therefore it looks permissable for the Latin Church, in such a situation, to adopt laws from the Code of Canons of the Eastern Churches; the more so since in both cases, the Pope is the legislator.

The following rules for proper governance are all derived from papal and episcopal law in the church. It is suggested to extend them to other cases for which they were not foreseen. None means impairment of church authority power.

3. Procedural Rules in Church Councils

Church councils, which should truly reflect the entire community (cf. can. 512 §2), generally discuss proposals of diocesan policy, which may end in general decrees by the bishop. This might be the case in a particular council, a diocesan synod, a council of priests, or a diocesan pastoral council (can. 443 §1; 466; 500 and 514 §1). The deliberative or decisive vote of a church superior in these ecclesiastical assemblies can, in various ways, be brought into good perspective with the merely consultative vote of the others present. One way is that the superior, prior to the vote, puts forward his own views. Another way could be, should he not accept the majority view, to present his opinion with his own considerations. A supplementary possibility is to have a new deliberation, followed by a new vote; or a committee might be formed to draw up a new proposal acceptable to both the bishop and the others[14].

The advantage of these rules, found in particular law, is that the parties concerned are invited not to think in terms of power positions, but to

---

[14] Cf. E. HANGARTNER-EVERS, *Synode 72. Vom II. Vatikanischen Konzil zur Vorbereitung und rechtlichen Ausgestaltung der Synode 72*, Luzern, 1977, p.104 and pp.128-129; K. HARTELT, *Die Diözesan- und Regionalsynoden im Deutschen Sprachraum nach dem Zweiten Vatikanum. Rechtshistorische und rechtstheologische Aspekte der Verwirklichung des Synodalprinzips in der Struktur der Kirche der Gegenwart* (Erfurter Theologische Studien, 40), Leipzig, 1979, pp.136-138 and p.271.

enter upon a course of mutual and reasonable deliberation based upon analyses and arguments. In this context attention should be paid to a superior's duty to provide necessary information to church councils. Canon 1292 §4 of Book IV: *The Temporal Goods of the Church* of the Code of Canon Law rules that "those who must give advice about or consent to the alienation of goods are not to give this advice or consent until they have first been informed precisely both about the economic situation of the juridical person whose goods it is proposed to alienate and about alienations which have already taken place". Advice or consent presupposes adequate knowledge. Canon 127 §3 of Book I, Title VII: *Juridical Acts* rules: "All whose consent or advice is required are obliged to give their opinions sincerely". The Code of Canons of the Eastern Churches supplies an important addition in canon 934 §3: "To those whose consent or advice is required the authority requesting consent or advice is to supply the necessary information".

Another way of improving communication within the church is regular reporting. A church superior can supply regular reports of his activities, policy and general decrees to his councils and committees as well as to the community. It is church custom to present annual financial and economic reports on income and spending (can. 493), or give an annual account to the ecclesiastical superior. "The administrators, both clerical and lay, of ecclesiastical goods are bound to submit each year to the local Ordinary — Bishop — an account of their administration" (can. 1287 §1). Canon 399 §1 rules that "every five years the diocesan Bishop is bound to submit to the Supreme Pontiff a report on the state of the diocese entrusted to him". The Code of Canon Law mentions a single case in which an authority is to give an account to the community. "Administrators are to render accounts to the faithful concerning the goods they have given to the Church" (can. 1287 §2). There is nothing to prevent any ecclesiastical authority to give much wider publicity to the reports they are expected to send to their superiors, or any other report for that matter. Thus interest in church policies is stimulated, and active participation of the faithful is improved.

4. Singular Decrees or Procedures

Church authority can decide that it will, in due course, provide an answer to a request made to it, or else it will announce a delay. More often than not faithful send requests to church authorities without ever receiving any reaction. These requests are based upon canon 212 §2:

"Christ's faithful are at liberty to make known their needs, especially their spiritual needs, and their wishes to the Pastors of the Church". Canon 57 §1 rules: "Whenever the law orders a decree to be issued, or when a person who is concerned lawfully requests a decree or has recourse to obtain one, the competent authority is to provide for the situation within three months of having received the petition or recourse, unless a different period of time is prescribed by law". Here the superior is, by law, subjected to a term of answer.

There is no juridical ground to prevent this rule being applied in cases, unforeseen by law. The Code of Canons of the Eastern Chuches correctly contains a rule for this. Canon 1518 rules: "The authority is to issue a decree within sixty days of having received the petition to obtain a decree". The *Apostolic Constitution on the Roman Curia Pastor Bonus* (1988) rules in Art. 26,3: "Questions brought before the dicasteries are to be diligently examined and, without delay, an answer or, least a written acknowledgement of receipt, insofar as this is necessary, should be sent".

The Code of Canon Law rules in canon 50: "Before issuing a singular decree, the person in authority is to seek the necessary information and proof and, as far as possible, is to consult those whose rights could be harmed". The Code of Canons of the Eastern Churches rules in canon 1517 §1, following "the necessary information and proof": "he should hear or consult those who have a right to be heard or consulted; he should hear those whom the decree concerns directly, and especially those whose rights could be harmed". The Code of Canon Law could profit by this, because an extensive and elaborate consultation is prescribed.

In the Code of Canons of the Eastern Churches canon 1517 §2 mentions another detail, unknown in the Code of Canon Law: "The authority should provide both the petitioner and the lawful opponent with the information and proof, which can without public or private harm be divulged; it should also provide counter-arguments, if any. He should be enabled to respond, also with an advocate's assistance, within the term fixed by this authority". It is ruled here that, prior to the decree, the person concerned can obtain the information needed, and can defend himself. This is a guarantee that church authority can, subsequently, issue its decree as objectively as possible. In juridical terms this looks like a better solution than what is ruled in the Code of Canon Law canon 1733. There finding "an equitable solution" with the help of "serious-minded persons" or of a "permanent office or council" does not take place in dioceses until after the decree has been issued.

The Code of Canon Law canon 51 rules that "a decree is to be issued in writing. When it is a decision, it should express, at least in summary form, the reasons for the decision". Commentaries do not agree on the exact difference between a decree and a decision. The decision is defined in various ways. It can responsibly be assumed that a decision, as meant in canon 51, is understood to be a decree within a recourse against administrative decrees (can. 1732-1739)[15]. This can be the decree by which a superior decides on a request of revocation or amendment of his earlier decree (can. 1734 §1). It can also refer to a decree by a hierarchical superior (can. 1737 §1), by which he decides on someone's recourse against a lower authority. The rule about this decision is: "In so far as the case demands, it is lawful for the Superior who must decide the recourse, not only to confirm the decree or declare that it is invalid, but also to rescind or revoke it or, if it seems to the Superior to be more expedient, to amend it, to substitute for it, or to abrogate it" (can. 1739). Since they qualify for further recourse of appeal, decisions in a recourse must have an argued foundation. Otherwise they could not possibly be assessed by the hierarchical superior or the judge.

If this interpretation of decision in canon 51 is correct, it would mean: only in the context of a recourse against a decree by a superior, who made it, he is obliged to state the reasons for his decree, not earlier. It is regrettable that the Code of Canon Law should have no general rule about motivation for the many ordinary decrees in the life of the church. These can be made without giving the arguments. The Code of Canons of the Eastern Churches, however, rules in canon 1519 §2, regarding all decrees, including those made outside a recourse or appeal: "In the decree the reasons should, at least in summary form, be expressed". This rule, too, could be copied by ecclesiastical superiors of the Latin Church.

5. The Removal from an Office or Function

A person's removal from an office or function against his will is a most sensitive affair. The rights of the office-holder must be carefully weighed against the reasons church authority is having to remove him. This concerns offices within the ecclesiastical organization of dioceses, deaneries and parishes. These also include offices or functions in Roman-Catholic organizations which are part of the church or are

---

[15] Cf. R.G.W. HUYSMANS, *Algemene Normen van het Wetboek van Canoniek Recht. Normis Generalibus* (Novum Commentarium Lovaniense in Codicem Iuris Canonici Liber I), Leuven, 1983, pp.152-159.

attached to her by statute, such as institutions for education and research, for medical care, for mental health care and for other social assistance. The degree to which these are subjected to Canon Law or/and to the diocesan bishop's authority differs countrywise.

The removal from office by order of church authority requires procedural rules and safeguards. For the transfer from one office to another by the same authority, canon 190 §2 rules: "A grave reason is required if a transfer is made against the will of the holder of an office and, always without prejudice to the right to present reasons against the transfer, the procedure prescribed by law is to be observed". For a removal "grave reasons" are required, and it should take place "in accordance with the procedure defined in law" (can. 193 §1 and 2). The Code of Canon Law mentions a *Procedure for the Removal* for parish priests only (can. 1740-1747), not for other offices or functions. In case of other functions the procedure of removal is determined by the preliminary investigation of canon 50 [16], and by the written decree of canon 51 [17] which need not mention reasons.

It is characteristic for the *Procedure for the Removal of Parish Priests* that it is based upon reasons and grounds, and that it has a right of reply. Moreover, "the Bishop is to discuss the matter with two parish priests chosen from a group stably established for this purpose by the council of priests at the proposal of the Bishop" (can. 1742 §1). Consultation with two peers, a kind of 'peer-judgment', takes place. In a similar way canon 1280 of *The Administration of Goods* rules that "every juridical person is to have its own finance committee, or at least two counsellors, who are to assist in the performance of the administrator's duties, in accordance with the statutes". Here, too, the wisdom of at least two other persons is called for. The Code of Canon Law does not forbid to adapt the *Procedure for the Removal of Parish Priests* for application in other church offices or functions, and to enable a more elaborate procedure than the ones meant in canon 50 and 51.

In the Code of Canon Law canons 694-704 deal with *The Dismissal of Members* of an institute of consecrated life, of a religious person. Canon 700 rules: "For validity the decree of dismissal must indicate the right of the person dismissed to have recourse to the competent authority within ten days of receiving notification of the decree. The recourse has a suspensive effect". Here it is ruled that a superior must inform the religious person about the means to appeal against the decree, and what

---

[16] Cf. *supra*, p.190.
[17] Cf. *supra*, p.191.

the juridical consequence is. It is a sign of good governance by church authority whenever this is done with regard to a decree that is hard for the person concerned[18]. Although "ignorance is not presumed about a law" (can. 15 §2), yet there is a wide-spread, though irreprehensible ignorance within the church about her laws and procedures.

6. Judging People in Serious Cases

Canon 221 §2 rules: "If any members of Christ's faithful are summoned to trial by the competent authority, they have the right to be judged according to the provisions of the law, to be applied with equity". Only very rarely are faithful summoned by competent authority to stand trial according to the rules of Book VII: *Processes* of the Code of Canon Law. However, quite regularly faithful and, particularly, holders of an office or function are called to account by church authority in an administrative manner. The very same superior formulates the objection, passes judgment on the person concerned and finally takes a decision. The reasons are that a person's life style, doctrinal statements or pastoral behaviour are supposedly not up to the church's requirements. For cases like these, in which no judicial trial is called for, the Code of Canon Law has no rules, except those of canon 50 and 51, and those of the closing words of canon 221 §2 about equity. Supplementary rules for a brief administrative procedure have to be made in the dioceses.

At the very least this procedure consists in the expression by church authority of the suspicion against a person, the disclosure of the sources for this, the hearing of the person concerned, the opportunity of defense with the right of reply, the help of an advocate (cf. can. 1738), and finally, a written decision. The case is best served by a written and signed record of the several phases. But even more securities can be built in by, e.g. making use of the wisdom and knowledge of others. The Code of Canon Law prescribes this more often. Canon 500 §2 rules: "The diocesan Bishop is to consult the council of priests in matters of more serious moment". When removing a parish priest from office he requires the assistance of two fellow parish priests. An administrator of a juridical person requires the assistance of at least two counsellors [19]. So according to the law a superior should, in certain cases, make use of the wisdom and expertise of others in the church, who are his subjects.

---

[18] In German: *Rechtsmittelbelehrung.*
[19] Cf. *supra,* pp.191-192.

The form of such a supplementary procedure has two fundamental alternatives. The first has just been described: Church authority consults at least two Roman-Catholics, whether qualified or not, for the assessment of persons or cases. The other line is: both the superior and the person to be judged appoint one or two persons in a committee, presided over by an independent chairperson, to prepare a well-argued advice to the superior. The person concerned can agree or oppose it. Around these two alternatives some precise rules can be arranged. In either case the final decision is lawfully due to the competent church authority. It is a good thing for the dioceses to have publicized procedures for administrative, non-judicial judgment of persons against whom suspicion has been raised.

For the judicial judgment of persons canon 221 §2 orders the application of equity[20]. This is a characteristic feature of Canon Law. When persons are liable to be treated with severity equity is required. Canon 1752, the last of the Code of Canon Law, rules that, next to care for the salvation of souls, canonical equity is always to be observed. In the *Preface* of the Code of Canon Law *Principle* no. 3 of the *Ten Principles Which Govern the Revision of the Code of Canon Law* (1967) is defined as follows: "To favour the pastoral care of souls, the new law must provide not only for justice, but there must be a place for charity, temperance, humaneness, and moderation by which fairness — equity — shall be found not only in the application of the laws by pastors but also in the legislation itself".

In short, canonical equity means that he who is about to take severe measures against another person, should try and identify with him and should, from this position, try and realize what he is about to do. This is the application of the *positive golden rule*, taken from St Matthew's Gospel: "Do to other men all that you would have them do to you; that is the Law and the Prophets" (Matt. 7:12; Luke 6:31). Such equity cannot be forced. She cannot be further defined by law either. It is part of the real relationships of people within the church, and can only be applied according to the circumstances. This is no optional matter, for the Code of Canon Law prescribes it.

7. Without Procedural Rule

Regrettably a church superior occasionally happens to take a harsh decision about someone within the church without a procedural rule to

---

[20] Cf. R.G.W. HUYSMANS, *Algemene normen*, pp.106-109.

guarantee a careful preparation. My advice would be the following. If a church authority reproaches a person for having acted against an ecclesiastical duty, it is advisable to find out if there might be a right in the same field. For most duties under the Code of Canon Law also contain a right, implicitly or explicitly. The reverse is also true. The duty "to lead a holy life" (can. 210) presupposes "the right to be assisted by the Pastors from the spiritual riches of the Church, especially by the word of God and the sacraments" (can. 213). The duty "to show christian obedience to what the sacred Pastors declare as teachers of the faith" (can. 212 §1) contains the right that "the mystery of Christ is to be faithfully and fully presented in the ministry of the word, which must be founded upon sacred Scripture, Tradition, liturgy and the magisterium and life of the Church" (can. 760). It is a good thing to keep an eye on the right, connected with the duty, and recommend it to a church authority.

Then, if a person should be summoned (cf. can. 221 §2) by some church authority, it is advisable to try and structure juridically the relationship to the superior. This means to request, if necessary through a canonist or lawyer, that at least canons 50 and 51 of the Code of Canon Law — with supplementary ruling from canons 1517 and 1519 §2 of the Code of Canons of the Eastern Churches — be observed[21]. The elements mentioned under 'Judging People in Serious Cases' may also be insisted upon. In view of possible publicity church authorities may be sensitive to requests for these elementary procedural rules. This privately undertaken juridical structuring of the relationship to the church authority may not always be easy and agreeable, but in a number of cases it appears to be succesful.*

---

[21] Cf. *supra*, p.193-194.
* Translation by M. van Buren.

DEMOCRACY IN THE CHURCH

MARIE ZIMMERMANN

While expressing it discretely, the Roman Catholic Church now feels a certain pride in having played a role in the recent fall of the so-called 'popular democracies' of Eastern Europe. By contrast, it more overtly commends the 'democracy' of other modern states which have committed themselves to 'freedoms', even if its public pronouncements sometimes allude only to religious liberty. This represents significant progress in the church's reception of the idea of democracy since "Mirari Vos", the 1832 encyclical letter of Pope Gregory XVI which condemned modern liberties and challenged the claims of 'lay' Christians with the heavy hand of ecclesiastical authority. But, according to the French canonist Marie Zimmermann, this progress is found entirely in the church's 'external relations'.

The idea that Christians other than the hierarchy of clergy may be involved in the internal organization of the church still elicits a negative reaction among its hierarchy. Cardinal Joseph Ratzinger, the current prefect of the Vatican Congregation for the Doctrine of the Faith, once treated the issue this way:

"No doubt the upcoming (diocesan) synods will have an important role to play in the situation of the contemporary church. One hears complaints that the large majority of the faithful have but scant interest in their preparation. I must confess that this reservation strikes me as a healthy sign. Those with a Christian mentality, that is, those particularly grounded in the New Testament, have discovered that they have little to gain from men who passionately gather to discuss the problems of a synod. No one becomes a sportsman simply by claiming a role in the development of rules for the International Olympic Committee. It is understandable that a zeal to talk about the apparatus of the church is becoming, little by little, of little interest to men. Objectively speaking, this reaction corresponds to that which is essential in the life of the church.

We should not wish to be informed in detail about the methods used by bishops, priests and lay Catholics who hold official positions to apportion their responsibilities. We should want to know what God desires and does not desire of us in the course of our lives and at the moment of our death. In responding in this way, these bishops, priests and lay Catholics are not on the right path, for a church which causes itself to be talked about is not talking about that which it has a duty to talk about. From this point of view (and it is not the only one), one is sadly obliged to note today a decadence in theology and its popularized forms. The struggles which it leads in order to arrive at new ecclesiastical structures appear distanced from the proper object of theology... These reflections do not mean to imply that functions are without importance in the church... (but) the type of function which conforms most closely to the Gospel is that which remains most faithful to the particular (hierarchical)[1] rights which the church possesses... The notion of fraternity raises a determinant imperative for each Christian development in the institutional order, but this notion does not in itself offer a model of institution."[2]

With a certain hierarchical cynicism which ignores current dysfunctions in the church[3], and with its clerical, moralistic language, the Ratzinger text on the synods which are often considered a form of democratic advancement[4] in the church is precisely a prototype of what is problematical in her current institutional form. Nonetheless, it also points to the *raison d'etre* of a church firmly oriented toward the world. It is precisely for this reason, it seems to us, that christians, including our brothers in the hierarchy, have the obligation to pay attention to their motivations. Why is it, we wonder, that whenever christians speak of democracy or democratization in the church, or whenever they get involved in the church's institutional activity, the highest ecclesiastical authorities are so quick to raise their shields defensively?

To address this dilemma, we will first attempt to situate the term democracy, so that we can subsequently appreciate its eventual capacity

---

[1] Parenthesized words are our own. The term 'hierarchy' is generally made more explicit when reference is made to constitutional law in the church. But here the reference is strictly her initiated members, so there is no need to be more explicit. On the notion of fraternity, see the very severe critique of the Catholic Church by E. DREWERMANN, *Kleriker: Psychogramm eines Ideals,* München, 1989, p.905. The author is particularly severe on a church which preaches a message of love and fraternity, but is incapable of putting it into practice.

[2] J. RATZINGER, *Démocratisation dans l'église,* Paris, 1971, pp.21-23.26.

[3] H. TINCQ, "Des catholiques contestaires dénoncent les blocages crées par la réduction du corps ecclésiastique," in *Le Monde* (February 6, 1993) p.14. The article cites in particular the growing number of ecclesiastic assemblies without a priest, i.e. without Eucharist, which now number over 2000 in France on a typical Sunday.

[4] M. DELBERGHE, "Lyon. Laboratoire d'église, solidarité, coresponsabilité, synode," in *Le Monde* (April 13, 1993) pp.1.9.

or incapacity to inform, both in theory and in practice, ecclesiastical structures.

1. Definitions

When Ratzinger maintains that it is inopportune for christians to concern themselves with ecclesiastical institutions, he rightly refers to the primordial relationship of the church to the Gospel. However, insofar as the Gospel imperative is not a saying but a doing (the action of God on behalf of humankind), it cannot be detached from human action in general and from one specific human action: the action of God realized through the action of the man Jesus.

The human reality acquires a genuine importance when it involves the church; it is not indifferent. In other words, it is legitimate to be concerned about the social structures of church institutions, and to speak of them in terms of monarchy, oligarchy, democracy, etc. Such speech is not an attempt to give a definition to the church, but simply to examine its human form, or the human form of its actions. One cannot maintain, as do many authors (particularly canonists), that talk of democracy in the church misses its 'essence', its 'profound reality' or even its 'very self'. In fact these essentialistic or 'personalist' terms are used by specialists in Roman Catholic Church law to push aside all questioning of her anti-democratic, institutional form. In this context, it is not rare to hear simply and without supporting argument the blatant affirmation, "The church is not a democracy".

In fact, it used to be argued in the context of syllogistic reasoning that "the church is a state"[5] to affirm its sovereignty in relation to the organization of modern society. But if the church is a community/communion(?), it cannot escape the human forms it shares with the rest of society, or a sociological analysis of those forms. Its communal actions are therefore understood to manifest themselves in structures demonstrable according to the paradigms of all human social structures[6]. There is no authority to limit this organization to the activities of those 'at the top' of the church. This being the case, and accepting Ratzinger's contention that the interest of most christians in the institutional form of their

---

[5] M. ZIMMERMANN, *Structure sociale et église*, Strasbourg, 1989 (3rd ed.), p.45.

[6] H. Heimerl specifically observes that christian action is not limited to the actions of a few individuals at the top, and that this must translate into the concrete organization of church institutions. Cf. "Das Kirchenrecht im neuen Kirchenbild," in *Ecclesia et ius. Festgabe Scheuermann,* München/Paderborn/Wien, 1968, p.17.

church is underdeveloped, what does the term "democracy" mean to those for whom this (the structural organization of the church) is a vital concern?

Immediately, we understand that the term refers to power and its legitimization. We also instinctively return to the 18th century French *philosophes* (especially Rousseau) to recall that the idea of democracy is connected to the sovereignty of the nation, of the citizens as equal individuals, and also to protest the usurpation of the "rights" of God. Power in the church, as it had been in society, belongs to God. The shift in the attribution of power from God to man (atheism) is spontaneous, although the 1791 French Constitution was not explicitly atheistic. Certainly, the August 26, 1789 *Declaration of the Rights of Man and of the Citizen* adopted by the National Assembly in 1791 had something to say about the beliefs of citizens, but it was not antireligious[7].

Opponents of democracy in the church, particularly canonists[8], rightly point out that democracy as defined by the 18th Century *philosophes* has never had, nor can it ever have, any concrete application, since it is impossible to establish all citizens into a continuously governing authority. But the *philosophes*, who excluded women from their citizenry, never envisioned this type of direct civic participation[9]. Even more to the point, the evolution of the Roman Catholic Church which now integrates 'the republic' into its concept of the modern state proves that 'divine right' is not necessarily breached by power exercised in democratic form. To say that "power resides in the people" is not yet a statement about the origins of power itself[10], although one can sanctify the people as sovereign, as Gallicans and Anglicans did with 17th Century royalty to better combat the secular power of the Papacy.

In the end, the idea of democracy is multi-formed and locally determined: it can serve either an absolutist liberalism as well as the despotism of a Soviet-style gulag. Recently an American author placed certain

---

[7] *Les Constitutions de la France depuis 1789,* présentation par J. GODECHOT. Paris, 1973, p.33. The June 24, 1793 constitution was the first to be democratic in this sense by endeavoring "to have the maximum number of citizens involved in the power" of the state. Of course, this was limited to male citizens.

[8] The canonist most determined to demonstrate the practical incompatibilities of democratic theories is: G. MAY, *Demokratisierung der Kirche: Möglichkeiten und Grenzen,* Wien/München, 1971, p.205. Along the same lines, see: A. MÜLLER, N. GREINACHER and K. LEHMANN, *Editorial* in *Concilium* 1971, no.7, pp.7-9.

[9] Only a few timid voices proposed suffrage for women in 1793. See *Les Constitutions de la France,* p.73.

[10] See the treatment of Abraham Lincoln's Gettysburg Address of 1863 by K. TUDYKA, "The Meaning of Democracy Today," in *Concilium* 1992, no.5, pp.3-13.

social gains, particularly those of American feminism, into question with a liberal definition, the key point of which is the absolute equality of every citizen under the law. Thus he defines democracy as "a social order in which most governmental decisions conform to the will of the people, and which assures individual freedoms to the maximum extent possible... Democracy guarantees equality of rights, equality of liberties, equality of opportunity... and nothing more"[11]. The author goes further in asserting a right to discriminate in the private sector[12]. However, this anthropological option relies upon an absolute confidence in education: it is supposed that in American society education is sufficiently developed to establish the most broad individual liberties, whatever the risks[13]. In a word, the democracy elaborated by Levin, both as societal attitude and as organizational structure of society, is linked to undemonstrated, if not undemonstrable, anthropological options. Can one apply this assertion to both defenders and detractors of the idea of applied democracy in the Roman Catholic Church?

2. The Church as an 'Organic Body'

Whenever the idea of democracy is applied to the Roman Catholic Church with the consent of the clergy (hierarchy), one can say that it has been stripped of its very substance. The idea of democracy is today expressed in the yearning for "the greatest possible amount of self-determination and the least amount of external determination... and it can be expressed and institutionalized on various levels and in different forms"[14]. This implies a concept of man as 'agent' and of the world as a constructed reality. But the church through its official teaching of Vatican II tends to conceive of the "people of God" as above all a given reality concretized in rituals, particularly those of the gathered assembly. A few basic principles govern this passive, anti-democratic attitude.

---

[11] M. Levin begins with the individualistic anthropology that underlies the definition of democracy to criticize the 1970 decision of the U.S. Congress to amend the 1965 *Civil Rights Act* to include women. See "Feminism vs. Democracy," in *The St. Croix Review* 26 (1983) nr.5, p.39. The author uncritically revives Aristotle's distrust of democracy as the road to anarchy and tyranny.

[12] *Ibid.*, p.40.

[13] *Ibid.*, p.47.

[14] B. KOPETZKY and R. BAER, "Students and the Democratization of the Church," in *Concilium* 1971, no.7, pp.144-158.

The term 'organic'[15] is reflected in the Gospels only in common image of the human body. In the common imagery of pre-scientific societies, it is assumed that the head is the functional equivalent of authority in society: not only the 'superior part' of the body, but the very seat of life. However, no one ever demonstrated what brain death meant in terms of the absence of life. Implicitly, the overvaluation of the head in relation to the body leads to the practical denial of value to the governed, who become workers and listeners best appreciated when they are most docile. This was clearly stated in a recent document of the French bishops' conference which alluded to "the primacy of the role of the priest"[16]. The use of the term 'organic' in the ecclesiological or canonical tradition of the Roman Catholic Church is practically synonymous with the idea of hierarchy as the essential life force in the society of the church.

Beginning with the body as a hierarchically organized (ordered), closed universe, the Greek philosophers Plato and Aristotle, in opposition to the Atomists, imagined a closed world of nature endowed with a hierarchically organized structure (order). Like the organs of the human body, every being in the universe has a fixed place in this world, and for each there is a corresponding function. Like the Bible, this school of Greek thought placed man at the summit of the hierarchical order. Ecclesiology and the canonical tradition uncritically took up this image and applied it to another body — the church. She needed a head: Christ or his *alter ego* (the clergy) possessing that which only the head can possess, i.e., the impulse of life, from which power must flow. Grace thus finds channels in search of its 'receptacles'. Astonished by what has happened to them, the receptacles are overwhelmed with gratitude. This representation of the body of the church has found its expression for the last fifty years in the doctrines of Western canon law known as the "law of word and documents."

Given a certain official status by its acceptance into the Code of 1983, the law of word and documents finds its ideal expression in ritual, a ritual reserved to sacerdotal power. The adage "the church makes the Eucharist, and the Eucharist makes the church" operates within this closed theory of an organized body. Considered carefully from a logical

[15] For the context in which this term was developed, see D. FURLEY, *The Greek Cosmologists: 1. The Formation of the Atomic Theory and its Earliest Critics*, Cambridge, 1987, pp.7-8. For other accepted uses of the word, see M. ZIMMERMANN, "Théologie du droit ou idéologie du droit?" in *Revue de droit canonique* 39(1989) pp.55-63.

[16] See *Le Monde* (March 18, 1993) p.10. In order that letters of mission or delegation to lay persons would not question, "...the primacy of the ordained ministry".

point of view, the theory makes no sense: If the church makes the Eucharist it is because its exists before the sacrament; the eucharist cannot be its own source. And if one reverses the formula, the Eucharist can not possibly be realized when there is no church, i.e. no hierarchy, empowered to 'make' the Eucharist. Here the closed world is only guaranteed by a circular reasoning which in turn only finds meaning in a totality that is closed upon itself.

Beyond the fact that the formula "the church is born in the Eucharist" has no meaning in the world of action, it specifically repudiates all forms of democratization, that is to say, the attribution to man of the fundamental power which can constitute humanity as an action. For here the priest does not really act; he substitutes for another, as expressed in the doctrine of action *in persona Christi* (in the person of Christ). In the end, the priesthood loses all of its own substance in order to identify with the head in a supreme act of submission. The rite totally drains it.

We now address the theory of the 'assembled people' which is simply identified with the liturgical assembly. Constituent power is simply transposed to ritual. The sacrament[17] then tends to take on a dimension which tends to nullify the value of all human activity, whether individual or communal. But if, as christian doctrine states, salvation is acquired through death and resurrection, ritual cannot constitute it nor exhaust it. It can merely re-present in dramatic form the mediating act, not its disappearance. Thus human action remains, in the biblical context of the doctrine of the covenant, a co-action, including the building up of that entity which we call church. And this action must find a visible form of expression in order to be recognized separately.

An example will serve to illustrate the need for a doctrine which takes into account human action. When Pope John Paul II was asked by a young man in France about what day the pontiff would call "the most beautiful in his life,"[18] his response that it was the day of his ordination to the priesthood was 'heretical', no matter how it is interpreted. In one scenario, the pope is situated in the closed cycle of a ministerial priesthood with its theory of magisterial teaching, and he is conveying an official Christian message. In this context only the day of one's baptism can be presented as the most beautiful (fundamental) day for a Christian. In another scenario, the pope is situated in a psychological context of

---

[17] "Sakramentale, theokratische und demokratische Kirchen. Zitate aus Paul Tillich, Die Bedeutung der Kirche für die Gesellschaftsordnung in Europa und Amerika (Gesammelte Werke III, Stuttgart, 1965)," in *Una Sancta* 25(1970) pp.379-382, p.380.

[18] Papal trip to Paris.

personal emotion and he is not conveying an official Christian message. But here he has stepped outside of his teaching ministry, which is his particular magisterial role. How then can the pope's words be linked to doctrine? We will return to this point; but let us for now simply note that human action is an integral part of the church, and as such must be recognized and valued as to its form.

3. The Distinction Between Clergy and Laity

Canon 207 §1 of the 1983 Code of Canon Law, the most recent legislation in the western church, affirms: "Among the Christian faithful by divine institution there exist in the church sacred ministers, who are also called clerics in law, and other Christian faithful, who are also called laity."[19]

Let us first recall that the term cleric/*cleros* in Greek was first applied to the whole Christian people as the Elect[20]. As for the term laity, so much a part of the question in addressing democracy in the church, it does not even appear in the 1923 *Dictionnaire de Théologie Catholique*. Going further back in Christian history, we find that there is no exact corresponding term in the Gospels: the closest Greek term is *laos*, which signified Jews other than priests and Levites in the Old Testament, or people in general in the New Testament[21].

It is here that the ecumenical tradition differs from the Catholic Church in the role that is gives to the laity, underscoring particularly the negative characterization which it gives to the term itself: "non-ordained members of the church"[22]. The Code of Canon Law of the Roman Catholic Church returns to precisely this negative definition in Canon 207 §1.[23] Might one here detect a post-Vatican II regression compared

---

[19] Cf. also Canon 129 §1.

[20] R. NAZ (ed.), *Dictionnaire de droit canonique*. T. 3, Paris, 1942, p.827. We note that the *Dictionnaire de théologie catholique* published under the direction of A. VACANT, E. MANGENOT and E. AMANN of 1923 does not mention this understanding of the term 'cleric' in favor of a more recent understanding where the cleric/lay distinction had already taken form in the post-apostolic tradition. The same occurs in the *Nouvelle encyclopédie catholique*, Paris, 1989, pp.557.1048. Is theology more "orthodox" than canon law? The ecumenical tradition does not speak of clergy but of ministries in the church, except to use the comparison laity/clergy as a method of noting how these notions are used in a variety of ways by various denominations. See *Dictionary of the Ecumenical Movement*, Geneva/Grand Rapids, 1991, p.585.

[21] *Nouvelle encyclopédie*, p.547. This understanding of the term does not appear in the *Dictionnaire de Droit Canonique*, pp.329-331.

[22] *Dictionary of the Ecumenical Movement*, pp.580-584 (E. Adler).

[23] See, for example, index page 333 of the approved 1984 French translation of the code.

to the attitude of previous popes? Pope Pius XI called upon the laity to participate in the apostolate of the hierarchy in 1922, and Pope Pius XII in 1946 spoke in terms of *being*, rather than simply *belonging* to the church. One might also cite the 1959 creation of a permanent committee for international conferences on the apostolate of the laity.

The Dogmatic Constitution of the Church of Vatican II focused attention on a definition of membership in the church as gained through baptism: the church is the people of God, a holy priesthood (1 Peter 2:4-10). But Pope John Paul II, in his 1989 apostolic exhortation following the 1987 Synod of Bishops, recalled the necessary distinction between clerics and lay persons: the best apostolate of the laity being realized in obedience to the church and in dependence upon the clergy[24]. It is as if Vatican II ratifies not only the attention given to baptized Christians by a theology often ignored if not indirectly attacked by the highest levels of the magisterium[25], but also another tradition centered on sacramentality in its ritualistic sense.

If Ratzinger has rejected the distinction between ordinary ordained and non-ordained sacred power in favor of priesthood, the 1983 code goes even further by placing this sacred power in the clergy. Its redactors knew how to take advantage of Vatican II in another way by borrowing the notion of sacred power/*potestas sacra*, which does not make the distinction between the power of orders and the power of jurisdiction. For Ratzinger, "a full power which does not derive from priesthood would lead to the destruction of the hierarchical structure of the church. There would therefore be no further reason to transform councils into decision-making bodies"[26].

Even if all of the redactors of the code did not share in the radicalism of the Prefect of the Congregation for the Doctrine of the Faith, the 1983 code would speak of the "non-ordained" only in terms of their participation through service to governance/*munus regendi*, not through their participation in sacred power/*potestas* as Vatican II presented it, or as hoped for by the non-ordained who are already fulfilling functions of

---

[24] Pope JOHN PAUL II, "Pastores Dabo Vobis: Post-Synodal Apostolic Exhortation on the Formation of Priests in the Circumstances of the Present Day," in *Origins* 21(1992) pp.717-759.

[25] Ratzinger rejected preliminary drafts of Canons 126, 244 and 1373 §2 which distinguished between "the ordinary sacred power which derives from orders and the ordinary sacred power which does not derive from ordination".

[26] *Pontificum Concilium de Legum Textibus Interpretandis, Congregatio Plenaria, Diebus 2-29, Octobris 1981 habita*, Citta del Vaticano, 1991, pp.35-97.

this type in the church[27]. These lay persons tend to speak in terms of participation or co-responsibility; while the church's supreme authority, Pope John Paul II, prefers to speak of "the co-presence or the collaboration of lay persons"[28].

The fundamentally anti-democratic attitude of the highest church authorities is largely shared by the specialists in church law who enjoy the favor of the magisterium in such a radical way that they do not see that the quality of being a christian is necessary for a non-ordained person to fulfill a function in the church. Aymans stated at a 1987 canon law convention in Ottawa that an instructed Muslim could perform strictly technical duties, such being a notary, as well as a christian in an ecclesiastical court. In other words, all active participation by a non-ordained christian, a lay person as opposed to a cleric, in ecclesiastical activity has no human or religious meaning: it is lost within its materiality or its execution. Nor does it therefore have any meaning in the building up of the church, which the Docetist-like theology of the canonical milieu in any case tends moreover to cloak in mystery. From these inaccessible heights, the human denseness of the church is merely an illusion; only the cleric acts, and he, only through another, *in persona Christi.*

Human science labels as 'archaic' a mentality that is incompatible with a democratic approach to society[29], and therefore to the church. Here the human is 'taboo'[30], that is to say, it is reduced to nothingness within the divine only to rise up again in the use of power as interdict. But is the denunciation of this taboo by certain canonists for the last 20 years driven by an admitted ignorance, by fear of mystery or by political will? This is what we must now examine.

[27] See for example, Y. BERGERON, *Partenaires en église. Femmes et hommes à part égale,* Montreal, 1991, p.105. And for the point of view of one in authority, see Bishop R. LEBEL in *Revue Notre Dame* 8(1992) p.27: "Il faut que l'on cesse dans l'église de lier aussi étroitement qu'on le fait autorité et ordination" ("It is necessary in the church to stop linking so closely authority and ordination as it is done.")

[28] Pope JOHN PAUL II, Apostolic Exhortation "Christifideles Laici," in *Origins* 18(1989) p.561-595.

[29] W. ORBIST, "A Consecrated Hierarchy — An Obstacle to a Democratizing of the Catholic Church," in *Concilium* 1992, no.5, pp.27-37.

[30] See "La démocratie dans l'église: Un tabou?" title of *Concilium* 244, 1992. But the term was already used by H. HERMANN in *Zu nahe Getreten: Aufsatze 1972-1978,* Frankfurt am Main, 1979, p.304.

4. The Test of Democracy

If a certain cultural form necessarily precedes democratic attempts at the organization of power, then it is necessary to understand that which in the Roman Catholic Church fosters an anti-democratic mentality. The institutional (ecclesiology and canon law) literature of the Roman Catholic Church is generally striking in its negative approach to humanity. Even if God has saved the world, sin is still omnipresent in it. What's more, human "nature" is likened to "the world" understood as sin, or to "the crowd" as the unconscious and rebellious force within oneself.

From this reasoning, truth, knowledge and action then become a sphere reserved for an elite, whose ideal expression is the cleric. Himself placed in a hierarchy within the clerical corps, he has no other perspective but to aspire to the fullness given by decree. Ratzinger[31] rightly notes that this notion of an ascension within the priesthood to its fullness reached a certain fulfillment in the theology of Vatican II: it was the council that recognized priesthood as the sole source of ecclesiastical power. Nonetheless, we must recall that the council did not intend to be dogmatic and the Code of Canon Law reserves power to the cleric, which it does not at all confuse with priesthood. In other words, in the Roman Catholic Church the human being, insofar as action and therefore measure of power is concerned, is viewed in only the most negative terms. The most developed form of this anthropological pessimism is its view of woman, who is seen as temptress or inciter of evil. She cannot therefore enter into the privileged sphere of the elite[32] which is protected from negativity. For she who is 'crowd', world or matter, salvation is ideally realized through the renunciation of all human power: obedience in all realms becomes her supreme virtue as it is for the crowd.

Yet in order for this obedience to be fully expressed, authority must be removed from the human sphere of power and placed in another order (of ordination). It then acquires a status that is unaffected by all contingencies. The clergy enjoy an exorbitant privilege over all human thought and action. And as Ratzinger duly remarks[33], the law of the church is

---

[31] See note 2. Cf. also G. THILS, "Le Pape et le Gouvernement de l'Eglise" in *Revue théologique de Louvain* 24 (1993) pp.70-76 for a more recent work on this topic.

[32] C. DIBOUT and A. FAIVRE, "Les chrétiennes. Entre leurs devoirs familiaux et le prestige de l'épiscopè. Un dilemme aux sources de la documentation canonico-liturgique," in *Laval théologique et philosophique* 49(1993) pp.69-92. This exclusion was also made by other religions such as Judaism in the same era. Cf. J. WEGNER, "Le Statut de la Femme Juive," in *Praxis juridique et religion* 10(1993) pp.5-35.

[33] See note 2.

statutory and elitist, concerning itself exclusively with matters that do not concern the crowd. As for the crowd, it finds its salvation in submission order, where it is allowed to exercise devoid of any structural control, i.e. of any democratic notions. At the most, this order can have at its disposal a measure of truth, likened in the code of canon law to knowledge in order to better assure its proper functioning.

For a long time, knowledge was commonly likened to the accumulation of facts; to know was to possess a treasure. God himself thus became an object of knowledge. But knowing facts presupposed favorable conditions: time, accessibility to the treasure troves from which one draws. In other words, knowledge was elitist and separated; it was not long before it was transformed into a reserved, that is to say anti-democratic, knowledge. By contrast, in the idea of knowledge as 'understanding', that which, in one way or another, is already accessible has democratic traits.

In the Roman Catholic Church, the idea of dogma places knowledge in a sphere reserved to an elite, both in knowledge itself and in power. Certainly, this idea is not in itself restrictive in that which concerns the christian community. One can, (and non-official Roman Catholic theology offers many examples[34]), link dogmatic pronouncement to pronouncement of 'the people'. This implies participation by christians in the enunciation of faith. This is a form of knowledge which is understood as an 'understanding'. It is open to a broad field of investigation and to a true democratic process. This is certainly not the orientation given to knowledge by the hierarchy. The pope and a large part of the episcopal corps — those clergy possessing the fullness of the priesthood — exercise a very coercive control over the collection of 'facts', and their transmission. And to better guarantee dogma, i.e. authoritative doctrine approved[35] if not initiated by them[36], the 'sphere' of dogma is extended to all teaching emanating from a magisterium ordained to protect it at all costs.

---

[34] Just to limit ourselves to a more recent article, see J. BURKHARD, "Sensus Fidei: Meaning, Role and Future of a Teaching of Vatican II," in *Louvain Studies* 17(1991) pp.669-711. In a more specific sense, see J.L. Segundo, *The Liberation of Dogma: Faith, Revelation and Dogmatic Teaching,* Maryknoll (NY), 1992.

[35] See article on "Dogme" in *Dictionnaire de théologie catholique,* T.4.2, pp.1574-1650. Also Congregation for the Doctrine of the Faith, "Litterae ad catholicae ecclesiae prout est communio," in *Observatore Romano* (French edition), (June 15-16, 1992) pp.7-8 and B.D. DE LA SOUJEOLE, "A propos de l'église comme communion," a note in *Revue Thomiste* 93(1993).

[36] F. MORRISEY, *Les documents pontificaux et la curie: leur portée canonique à la lumière du code de 1993,* Ottawa, 1992, p.50. The author cites many places where the documents are particularly ambiguous in their juridical nature. Among other things, he cites instances where their form do not correspond to their content.

Certainly, the assent imposed by the ordinary magisterium is distinct from that claimed for dogma. Nonetheless, the submission of thought and practice often required by written professions of faith[37] leads in fact to the exclusion of all tradition not supported by the clergy. This process is particularly reductionist when it is accompanied by a political will for the establishment of a hierarchy which actively supports a schema separating clergy/laity which cannot claim to be rooted in the primitive church[38]. This knowledge transformed into power will necessarily collide with other knowledges organized as teaching or preaching in conflicts which are by definition unequal. One can immediately doubt the outcome of these conflicts, regardless of the juridical form used. The law of the church cannot adopt democratic forms for the structure of the church itself while denying their underlying presuppositions. The democratic attitude with its moral components must precede the establishment of institutional structures.

In conclusion, it is easy to note that democracy is grounded in an ideal of life — an ethic — that is both personal and communitarian. Within the church as in society, it will win or lose according to how it is defined. As a work of human beings, democracy will not become a crowning glory of the church until it agrees not to lose its human face in an institutional Docetism, where the role of a human being will no longer be just a pale shadow of what certain canonists call its "true essence," the only essence worth consideration. Perhaps this aspiration amounts to an idle dream, and the power structure does not live easily with dreams.*

[37] This written profession of faith is used in the granting of canonical degrees.

[38] A. FAIVRE, *Ordonner la fraternité: pouvoir d'innover et retour à l'ordre dans l'église ancienne,* Paris, 1992, p.550. See also by the same author: *The Emergence of the Laity in the Early Church.* New York, 1990, p.242.

* Translation by B. Pomerleau

INFORMATION ABOUT THE AUTHORS

Raffaele Botta (Italy, 1947) is Professor of Roman Canon Law and Canon Law in the Law Faculty of the University of Modena and Bologna. He is also manager of the Juridical Science Department in Modena. He has written several publications, among others: *Il lavoro dei religiosi* (Padova, 1984); *Sentimento religioso e Costituzione repubblicana* (Torino, 1990); *Codice di diritto ecclesiastico* (Milano, 1990).

Erik Borgman (the Netherlands, 1957) studied Systematic Theology at the Catholic University of Nijmegen (NL). In 1990 he published a thesis on the relationship between liberation theology and western academic theology: *Sporen van de bevrijdende God.* He works as research fellow for the Dutch province of the Dominican Order, on a project about the development of the theology of Edward Schillebeeckx in relation to its context.

Bert van Dijk (the Netherlands, 1946) studied Community Development in Sittard and Social Theology at the Catholic University of Nijmegen (NL). He is staff member of the Eighth of May Movement, a Dutch catholic renewal movement, and a member of the European Conference for Human Rights in the Church. He is also a member of the Board of the National Committee for Development Education (NCO).

Peter Hebblethwaite (England, 1930) has been reporting on the Vatican since 1965 when he attended the fourth and final session of the Second Vatican Council for the British Jesuit review, *the Month.* Since 1979 he has been Vatican Affairs Writer for *The National Catholic Reporter.* He also writes frequently in *The Guardian, the Independent* and *The Times Literary Supplement.* He has published fourteen books. His latest book is on Pope Paul VI (*Paul VI. The First Modern Pope,* Harper Collins, 1993).

Ad van der Helm (the Netherlands, 1962) is a priest of the diocese of Rotterdam who studied Theology at the Catholic University of Amsterdam (KTUA). In 1987 he followed a human rights summercourse in Strasbourg (France) where he also studied Canon Law and obtained a doctorate in 1993. He published *Comparer en droit* (Strasbourg, 1992) and recently a comparative study on the pastoral activities of laypersons in the Roman Catholic Church, *Un clergé parallèle* (Strasbourg, 1993).

Jan van Hooydonk (the Netherlands, 1954) studied Political Science at the Catholic University of Nijmegen, and Theology at the Catholic Theological University of Utrecht (NL). He is editor at the catholic opinion weekly for church and society *de Bazuin,* and a member of the Working Group for press, publicity and communication of the Eighth of May Movement. He is co-founder and member of the *Werkverband van Katholieke Homo-Pastores* (Working Group of Catholic Gay Pastors). In the field of spirituality he feels related to the religious movement of Saint Dominic.

Ruud Huysmans, (the Netherlands, 1935) was ordained priest in 1959 for the Diocese of Rotterdam (NL). From 1960 till 1966 he studied Canon Law and Roman Law at the Pontifical Lateran University in Rome. Since 1967 he is professor of Canon Law at the Catholic Theological University of Amsterdam, since 1992 in Utrecht. He recently published a book on Canon Law: *Liber I. Algemene Normen van het Wetboek van Canoniek Recht. De Normis Generalibus* (Novum Commentarium Lovaniense), Leuven, 1993.

Jan Jans (Belgium, 1954) studied Religious Sciences and Theology at the Catholic University of Leuven (Belgium). Since 1991 he is teaching Moral Theology at the Theological Faculty of Tilburg (the Netherlands). He published several articles on personalism and bio-medical ethics.

K. Lüdicke (Germany, 1943) studied Catholic Theology, Civil Law and Canon Law at the universities of Münster and München (Germany). He currently is professor of Canon Law at the *Institut für Kanonisches Recht* of the University of Münster and Judge in the Diocesan Tribunal of Münster. His most important publications are: *Psychisch bedingte Ehe-unfähigkeit* (Frankfurt, 1978), *Familienplanung und Ehewille* (Münster, 1983) and the commentary on Sacramental Law, Matrimonial Law, Penal Law and Procedural Law in *Münsterischer Kommentar* zum Codex Iuris Canonici (Essen, since 1984).

Karl-Wilhelm Merks (Germany, 1939) studied Theology, Classical Philology and Philosophy in Bonn (Germany), Freiburg (Switzerland) and Toulouse (France). He has been an Assistent at the *Moral-theologischen Seminar* of the University of Bonn and is since 1981 Professor of Moral Theology at the Theological Faculty of Tilburg (the Netherlands). He currently is member of the researchproject on Human Rights in Tübingen, headed by Prof.Dr. J. Schwartländer. He is the author of *Theologische Grundlegung der sittlichen Autonomie,* Düsseldorf, 1978 and was the editor of *De moeilijke waarheid. Sociaal-ethische aspecten van waarachtigheid en leugen,* Baarn, 1992.

Ida Raming (Germany) studied Philosophy, Pedagogy, Theology and Germanics in Münster/Westfalen and Freiburg (Germany). She obtained her doctorate in Catholic Theology in 1970 with a thesis on *The Exclusion of Women from the Priesthood - Divine Law or Sex Discrimination?* (Scarecrow Press, Metuchen (NJ), 1976. Original in German: *Der Ausschluß der Frau vom priestlichen Amt - gottgewollte Tradition oder Diskriminierung?* Köln/Wien, 1973). She has also published several studies and articles on Women and the Church and on the history of the Women's Movement, most recently: *Frauenbewegung und Kirche. Bilanz eines 25jährigen Kampfes für Gleichberechtigung und Befreiung der Frau seit dem 2. Vatikanischen Konzil,* Weinheim, 1989; 1991 (2nd ed.).

Theo Salemink (the Netherlands, 1946) studied social theology and in 1980 wrote a thesis on Catholic thinking in the Thirties: *Crisis en confessie.* He teaches history of church and society at the Catholic Theological University of Utrecht (the Netherlands), and is chairman of DISK, the Dutch ecumenical organisation for church presence in the world of industry. In 1991 he published a handbook on catholic social teaching: *Katholieke kritiek op het kapitalisme 1891-1991.*

Antoon Schoors (Belgium, 1934) was ordained in 1959. He studied Philosophy and Theology at the Catholic University of Leuven and Biblical Sciences at the Pontifical Biblical Institutes of Rome and Jerusalem. He has been Assistant Professor since 1965 and Professor of Hebrew, Aramaic, Ugaritic, Syriac and Archaeology of Syria-Palestine since 1973. He married in 1971 and is president of *Inspraak,* the Flemish organization of married priests.

Caroline Vander Stichele (Belgium, 1959) studied Religious Sciences and Theology at the Catholic University of Leuven (Belgium). From 1988 till 1993 she has been a teacher of New Testament Exegesis at the University of Utrecht (the Netherlands) and since 1993 at the Faculty of Theology of the University of Amsterdam (the Netherlands). She wrote several articles and edited a book on the situation of women in the Catholic Church in Flanders: *Het zwijgen doorbroken. Vrouwen over vrouwen en kerk,* Tielt, 1989.

Rik Torfs (Belgium, 1956) studied Law and Canon Law at the Catholic University of Leuven and is currently Professor at the Faculty of Canon Law in Leuven. He is the author of several books on Canon Law: *De vrouw en het kerkelijk ambt. Analyse in functie van de mensenrechten in Kerk en Staat,* Leuven, 1985; *Het huwelijk als levensgemeenschap. Een kerkrechtelijke benadering,* Leuven, 1990; *Congregationele gezondheidsinstellingen. Toekomstige structuren naar profaan en kerkelijk recht,* Leuven, 1992; *Mensen en rechten in de Kerk,* Leuven, 1993. He also wrote numerous articles in this field.

Svetko Veliscek (the Netherlands, 1931) is secretary of the committee on Human Rights in the Church of the Eight of May movement in the Netherlands

Knut Walf (Germany, 1936). He studied Philosophy, Roman Catholic Theology, Law and Canon Law in Munich and Fribourg (Germany). He obtained his Ph.D. in 1965 and 'Habilitation' in Canon Law in Munich (1971). He was a lecturer from 1972 till 1977 at the University of Munich, and in 1977 he was appointed Professor of Canon Law at the University of Nijmegen in the Netherlands. Since 1985 he is also Professor in Canon Law at the Faculty of Theology in Tilburg (the Netherlands). He is the author of numerous publications in Canon Law, on the changes in religious consciousness (*Stille Fluchten,* 1983), and in Taoism (*TAO für den Westen,* 1989/ *TAO voor het Westen,* 1991; *Westliche Taoismus-Bibliographie/Western Bibliography of Taoism,* 1992 [third ed.])

Luciano Zannotti is researcher of Ecclesiastical Law at the University of Florence (Italy). Recent publications of his are: *Riforma della legislazione scolastica e nuovo Concordato,* in *Concordato e Costituzione. Gli accordi del 1984 tra Italia e Santa Sede,* a cura di S. FERRARI, Bologna, 1985, pp. 197-211; *Stato sociale, edilizia di culto e pluralismo religioso. Contributo allo studio della problematica del dissenso religioso,* Milano, 1990; *Le cerimonie religiose nella scuola pubblica,* in *Il diritto ecclesiastico,* 1993, II, pp. 215-227.

Marie Zimmermann (France, 1936) is researcher of the CNRS (Centre National de la Recherche Scientifique) in Strasbourg and director of CERDIC (*Centre de recherche et de documentation des institutions de croyances religieuses*). She studied Theology, Canon Law and Philosophy. She published a book on the relations between church and state (*Structure sociale et église,* Strasbourg, 1983) and on mariage and alternative couples (*Couple libre,* Strasbourg, 1983).

DRUKKERIJ ORIENTALISTE, KLEIN DALENSTRAAT 42, 3020 WINKSELE-HERENT